Improving
Reading and Literacy
in Grades 1-5

Improving
Reading and Literacy
in Grades 1-5

A Resource Guide to Research-Based Programs

Edward P. St. John
Siri Ann Loescher
Jeffrey S. Bardzell

CORWIN PRESS, INC.
A Sage Publications Company
Thousand Oaks, California

KH

For information:

Corwin Press, Inc.
A Sage Publications Company
2455 Teller Road
Thousand Oaks, California 91320
www.corwinpress.com

Sage Publications Ltd.
6 Bonhill Street
London EC2A 4PU
United Kingdom

Sage Publications India Pvt. Ltd.
B-42 Panchsheel Enclave
Post Box 4109
New Delhi 110 017 India

Printed in the United States of America

Library of Congress Cataloging-in-Publication Data

St. John, Edward P.
Improving reading and literacy in grades 1-5 : a resource guide to research-based programs / Edward P. St. John, Siri Ann Loescher, Jeffrey S. Bardzell ; with reviews by associated authors.
    p. cm.
Includes bibliographical references (p.   ) and index.
    ISBN 0-7619-4647-0 (cloth) -- ISBN 0-7619-4648-9 (paper) 1. Reading (Elementary)--United States. 2. School improvement programs-United States. 3. Literacy-United States. I. Loescher, Siri Ann. II. Bardzell, Jeffrey. III. Title.
LB1573.S8217 2003
372.4'0973--dc21
2002156120

This book is printed on acid-free paper.

03   04   05   06   10   9   8   7   6   5   4   3   2   1

Acquisitions Editor:	Faye Zucker
Editorial Assistant:	Stacy Wagner
Copy Editor:	Patterson Lamb
Production Editor:	Sanford Robinson
Typesetter:	C&M Digitals (P) Ltd.
Indexer:	Karen McKenzie
Cover Designer:	Michael Dubowe
Production Artist:	Janet Foulger

10/25/04

Contents

Acknowledgments

Improving Reading and Literacy in Grades 1–5: A Resource Guide to Research-Based Programs developed out of Improving Early Reading: A Resource Guide for Elementary Schools, supplemented by understandings reached from evaluation studies that used the framework developed in the guide. The earliest version of the Improving Early Reading guide was developed as part of an evaluation study on reading interventions by the Indiana Education Policy Center (IEPC). The original guide can still be accessed at the IEPC Web site: www.indiana.edu/~iepc.

The framework used in both guides was developed initially as part of a study of Indiana's Early Literacy Intervention Grant Program, which has supported interventions in Indiana's schools since 1997. Then the framework was expanded to include comprehensive school reform (CSR) in a project conducted for the Minnesota Department of Children, Families and Learning (MDCFL) in collaboration with the North Central Regional Educational Laboratory (NCREL). This collaboration and support is gratefully acknowledged. The opinions expressed in this Guide are the authors' and do not represent official policies or positions of the Indiana Department of Education, NCREL, or the MDCFL.

Several individuals helped make possible the reviews and research reported in this volume. We especially thank several individuals at the Indiana Department of Education and NCREL. Dr. Suellen Reed, Indiana superintendent of public instruction, provided leadership and funding of the Early Literacy Intervention Grant Program. Dr. Earlene Holland, associate director of professional development, served as project officer for several of the studies summarized in this book. Phyllis Usher, assistant superintendent for professional development, and Terry Spradlin, legislative liaison, provided guidance and reviews. Lawrence B. Freidman served as NCREL's project officer for the studies in Minnesota, Wisconsin, and Michigan. Matthew Mohs, federal education programs and policy specialist in MDCFL, provided guidance on reviews of CSR models and the linking of the review method to reading standards in Minnesota and other states.

We also owe thanks to members of the advisory committee who reviewed prior versions of this Guide. Committee members from Indiana University included Roger Farr, professor emeritus of reading education; Beth Greene, associate scientist in language education; Carl B. Smith, director of the ERIC Clearinghouse for Reading and Family Literacy; and Leo Fay, professor emeritus, language education. Marie McNelis, reading specialist, Washington Township Schools (Indiana), and Jack Humphrey, director of the Middle Grade Reading Network (Indiana) also contributed as members of the review committee.

Corwin's version of the *Guide* integrates new understandings reached from several years of evaluation research on early reading and school reform. It combines the systematic reviews from the earlier guides with insights from the evaluation studies. Several faculty members at the Indiana University School of Education contributed to the design of the research. Genevieve Manset-Williamson, associate professor of curriculum instruction, and Jonathan Plucker, associate professor of educational psychology, served as reviewers in the early stages of the project and as co-principal investigators (with Edward St. John) for reading studies. In addition to reviewing reform models, Amy Seely Flint, assistant professor of language education, and Mitzi Lewison, associate professor of language education, helped us develop an integrated approach to the study of reading and literacy outcomes. Carol Anne Hossler, lecturer in curriculum and instruction, collaborated on site visits in Michigan and helped us refine our conceptualization of professional development.

Colleagues in the Indiana Education Policy Center also helped with the research process. Genevieve Manset-Williamson and Robert Michael helped direct some of the studies reviewed here and were also co-authors of the survey instrument. Kim Manoil, Stacy Jacob, Osman Cekic, and Glenda Droogsma Musoba contributed to the reviews of reading reform models and conducted site visits. In addition Kim & made a substantial and direct contribution to the framework used in this book. Their contributions are gratefully acknowledged.

In addition, Ada B. Simmons and Gayle Hall helped coordinate the research projects that provided the basis for the *Guide*. Margaret Clements, Eric Asker, Kimberly Worthington, and David Gordon assisted with literature reviews and co-authored related research reports, along with others noted above. D. Leigh Kupersmith served as typist and publication coordinator for these earlier publications and also provided word processing support for the *Guide*. This book would not have been possible without their competent and professional support.

In addition to serving as co-authors of this volume, Siri Loescher and Jeffrey Bardzell played central roles in the conceptualization of the framework and in the evaluation studies. When he was publications coordinator and writer at the Policy Center (1997–2000), Jeffrey helped conceptualize the initial framework. While serving as a consultant to the Center (2000–2002), Siri helped expand the framework to include CSR models and to link the framework to reading standards. They also continued to collaborate on the development of the new text material after leaving the Policy Center, exhibiting a high professional standard.

Finally, we would like to thank educators who have filled out surveys, model providers who answered interviewers' questions about their model designs, and the school children who inspire them. Without their responsiveness, this book would not have been possible.

Edward P. St. John
Professor of Education
Indiana University

About the Authors

Edward P. St. John is professor of educational leadership at Indiana University and was director of the Indiana Education Policy Center. His research focuses on policy issues in K–16 education (1998–2002). At the Policy Center, he has directed several studies of the impact of early reading programs and comprehensive school reform. His other collaborative books on topics related to school reform include *Accelerated Schools in Action* (Corwin), *Families in Schools* (Heinemann), and *Reinterpreting Urban School Reform* (SUNY Press).

Siri Ann Loescher is an educational specialist and served as a policy analyst for the Indiana Educational Policy Center, and currently works as a consultant. She has an M.A. in administration and policy analysis from Stanford University where she completed advanced course work. She has worked as an alternative educator in an urban school district, and an instructor and teacher program coordinator with a Washington, DC, based experiential civics education program. She spent four years working for the National Center for the Accelerated Schools Project as a coach and liaison for special programs in an urban school district. She currently serves as a leader on the founding board of a proposed charter school to serve at-risk youth.

Jeffrey Bardzell, founder of Allecto Media, an eLearning consulting and development company, is a Ph.D. candidate at Indiana University, where he also works as a trainer and multimedia instructional developer. He is also an eLearning Web developer, author, and instructor. Among his technical publications are *Macromedia MX eLearning: Advanced Training From the Source* and *Special Edition Using Fireworks MX.* Jeffrey honed his learner-centered approach through seven years of teaching literature and composition. He has also worked for three years as a policy analyst for the Indiana Education Policy Center. His education and academic publications cover such topics as early literacy instruction, school finance reform, and epic poetry.

Contributing Reviewers

Stacy Jacob, a Ph.D. candidate in higher education at Indiana University, was a research associate on the Policy Center's studies of early reading.

Kim Manoil, a Ph.D. candidate in educational psychology at Indiana University, was a research associate on the Policy Center's studies of early reading.

Amy Seely Flint, Assistant Professor of language education at Indiana University, consulted on the Policy Center's studies of early reading. Her research specialization is in critical literacy and learning communities in schools.

Mitzi Lewison, Associate Professor of language education at Indiana University, consulted on the Policy Center's studies of early reading. Her research specialization is in teacher inquiry and critical literacy.

Glenda D. Musoba, a Ph.D. candidate in higher education at Indiana University, is a senior policy researcher in the Policy Center. She has collaborated on studies of reading, comprehensive school reform, and college access.

Osman Cekic, a Ph.D. candidate in higher education at Indiana University, was a research associate on the Policy Center's studies of early reading and comprehensive school reform.

1

Introduction

Early reading and literacy have become a focus of policymakers. Early reading should also be a concern of teachers in Grades 1–5 because children have a substantially greater risk of failure and dropout if they cannot read for understanding by the end of elementary school. Thus the renewed emphasis on early education represents a challenge and opportunity for elementary school teachers. *Improving Early Reading and Literacy in Grades 1–5* provides a resource guide for teachers. It is designed to help them assess their current approaches to reading and language arts education, compare their practices to major reform models, and collaborate in systematic change processes within schools that focus on improvement in early reading. Our primary assumption in writing this book has been that it is crucial for teachers to become more involved in planning for reforms in early reading because they are responsible for the instruction and other classroom practices that will foster improvement in literacy outcomes. The book provides a cohesive framework with an integrated set of reviews of reform models.

This introduction starts with a brief overview of the changes in educational policy that have led to the current focus on early reading and literacy in elementary schools. Then a process approach to early reading reform is introduced that teachers can use to (a) assess their own practices in early reading instruction, (b) review alternative approaches to early reading and literacy reform, and (c) collaborate in school decision processes aimed at improving reading outcomes. Individual teachers make daily decisions about early reading instruction that influence student outcomes, which means reading should be of concern to all teachers. Yet teachers in elementary schools need to coordinate their practices in ways that foster the development of children's reading and comprehension skills as they progress through elementary school. Thus improvement in early reading programs requires collaboration among teachers. Therefore we suggest that teachers collaborate in the process of developing reading reforms. This introduction concludes with an overview of the resources in this *Guide* that teachers can use in support of their planning processes.

■ PUBLIC POLICY AND READING REFORM

If teachers are to flourish in this context of intensive government interest in reading, they need an understanding of the intent of federal education policy. State and federal policymakers focus on education because most voters are concerned about education. However, when legislators and educational officials advocate different types of programs, they do so within a political context.

Local boards and district officials have substantial influence on educational practice. Historically, education in the United States was locally controlled. Even before the American Revolution, local communities taxed themselves to support schools (Burrup, Brimley, & Garfield, 1988), a pattern that continues in the twenty-first century. Whereas states have taken a more substantial role in funding and in setting parameters for curriculum, the local boards and district officials continue to exert influence on curriculum. School boards offer the initial opportunity for entry into electoral politics. Many school board members eventually become state legislators. Thus many of the most basic decisions about curriculum, including decisions about reading reform strategies, are made locally and are often politically constructed. Yet state and federal policies guide and constrain the available choices.

States also exert substantial influence on curriculum and teaching. In the late 1800s, many states began providing financial incentives to local school districts to extend their school days, increase the number of days in the school year, and promote a common curriculum in schools within the states. And while the federal government now provides substantial funding for special programs, states administer most federal funds and, as a result, exert substantial influence on the regulations that guide the implementation of federal programs. Thus states exert a large influence over the curriculum of schools, even though local districts retain control over many educational decisions.

For the past forty years, federal education policy in the United States has focused on education for students in situations that put them at risk of failure. While there was a fundamental shift in the underlying philosophy of education policy after 1980, from emphasizing equal opportunity to emphasizing excellence for all, federal education programs have continued to focus on the students at the greatest risk of failure. Both of these foundational beliefs—equalizing educational opportunity to learn and academic preparation for all—exert a substantial influence on government policy in reading.

Although government initiatives influence curriculum, teaching remains the responsibility of teachers. We examine major philosophies embedded in government policy below to provide more background for teachers.

Equal Educational Opportunity

The Elementary and Secondary Education Act (ESEA) of 1965, the first federal legislation to create sustained national education programs, had a substantial focus on equalizing education opportunity. In the 1950s, the federal government had taken a more activist role in education as a consequence of federal court decisions about desegregation. The ESEA funded special education programs and also introduced a new program under Title I that provided supplementary resources to schools serving large percentages of low-income students.

While the early Title I program was initially relatively flexible, it later emphasized pulling children with learning difficulties out of the classroom to provide them supplemental reading instruction (Wong, in press). There was experimentation with the involvement of parents and instructional aides through Title I and some instructional programs were developed (e.g., Ellson, Barber, Engle, & Kampwerth, 1965; Ellson, Harris, & Barber, 1968), but Title I did not promote a specific curriculum. Rather Title I originally provided additional resources for schools serving children from low-income families.

While the percentage of students graduating from high school steadily increased from 1960 through 1980 (National Center for Education Statistics [NCES], 2000), indicating increasing efficacy of programs that promoted equal educational opportunity (St. John, in press), the early federal programs were subjected to frequent criticism. Whether increasing high school graduation rates in the 1970s (NCES, 2000) was attributable to the resources provided by Title I and other federal programs remains subject to debate, but the fact that subsequent policy became more curriculum focused is beyond dispute. Further, the focus on providing educational opportunities for students from low-income families and in other situations that put them at risk of failing educationally remained central to educational policy. However, high school graduation rates have not improved since 1980 (NCES, 2000), indicating equal opportunity has not been the underlying concern of policymakers (St. John, in press).

Academic Preparation for All

The publication of *America at Risk* in 1983 focused public attention on the educational process. During the 1980s and 1990s state and federal education policy emphasized testing and standards. State and local policy increasingly focused on improving pass rates on standardized tests. Many states have implemented high-stakes graduation tests, a pattern that complicated efforts to educate students with special needs (Manset-Williamson & Washburn, in press) and low-income students (Jacob, 2001). The intensive focus on standards and testing corresponds with improved college enrollment by high school graduates since 1980 (NCES, 2000; St. John, in press), but dropout rates worsened.

There were also substantial changes in the programs that served students in at-risk situations during this period. In the 1980s, independent reformers began to experiment with school-wide reform models that engaged the entire school in the reform process (e.g., Hopfenberg, Levin, & Associates, 1993; Slavin, Madden, Karweit, Dolan, & Wasik, 1992). By the early 1990s, the Title I program began to encourage schools with high percentages of low-income students to try out these models as part of the school-wide reform option under Title I. In the early 1990s, the federal government funded a number of new reform initiatives in an attempt to create new models for schools. Then in 1997, the Obie Porter legislation provided funding for more schools to undertake these comprehensive reforms. Many of the schools that adopted these reforms improved the percentage of students who continued on grade level as well as the percentage of children passing standardized reading tests (St. John et al., in press).

The Reading Excellence Act of 1998 provided funding for states to undertake reading reforms that were "research based." States funded through this federal program developed distinctive state programs to promote improvement in early reading and literacy program. However, some states developed programs that focused on early literacy even before the new federal legislation was passed. The National Research Council's report, *Preventing Reading Difficulties in Young Children* (Snow, Burns, & Griffin, 1998), had focused attention on early reading as a national priority. These developments set the stage for the most recent wave of reform.

Focus on Early Reading

The 2001 reauthorization of *ESEA,* the *No Child Left Behind* Act, both expanded the emphasis on early reading and supported comprehensive reform in high-poverty schools. The increased focus on reading in educational policy can be viewed by teachers as an intrusion or an opportunity. Early research on these new initiatives indicates they have potential for improving learning opportunities for children in at-risk situations as well as for all children in schools that engage in these reforms (St. John, Manset, Chung, Simmons, & Musoba, 2001). Increasingly states and the federal government are creating opportunities for elementary schools to apply for grant funding for improvement in early reading and comprehensive reform. The new policy environment creates an opportunity for teachers who are willing to seize it.

■ READING AND LITERACY REFORMS THAT WORK

This *Guide* provides a resource for educators—teachers in Grades 1–5 and school administrators—who are interested in improving early reading programs. It can be used *instrumentally* (as an integrated set of program reviews for schools selecting a reform model), *strategically* (as a process-driven reform approach to aid in the development of distinctive local reform models), and/or *communicatively* (as a basis for building a better understanding of learning processes among teachers in schools).

Criteria for Successful Reading and Literacy Reforms

While there is a broad consensus that early reading is critical to the eventual success children have in school, a wide range of strategies have been proposed for early reading interventions. There are also numbers of competing theories about how students actually learn to read. Our reviews of the research literature have identified five criteria that appeared essential for successful interventions in reading and literacy (St. John, Bardzell, & Associates, 1999). These criteria, or understandings, can help guide the reform process in schools.

Criterion 1: Recognize the Complexity of Early Reading. Reading demands and makes use of a remarkably diverse set of skills, experiences, and awarenesses. In addition to the well-documented importance of phonemic awareness and the ability to sound out unfamiliar words, children must have well-developed vocabularies, strong oral language comprehension, symbolic awareness, an ability to understand/translate between both local/family and standardized dialects, an awareness of different kinds of reading (i.e., genres, purposes, strategies), and an awareness of the social nature of reading.

There is a tension in the literature on early reading that is too often reduced to tension between phonemic awareness and direct instruction versus an emphasis on contexts, literature, language, and learning. In our view, both emphases are crucial. We use the term *reading* to apply to *readiness to read* (ready to understand the alphabetic principle), *decoding* as a phonemic process (*decoding*), and *comprehension*. We use the term *literacy* to refer to a broader construct that includes reading that emphasizes *emergent literacy* (an early understanding of language and texts), *composition* (integrating an emphasis on written language), and *critical literacy* (an ability to read to understand how texts relate to one's own context). While research that focuses on word recognition and reading comprehension consistently shows that the narrower definition is workable (Snow et al., 1998), programs that take the broader approach have success increasing the percentage of children who enter the educational mainstream without experiencing educational failure (Clay, 1991, 1993; Rowe, 1997).

Criterion 2: Use a Comprehensive, Balanced Approach. Given the complexity of reading and the variation in home experiences that children bring to the classroom, sustained attention to all aspects of reading is crucial to reach all students. Although the use of meaningful literature will enhance both motivation and sensitivity to different genres and purposes of written communication, a focus on code will help children internalize the code to gain accurate and automatic access to these meanings.

A focus on phonemic awareness helps students acquire an ability to decode words, but a broader, comprehensive, and balanced approach is needed to help students build understanding of texts and discern meaning from reading. Reading occurs within a broader system of communication. Many young children relate to reading when it integrates with their lives. Young children from families with parents who read aloud to them are more likely to be ready to read when they enter school than are children without such experiences. Consequently, successful preschool interventions emphasize literature and reading to children (e.g., Connors-Tadros, 1996; Levenstein, Levenstein, Shiminski, & Stolzberg, 1998). By extension, school-based programs that also include an emphasis on literature as well as decoding—programs that take a comprehensive approach—are also likely to reach a higher percentage of children in elementary schools. There is little disagreement about the fact that comprehensive programs, such as Success for All, enable students to acquire word recognition and comprehension skills, a point that is supported by the narrower research on phonemic awareness (Snow et al., 1998). The more emphasis teachers choose to place on literacy for all children—leading to reductions in grade-level retention and special education referral—the more important it is to develop interventions that are comprehensive (i.e., that include more than just phonics) and use a balanced approach to integrating decoding and texts.

Criterion 3: Focus on the Underlying Development of Children. Although language, reading, and literacy acquisition are nonlinear, some skills and awarenesses precede others. For example, phonics training will be lost on children who lack symbolic and phonemic awareness. On the other hand, some aspects of reading must be encouraged all along, such as comprehension and the sense of pleasure and accomplishment that comes with reading. All reading programs must be flexible enough to accommodate the nonlinearity of language acquisition while being coherent enough to offer a workable path (or set of paths) for all children to follow.

Childhood development theory has moved from a rigid emphasis on stages to a developmental concept that recognizes the different pathways children follow as they develop awareness of language and learn to read (Vygotsky, 1978). This more flexible, nonlinear view of language acquisition had a substantial influence on Marie Clay (1991, 1993) and the emergence of systematic and comprehensive approaches to reading acquisition and instruction, such as Reading Recovery (e.g., Rowe, 1997). This broader construct of child development helps illuminate the roles of symbolic awareness along with phonemic awareness as elements of reading readiness, of the joy embedded in the process of learning to read. These broader concepts provide a logical basis for the success attributed to programs that use the broader literacy concept. They also illuminate the need to have multiple learning pathways open to children within a school's literacy program.

Criterion 4: Use a Coherent Intervention Strategy. Features of reading programs need to be organized in such a way as to support each other. Examples of coherence include a program that sends classroom books home with children to read with parents. In this way, parent involvement supports classroom activity. Other examples include the use of ongoing professional development to support a theoretically rich program or strategic use of pullout instruction within a typical classroom-wide program to reach children with reading difficulties. Certain features are implemented to support and extend effectiveness of other features.

Our reviews have found that there are many common program features[1] across different reading interventions. Relatively few features of reading and literacy programs are unique to a single program. However, the specific set of features included in each of the reading and literacy program programs we have reviewed is unique. That is, each reading and literacy program combines features in a unique way. In fact, all the reform programs reviewed in this book include an array of features that support and reinforce each other. However, each reform program must integrate into a school's context—the existing features of the school—which may or may not support and reinforce the intended reform process. Indeed, some reforms depend on the preexistence of processes in schools. For example, Four Blocks, one of the classroom-based reform models reviewed in Chapter 5, does not include features related to professional development or parent involvement. Yet in Indiana where this model has been implemented with an emphasis on ongoing professional development, schools with the Four Blocks have shown a consistent pattern of improvement (St. John et al., in press). Thus it is important that educators consider the features of reform models, how well these features support and reinforce each other, and how well the features of the program fit with the processes currently in use in the school.

Criterion 5: Integrate Teacher Inquiry Into the Intervention Process. No matter how soundly an intervention is designed, its effectiveness will vary depending on the teachers and children actually participating in it. It is the school's responsibility to ensure that an implemented intervention is working for all children and to identify those aspects of the program that are not as successful as others.

Some reform models emphasize teacher inquiry; others do not. Yet given the diversity of schools, teachers, and children, there is a need to reflect of how well a program actually works. Teachers will likely need to adapt a model to fit the school. The example of Four Blocks in Indiana, described above, illustrates how adaptation can evolve. By emphasizing ongoing professional development as part of the reform process, the state evolved a workable and successful approach to Four Blocks. However, this capacity to reflect on what types of interventions are appropriate, on how well a chosen reform model is working, and on how to adapt the model to meet local needs is an essential ingredient of reading reform. As a means of encouraging this type of teacher inquiry, we suggest a process-oriented approach to reading and literacy reform.

A Research-Based Approach

This *Guide* was designed to support a research-based approach to the development of early reading and literacy programs in elementary schools. A systematic, theoretically grounded approach was used to review reform models and to develop a research approach that teachers can use to assess their own classroom practices, to compare their classroom practices and philosophies to possible models, and to engage in a reform process. There are three key elements of the research-based approach we recommend: (a) planning collaboratively in schools, (b) studying alternative reform models, and (c) integrating inquiry into reading and literacy reform.

Planning Collaboratively in Schools

The process approach has three phases: assessing current practices, setting a new direction, and designing an intervention strategy. The process can be used by individual teachers who are interested in improving reading instruction in their classrooms, as well as by teams of teachers in schools using collaborative approaches to reform in reading and literacy reform. The phases of the reform process (see Chapter 2) are as follows:

- **Phase I: Assess Current Practices.** A team of teachers will examine the reading-related outcomes of classrooms and the school as a whole, assessing classroom practices and identifying the challenges facing the school. Based on this initial assessment, teachers should have a good understanding of the types of reform that would be most appropriate for their school (e.g., targeted interventions, classroom-based interventions, or more comprehensive reform models).

- **Phase II: Set a New Direction.** The direction-setting process involves teachers in a process of building an understanding of the school's philosophy, as evidenced from teacher surveys; identifying the strengths and limitations of current practices; and identifying possible approaches. Teachers should be involved in this process to ensure their *buy-in* to the reform and to minimize teacher resistance to the reform process.

- **Phase III: Design Interventions.** With this base, it is possible to establish a direction, either selecting a reform that might help them address the challenges facing the school and individual teachers or designing an intervention locally.

Studying Alternative Reform Models

Early in the process of reviewing reading literacy reforms, we realized that there was not a common basis for comparing reforms. Much of the review literature focused on the debates about phonemic awareness and literature-rich approaches (e.g., Snow et al., 1998), but ignored many of the other features of reform models. Thus, it was necessary not only to identify criteria related to programs that work but also to develop a way to compare programs. We developed a framework that categorized the types of features that are included in various reform models (see Chapter 3) and used this framework to compare programs. We identified features related to systemwide processes, professional development, the embedded theory/philosophy, parent/community involvement, instruction, and organization/structure (including curriculum). When we examined the features of various reform models (i.e., the practice they advocate), we found that most features cut across reforms. This framework was then used to

- Provide an assessment instrument that teachers can use to compare their classrooms to the various models, inform their collaboration on the design of a reform model, and assess their progress on reform (see Chapter 2).
- Specify the program features associated with a large number of diverse reforms, providing a comprehensive approach to comparing reform approach (see Chapter 3).
- Compare the features of various reform models, providing reviews teachers can use to make informed choices about reform strategies in their schools (Chapters 4–8).

Integrating Inquiry Into Reading and Literacy Reform

Teaching students to read and comprehend the texts involves more than following any scripted approach to instruction, even scripted approaches that rely on phonemic awareness and use appropriate literature. Teachers should routinely assess how well their students are learning, adjust the materials and methods they use to meet the particular learning needs of students, and work on their own skills in assessment and teaching. Many of the reform models reviewed in this *Guide* include a formative assessment process that teachers can use to support early reading. However, even these systematic methods are not sufficient to ensure that every child will learn to read and that every teacher will reach her or his potential as a teacher. Chapter 9 concludes this *Guide* by providing guidance on using inquiry in the reform process. It focuses on using the inquiry cycle to improve classroom practices and using team approaches to build collaborative processes in schools that are using inquiry to support reform. Thus teachers can use classroom research and other collaborative inquiry processes to engage in reforms that improve the learning environments for all the children in their classrooms.

A RESOURCE GUIDE FOR EDUCATORS ■

This *Guide* provides a framework, reviews, tools, and methods that teachers can use to study their own practices as teachers as well as to engage in collaborative planning with other teachers in their schools, focusing on improving the learning environment for all the children in their schools. While we recognize that school districts and state agencies exert a substantial influence on reform strategies, it is ultimately the responsibility of teachers to work with students. Thus, this *Guide* is written for teachers, to provide them with the resources they need to improve their teaching.

When reform models are chosen by central offices, teachers must decide whether to resist the reform and teach in ways they think are appropriate or to adjust their classroom practices in ways that are consonant with the intent of the reform model. This *Guide* can help teachers to make these choices in an informed way, as well as help central administrators involve teachers in the report process. Not only does it provide teachers with the tools they can use to study and adapt their practices in virtually any type of reform environment, but it also provides guidance. Each chapter concludes with guidance for teachers, recognizing that the choices about reform models may be made in central offices. Therefore, we consider how our research can inform teachers in different types of reform environments. Ideally, a communicative environment can be created in schools that illuminates the complexities of central control of curriculum decisions in contexts in which teachers bear responsibility for improving learning outcomes. We hope this *Guide* can be used to facilitate the emergence of such shared understandings in schools.

Individual schools should have the freedom to choose the reform models and methods they use. Increasingly federal policy is moving in the direction of encouraging schools to choose either research-based models that have proven records or designs based on recent research. By encouraging a *buy-in* period before the reform begins, comprehensive school reform (CSR) and other federal reforms encourage collaborative planning. This text provides reviews of the designs used in various reading and literacy models. We have worked with state agencies (in Indiana, Minnesota, and Michigan) to identify reform models for review and to conduct reviews that help us link the designs of the reading components of the reforms back to the research. Teachers can use the reviews in this *Guide* to assess whether the design concepts used in various reforms would help them address the challenges they face. Further, a framework and process approach should enable teams of teachers to assess their practices, make informed choices about reform models, and evaluate their progress with the model compared to the design (and in some cases to research on schools that have used the model). Thus, this *Guide* provides a *resource* that teachers can use to make informed of strategic choices about reform strategies for the reading programs in their schools.

While most types of reform models for reading and literacy are reviewed here, the specific reforms examined are limited. The reforms presented in the *Guide* evolved through collaborations with state agencies. In Indiana, we developed two reform guides that reviewed the reading programs that were of interest to the Indiana Department of Education. In Minnesota, we worked with the state education agency and the North Central Regional Educational Laboratory to identify a set of reforms for review. Then, as part of our evaluation studies of CSR in Michigan we conducted further examination of reforms being used by Michigan schools so that we had common rubrics for research and evaluation. However, while this *Guide* reports on many of the reading and literacy reforms being used by these states, the set of reforms reviewed is far from exhaustive. Therefore, we are careful in the text to discuss contexts in which different types of reform strategies should be used as well as to suggest methods teachers can use to expand the range of models they consider. We treat these reviews as illustrative examples of reform models within generic approaches to reading and literacy reform.

Most of the reviews (in Chapters 4, 5, 7, and 8) examine program features of the interventions models, but discuss the research as part of the concluding section, Guidance for Educators. In the review of teacher-inquiry models (Chapter 6), the reviewers discuss the strengths and limitations of the models proposed. This additional step was used because of the emphasis these models placed on teacher research.

Ideally schools should be conceived of as learning communities of professionals who work together to create learning environments that enable students to read, comprehend, and solve problems of all types; equally important, they should support the personal and professional development of teachers. Learning communities of teachers can learn from various reform models. However, they can also learn from classroom-based reading reforms. By presenting our research results from the studies we have conducted for the states we have worked with, we add to the research base that schools can use to evolve coherent reform strategies. In particular, we summarize the results factor analyses that illustrate how different patterns of practice influence student outcomes. In fact, the *Guide* has been structured to help teachers build an understanding of the ways their practices relate to those in schools that have tried various reform models.

Thus this *Guide* is intended as a *resource* for teachers, administrators, and parents who are interested in collaborating within their school communities on strategies for improving reading and literacy instruction. It integrates a systematic review of reform models, a process-approach to change for elementary schools, and the findings from research on various reform models. The combination of information provides an integrated set of resources that teachers can use to refine the approaches they use in their early reading and literacy programs.

NOTE

1. Throughout this book we use the term *program features* to refer to the component parts of reading programs. The framework used to identify program features, along with the list of definitions of features, is presented in Chapter 2.

2

Planning for Reading and Literacy Reform

Schools and districts can choose from among a wide range of alternative approaches to early reading and literacy intervention. The reviews in this volume illustrate the range of choices, but this set of reforms does not exhaust all possible reform models. Educators who are considering interventions need to recognize that there are far more options available to them than we have reviewed. Schools can examine reforms as a step toward selecting a reform model or as a basis for developing a distinctive local reform. This chapter provides guidance for schools considering intervention options.

The processes of assessing the early literacy challenge, defining a new direction or vision, and selecting an intervention method are decision processes. They should involve teachers and administrators, and they should include input from parents. Ideally a group of teachers and parents should work together, as a team, to assess the early literacy challenge they face.

■ PHASE I: ASSESS CURRENT PRACTICE

Elementary schools are competing in an environment that emphasizes the educational "bottom line": how well the school compares to other similar schools. Most states use some type of standardized testing to compare schools. Many states have high-stakes testing for children, requiring them to pass standardized tests for promotion or graduation. Some states provide "report cards" to parents that compare similar schools. And most states have a policy that encourages or requires schools to change their curricula if they have poor educational outcomes. In this context, it is important to start with consideration of educational outcomes. However, this is only a start. It is also important to consider current educational practices—the features of the current early reading and literacy program—and challenges facing early primary teachers as they think about improving their early literacy programs. Therefore, we suggest three steps in assessing a school's early literacy program: (a) assess current educational outcomes, (b) assess the features of the existing program, and (c) compare these to state standards.

Step 1: Assess Current Educational Outcomes

When thinking about whether to undertake an intervention in early reading and literacy, a study team needs to start with an analysis of two types of outcomes: measures of attainment/opportunity (retention and special education identification) and measures of early reading achievement (first through fifth grades).

Opportunity to Achieve

When schools have large percentages of students who are referred to special education or who are retained in Grades K–5, the numbers could be an indicator of problems with the fit between the schools' literacy programs and the learning needs of children in the schools. However, since the percentages of students who are retained in schools is influenced by the extent of poverty (or percentage of children on free lunch) and the types of locale (with urban and rural schools usually facing the largest challenge), it is important that educators consider "similar" schools when assessing outcomes. The schools used for comparison should have similar rates of poverty and be in similar locale types within the same state. Many states have Web pages that provide teachers with comparative information on similar schools. Other states produce "report cards" for schools that provide peer comparisons. When beginning an assessment of the need for early reading intervention, the study team should ask:

- What percentage of students in Grades K–5 was identified as having learning disabilities? (Consider the past three years at a minimum.)
- How does this percentage compare to similar schools in the state? (Consider schools with similar poverty rates and in similar locale types.)
- What percentage of students in Grades K–5 was retained in grade level?
- How does this percentage compare to similar schools?

When the answers to these questions are compiled, the school will have an indication of the early reading and literacy challenge it faces. If both these indicators are below the average for similar schools, then the school has a strong program and a major restructuring may not be needed. There may be reason, however, to consider making refinements to the current program. If the school is close to the average for similar schools on these indicators, then there is room for intervention. These schools may have a sound targeted[1] program, but may also want to consider implementing interventions to help children read on grade level at the end of third grade. Finally, schools that have high percentages of students who are retained or who are referred to special education may want to consider a new classroom-wide approach to early literacy improvement or school-wide restructuring methodology.

Reading Achievement

Standardized tests provide another indicator of early reading achievement. However, the study team should consider how well low-achieving students are doing compared to low-achieving students at similar schools, as well as compared to the state average. Schools contemplating an intervention in early reading should consider the following questions:

- What is the school's pass rate on the state's test of early reading (i.e., state-mandated tests)?
- How does the pass rate compare to similar schools (by locale type and level of poverty)?

Test scores provide an indication of how well students are learning to read; the opportunity indicators (i.e., retention and special education referral) provide evidence of whether students are learning to read. Thus it is possible for a school to have high scores and high failure. If this is the case, some type of change may be needed.

If scores are high and both referral and retention are low compared to similar schools, the early literacy program is probably working well. There may be reason to continue with the assessment in order to reflect on where the school is now and how it can further improve. However, the goal for these schools is excellence! Teachers still may want to consider inquiry-based approaches that add to their professional development and to the learning opportunities (i.e., breadth and depth of student experience).

Finally, if schools have low scores as well as high special education identification and within-grade retention compared to similar schools, they face fundamental challenges. They should consider more substantial restructuring methods. Classroom-wide methods may be appropriate if the problem is reading and not math. If both indicators are problematic, the school may decide to seriously consider a comprehensive school reform model.

Step 2: Assess the Features of the Existing Program

Consideration of educational outcomes may provide visibility into the extent of the literacy challenge facing an elementary school, but it offers little insight into the specific nature of the problem. To explore the reasons for the challenge, the study team needs to understand the features of the current early reading and literacy program. We have attached a survey instrument that can be used to assess current practice (appended to this chapter). We suggest the following steps:

- All teachers and specialists who teach reading to students in Grades 1–5 should complete the survey.
- Tabulate the results: How did the teachers at each grade level respond?

- Analyze results: What were the similarities and differences in responses to the questions within grade levels and/or across grade levels?

The survey results provide a data resource that can be used in planning, and we provide further guidance for working with those results in the remainder of this *Guide*. However, as part of the initial analysis, it is important to consider these points:

- Are most early primary teachers using similar approaches in their reading and literacy instruction?
- Is a coherent approach evident across grade levels in the early reading and literacy program?
- Is the philosophy of teachers reflected in the classrooms?
- Is the approach balanced?
- Does it reflect strong systematic methods and a literature-rich approach?

Positive answers to these questions suggest cohesiveness in the early reading and literacy program. If these schools have problems with educational outcomes, then they may want to change the entire system—to try classroom-wide or school-wide methods. However, if there is great variation in the survey responses, there is reason to dig deeper, to consider how outcomes in classrooms are related to the methods used in classrooms. It is important for those who are engaged in the process to use an open and respectful process. Chapter 3 provides detailed definitions of the program features included in the survey, along with others included in various reform models.

Step 3: Compare Current Practice to State Standards

Once a profile of current practice has been compiled, consider how well current practices compare to state standards. A generic framework for relating reform features to generic reading standards was presented in Chapter 3. Consider the following questions:

- Which standards are currently being addressed (i.e., are a substantial portion of practices related to the standard frequently used)?
- Which standards are not adequately addressed? (If many of the features related to the standard are being used, consider whether the standard is being addressed by the practices that are being used.)

If there are gaps between classroom practices and the types of practices that relate to particular standards, then a challenge is to fill the gap. Teachers should consider alternative models that might help them address state standards.

Step 4: Identify Critical Challenges

Based on a review of these two data sources, it is possible to gain insight into the nature and extent of the literacy challenges facing an elementary school. This type of assessment provides information on the nature of the challenge facing the school. At this stage the study team should consider these questions:

- Are small refinements or large-scale changes needed?
- Who should review the assessment results?
- Who should be involved in the next phase of planning?

This first stage of assessment can provide an indication of the nature of the problem, but it offers no solutions. That is the work of Phase II.

■ PHASE II: SET A NEW DIRECTION

Planning for early reading and literacy intervention is appropriately viewed as a process that can build a consensus about the direction a school might take. One of the biggest challenges schools face in deciding on an intervention strategy is to choose a strategy that fits the school and has the support of teachers in the school. Therefore, the process of decision making and discussion needs to be open and to involve teachers in reflecting on their classrooms as well as on the changes in their classrooms likely to result from interventions. If this process is approached in a way that encourages communication about concerns facing teachers, parents, and children, then it is possible to build consensus on taking a new path in the early reading and literacy program. A suggested strategy is outlined below.

Step 1: Build an Understanding of the School's Philosophy

It is important that the school community consider the implemented philosophy of early reading and literacy. To get started, we suggest that the planning group reconsider the responses to the questions in Part II of the Early Literacy Intervention Classroom Survey. Each of these questions is presented as a continuum. They should reflect on the extent to which their classrooms

- Are teacher directed or student directed.
- Are child centered/developmental or prescribed/systematic.
- Are code/phoneme or meaning/comprehension oriented.
- Teach code/phonemes outside or inside context.

The responses to these questions will help to show the extent to which the school's early reading and literacy program is situated in a phonics tradition, a literature-rich tradition, or a balanced approach. Responses that are closer to teacher directed, prescribed/systematic, code/phoneme oriented, and teaching code/phonemes outside of context are more oriented toward the phonics tradition. The closer responses are to being student directed, child centered, meaning/comprehension oriented, and to teaching code/phonemes within context, the closer they are to the whole language tradition. Responses that are in the middle indicate balance. Consider these questions:

- Is a consistent philosophy used within grades? Across Grades K–5?
- Is the tendency toward phonics, literature-rich instruction, or a balance?
- Is a diversity of philosophies in use?

Understanding the school's philosophy provides a starting point for its planning process. The answers to these questions provide a critical source of information for making decisions about the intervention strategies and will also indicate whether there is a consensus in the school. If a school has respectable educational outcomes in relation to similar schools and a consistent philosophy, there may be no reason to change.

Current thinking—and a growing body of research—favors using a balanced approach. If a school relies more strongly on one philosophy (e.g., whole language or phonics) than the other and has poor educational outcomes, there may be a need to have an open discussion about the approach being used. In these cases it may be appropriate to consider moving toward a balanced approach. The advantage of this transition might be that it helps the school build a consensus. However, these questions relate to very basic values and beliefs held by educators and it is not desirable to try to force uniformity.

If the teachers in a school have diverse philosophies and students rate high on educational outcomes, school leaders are probably doing a good job assigning students to teachers whose philosophies match the students' learning styles. Certainly if a school finds itself in this situation, then the early primary teachers might want to share their insights about these issues.

Step 2: Identify Strengths and Weaknesses

The second step in the planning process should focus on strengths and weaknesses of the current approach. This involves getting into more depth about the program features related to structural/organizational (Survey Part I.A) and classroom instruction (Survey Part I.B). First review the results of the survey:

- What are the frequently and infrequently used structural/organizational features?
- What are the frequently and infrequently used instructional features?
- What patterns of frequently versus infrequently used features emerge? That is, do certain types of features cluster into groups of use/disuse?
- How well are the structural/organizational and instructional features aligned with philosophies used in the classrooms? (Individual teachers may want to reflect on this question for their own classrooms.)

Reflection on these questions provides an opportunity for teachers to consider their own values and practices in relation to each other. Ideally, the option of choosing an approach to improve the early literacy program should provide a chance for teachers to think about the strengths and weaknesses in their own classrooms. They may also want to consider the types of parent involvement that might be needed. The following questions can be helpful:

- When are current classroom practices (structural/organizational and instructional) closely aligned with the implemented philosophy?
- When are the classroom practices incongruent with the implemented philosophy?
- Are some classroom practices used too frequently or infrequently?
- How are classroom practices related to the educational outcomes of students in the classroom?
- Are there other practices that might merit more widespread use? Are there practices that you would like to learn more about?
- How can families be more involved in the early reading and literacy program?

Once teachers have had a chance to reflect individually on these questions, they should have a conversation. Share reflections! Consider what the strengths and weaknesses of the program might be. Such a conversation will provide a basis of information about the early reading and literacy program that can inform choices about the specific types of interventions that merit consideration in the school.

Step 3: Identify Possible Approaches

With this background, it is possible to identify a few interventions that merit more serious consideration. At this stage, teachers should reexamine the summary reviews of the interventions described earlier, other reading sources pertinent to the interventions that seem to be of interest, and additional related interventions. Consider how other schools have benefited from funding through state reading grants, comprehensive school reform, and other state and federal grant programs. The National Clearinghouse for Comprehensive School Reform (www.goodschools.gwu.edu) can provide access to recent evaluation studies. As part of this review, a planning team may want to consider these:

- Which interventions include the types of program features that the teachers would like to learn more about and try out?
- Which interventions are more consistent with the philosophies that predominate in the school (or that are desired, if there is agreement that change is needed)?

These questions should be openly discussed. Teachers should be encouraged to read more extensively about different methods when they have questions and to share their reflections on their reading. The chapters in this *Guide* review many reform models and suggest additional reading related to each reform model. The key issue is to choose a reform approach that makes sense to the school. It is possible that a single approach will make sense. It is also possible that none of the available methods will make sense for the school, in which case teachers may decide to develop their own approach.

PHASE III: DESIGN AN INTERVENTION ■

If there is a consensus around a method, it makes sense to proceed with the idea. This involves finding out where to get the professional development and other resources to try out the new method. However, if the school seeks to develop its own approach, it is time to start a more in-depth planning process. Ideally a planning team would be formed to develop an approach for the school.

Based on our research reviews, we have compiled a set of criteria to guide the design of site-based interventions for early reading and literacy programs (see Chapter 1). A step-by-step process for designing a local, research-based program using these criteria is outlined next.

Step 1: Recognize the Complexity of Early Reading

Using the assessment of educational outcomes, reconsider how well your school is doing on early reading and literacy:

- How well prepared are new students for learning to read? Do they enter school with emergent literacy skills? How well does the school help students develop these skills?
- How well does the school prepare children to decode texts?
- How well does the school prepare children to comprehend texts?
- How well does the school prepare children to compose texts in their early writing experiences?

The assessment of educational outcomes provides a baseline indicator of how well the school is doing on each of these outcomes. Teachers and administrators can use the assessment process to think through the current program and to identify the outcomes that need to be improved. These outcomes should be the target of the intervention design.

Step 2: Use a Comprehensive, Balanced Approach

Schools need a balanced approach to reading that combines (a) systematic and formative approaches to early reading instruction with (b) a literature-rich environment that provides texts that are meaningful to children. The assessment of classroom practices (the survey and discussion process outlined above) provides a baseline of information about the school's early reading and literacy program. Using these results, consider the following:

- Which philosophical approach to balancing decoding and literature-rich instruction should be used in the school?
- Which key features of the systematic and literature-rich aspects of the desired balanced approach are not being used frequently enough to bring balance to the classroom? Developing these features represents a challenge!

- Which key features of the systematic and literature-rich approach are currently being used? These features are strengths on which to build!
- What are the key features of a balanced approach that are needed in the school? In each grade level?

Thinking through these questions will provide insight into the existing strengths of the current early reading and literacy program as well as how the program might be strengthened. This list can be used as an input to the design of an intervention strategy.

Step 3: Focus on Underlying Development of Children

Children learn in different ways, but there is an underlying process of development that seems to guide the ways skills develop. However, given the diversity of ways that children learn, teaching early reading is not always as simple as laying out a prescriptive set of tests and processes. Before beginning to design an early intervention strategy, planners should think through the issues that seem to surface each year. Teachers who are involved in early reading and literacy instruction should consider these questions:

- What problems do they encounter each year at the start of the school year?
- What kinds of special learning problems do they frequently encounter during the school year? Are there some parts of the current curriculum that children have difficulty grasping?
- Do they have workable classroom strategies for dealing with differential rates of learning? Do children have ample opportunities to cooperate in the learning process and to learn from sharing with peers?
- Does the sequence of the curriculum work well for most children? When some children have problems learning or seem bored because they are ahead, are there alternative exercises and activities available to address individual learning needs?

Sharing reflections on these questions, along with related questions that surface during the process of discussing the curriculum, should provide insight into how well the flow of the curriculum matches the needs of children in the school. Further collective reflection on the following questions can lead to a set of design parameters:

- Are problems shared by teachers across the school, or do different teachers experience different problems each year?
- Are problems routinely encountered as children move across grade levels, or are there no clear patterns across the early primary grades?
- Are the biggest problems with the curriculum? Do most teachers feel as though enhancement and enrichment are more important concerns?

After teachers reflect together on these questions, they will have a better idea about whether they need to make fundamental, structural changes in the curriculum, or whether more teacher inquiry and reflection is the primary area of need. If, after reflecting on these questions, teachers agree there are shared, school-wide problems, then it makes sense to think about school-wide and classroom-wide intervention strategies. However, if the consensus is that the basic structure is workable but that each teacher needs to address specific issues, then an inquiry-based approach may be needed (within classrooms, in the school as a whole, or both, depending on the overall approach used).

Step 4: Use a Coherent Intervention Strategy

It is increasingly evident that the various parts of a school's early reading and literacy program must work well together. If one approach is used in a pull-out program and another approach is used in the regular classroom, for example, children will find it difficult to relate their learning experience in the one-on-one process to the regular process. While inclusion in special education and school-wide Title I have basic design approaches to overcome this difficulty, even these systematic approaches do not always work well for all children and all teachers. Therefore, as part of their collaborative-design process, teachers should reflect on questions about the cohesiveness of their approach to reading:

- How well do the curriculum and learning activities in pullout and regular classrooms complement and reinforce each other?
- How well do the methods used across the early primary grade levels enhance and reinforce each other?
- How well does the early primary reading and literacy program complement and enhance the learning environments of the upper-primary grades? Do students have the foundations in reading and literacy that they need to read on grade level by the start of grade 4? Does the upper-primary curriculum build on the skills of the lower grades or emphasize remedial processes that are redundant?
- Are there professional development opportunities for teachers that help them to identify their own professional challenges and to design strategies to address these challenges?

Reflecting on these and related questions provides a more concrete basis for a design. With this type of information, coupled with the insights from the earlier steps in this design process, teachers and site administrators can reflect on an overall design strategy: Which program features need to be more heavily emphasized in the early primary grades?

- Which approaches to these new programs will build on the current strengths of the school's early reading and literacy program?
- What do individual teachers need to learn to implement these approaches in the schools?
- What outside resources are needed? How can parents and the local community help?

- What types of professional development opportunities will be needed by teachers to make the plan work?

Chapter 3 provides a resource for teams of teachers who are involved in the planning process. It provides definitions of a large number of program features and identifies reform models that use these features.

Step 5: Integrate Inquiry Into the Intervention

One of the ways to help locally designed interventions work better is to integrate inquiry into the design. This should include focus on the intended outcomes of the intervention and the ways that the intervention is supposed to help children learn better. In addition, classroom inquiry can also enhance the ways individual teachers actually improve their educational practice. Therefore, reading and early literacy interventions need both evaluation of the program and inquiry by teachers in classrooms.

Schools that design their own intervention strategies will need well-defined action plans for implementation, along with well-defined evaluation plans. The implementation plans should include a focus on the professional development of teachers. This may require building in support from teacher educators at a local university. However, if the teams approach the intervention as an inquiry process, they will be better able to maintain a focus on professional development of teachers as well as on the educational outcomes of students.

■ GUIDANCE FOR EDUCATORS

The new wave of research-based reforms in early reading and literacy creates opportunities for educators to learn from proven methods when they plan for and develop site-based interventions. However, making good choices about intervention strategies is not a simple process. It requires assessing the educational needs, assessing the strengths and limitations of the school's early reading and literacy program, and developing an approach that addresses the most critical challenges.

This *Guide* provides a framework that can guide and inform school decisions about early reading and literacy interventions. The reviews of research-based programs offer resources to help choose a program, a sound design, and perhaps a solid confirmatory research base. Alternatively, the review can be used as an information base for developing a local intervention strategy.

NOTE

1. We define targeted interventions as reform models that focus only on children who are having trouble learning to read (see Chapter 4).

Early Reading and Literacy Classroom Survey

The position(s) of the person(s) completing this survey is (are):

Principal ○   Assistant Principal ○   Teacher ○
Reading Specialist ○   Other (please state) ○ _____

Grade Level:
| | | | | |
Pre-K ○   1st ○   3rd ○   5th ○   N/A ○
K ○   2nd ○   4th ○   6th ○

PART I.

Instructions: Please fill in the appropriate bubbles to indicate the extent to which the following features were used as part of the early literacy program in your school during the following years.

A. Structural/Organizational Features

Program Feature	Previous Year Extent of Use					Current Year Extent of Use					Description of Feature
	Never	Rarely	Occasionally	Often	Every day	Never	Rarely	Occasionally	Often	Every day	
1. Ability Grouping	○	○	○	○	○	○	○	○	○	○	Students assigned to groups based on ability.
2. Basal Readers	○	○	○	○	○	○	○	○	○	○	Series of graded readers.
3. Child-initiated Learning Centers	○	○	○	○	○	○	○	○	○	○	Materials kept in central area, allowing children to choose materials that interest them.
4. Independent Reading	○	○	○	○	○	○	○	○	○	○	Students read silently from materials they choose.
5. One-on-one Tutorial	○	○	○	○	○	○	○	○	○	○	Staff provides one-to-one instruction to student.
6. "Pullout" Instruction	○	○	○	○	○	○	○	○	○	○	Students leave their regular classroom for specialized instruction.
7. Small Groups, Teacher Directed	○	○	○	○	○	○	○	○	○	○	Students work in small groups led by teacher or other adult.
8. Systematic, Formative Evaluation	○	○	○	○	○	○	○	○	○	○	Students are tested frequently to monitor reading gains.
9. Ongoing Written Observations	○	○	○	○	○	○	○	○	○	○	Teachers keep records of and track progress on students' activities, books read, etc., on an individual basis
10. Trade Books	○	○	○	○	○	○	○	○	○	○	Uses literature-based books as the basis for reading instruction.

B. Classroom Instruction

Program Feature	Previous Year Extent of Use					Current Year Extent of Use					Description of Feature
	Never	Rarely	Occasionally	Often	Every day	Never	Rarely	Occasionally	Often	Every day	
1. Big Books	○	○	○	○	○	○	○	○	○	○	Oversized books students read together in class.
2. Cooperative Learning	○	○	○	○	○	○	○	○	○	○	Mixed ability groups working on a task, where student success is interdependent.
3. Creative Writing and/or Essays	○	○	○	○	○	○	○	○	○	○	Students write stories on their own or with some guidance.
4. Drama	○	○	○	○	○	○	○	○	○	○	Students stage a written selection, interacting with the text in the process.
5. Emergent Spelling	○	○	○	○	○	○	○	○	○	○	Students encouraged to write before mastering spelling rules.
6. Paired Reading	○	○	○	○	○	○	○	○	○	○	Pairs read to each other and are encouraged to help each other.
7. Phonics Assessment	○	○	○	○	○	○	○	○	○	○	Teachers regularly observe and record students' progress on exhibiting specified phonics skills.
8. Phonemic Awareness	○	○	○	○	○	○	○	○	○	○	Activities introduce students to and provide practice in oral, aural, and visual discrimination of letters and sounds.
9. Pattern Discrimination	○	○	○	○	○	○	○	○	○	○	Instructional activities engage students in identifying letter patterns and discerning words that match specified patterns.
10. Multi-Sensory Phonics Activities	○	○	○	○	○	○	○	○	○	○	Interactive approaches emphasize multiple senses (e.g. tactile, kinesthetic) to help students learn, recognize, and use phonics concepts.
11. Reading Aloud	○	○	○	○	○	○	○	○	○	○	Teachers read stories and other texts aloud to their students.
12. Reading Drills	○	○	○	○	○	○	○	○	○	○	Directly instructing students on reading sub-skills, using directly-targeted, repetitive, and exercises.
13. Worksheets/ Workbooks	○	○	○	○	○	○	○	○	○	○	Students fill out worksheets as part of the reading program.
14. School Library	○	○	○	○	○	○	○	○	○	○	Students use the school library for independent reading.

C. Parent Involvement

Program Feature	Previous Year Extent of Use					Current Year Extent of Use					Description of Feature
	Never	Rarely	Occasionally	Often	Every day	Never	Rarely	Occasionally	Often	Every day	
1. Book Distribution	○	○	○	○	○	○	○	○	○	○	Distribute books to households that may have limited reading materials.
2. Family Literacy	○	○	○	○	○	○	○	○	○	○	Literacy instruction provided to parents.
3. Paired Reading	○	○	○	○	○	○	○	○	○	○	Parents help children with reading.
4. Parent Conferences	○	○	○	○	○	○	○	○	○	○	Teachers meet with parents to discuss student progress.
5. Parent Volunteers	○	○	○	○	○	○	○	○	○	○	Parents volunteer their time to help directly in instruction.

D. Professional Development

Instructions: Please fill in the appropriate bubbles to indicate whether the following features were used as part of the early literacy program in your classroom during the following years.

Program Feature	Previous Year	Current Year	Description of Feature
1. Certified Training	○	○	Instructors in reading program are *required* to have reading specialist certification or other official affiliation.
2. Certified Specialist	○	○	A certified specialist comes to the school to assist with training of teachers and other participants.
3. Inservice Workshops	○	○	Teacher-attended workshop at the school provided by a topical expert.
4. Networking	○	○	Teachers meet with teachers from other schools who are involved in similar literacy approaches.
5. Opportunity for Collaboration	○	○	Teachers have release time for meetings, peer observations, etc.

Part II. Implemented Philosophy

Please indicate on the following scale (see example) the beliefs that <u>best</u> reflect your classroom's philosophy toward early literacy instruction for each year, K–3.

Example: The following would indicate a slightly higher emphasis on teacher directed instruction, compared to student directed instruction.

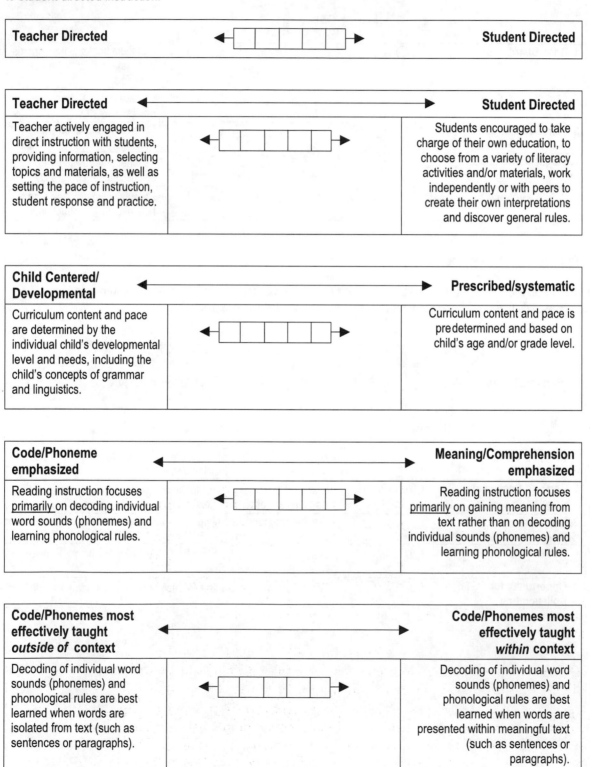

Teacher Directed		**Student Directed**

Teacher Directed		**Student Directed**
Teacher actively engaged in direct instruction with students, providing information, selecting topics and materials, as well as setting the pace of instruction, student response and practice.		Students encouraged to take charge of their own education, to choose from a variety of literacy activities and/or materials, work independently or with peers to create their own interpretations and discover general rules.

Child Centered/ Developmental		**Prescribed/systematic**
Curriculum content and pace are determined by the individual child's developmental level and needs, including the child's concepts of grammar and linguistics.		Curriculum content and pace is predetermined and based on child's age and/or grade level.

Code/Phoneme emphasized		**Meaning/Comprehension emphasized**
Reading instruction focuses <u>primarily</u> on decoding individual word sounds (phonemes) and learning phonological rules.		Reading instruction focuses <u>primarily</u> on gaining meaning from text rather than on decoding individual sounds (phonemes) and learning phonological rules.

Code/Phonemes most effectively taught *outside of* context		**Code/Phonemes most effectively taught *within* context**
Decoding of individual word sounds (phonemes) and phonological rules are best learned when words are isolated from text (such as sentences or paragraphs).		Decoding of individual word sounds (phonemes) and phonological rules are best learned when words are presented within meaningful text (such as sentences or paragraphs).

3

Comparing Reading and Literacy Reforms

Given the great diversity of intervention methods for early reading instruction, a framework is needed for reviewing and comparing different models. In a series of reviews and evaluation studies, we have collaborated on the development of a comprehensive framework for examining the features of specific intervention models. This chapter presents the framework used, defines the features associated with different reform models, discusses the outcomes of reading reforms and how they link to common reading standards, and provides guidance for educators who are interested in reviewing reform models.

FRAMEWORK ■

The reviews of the reform models included in this *Guide* use a common framework for comparison and common definitions of program features. This approach allows for a fair comparison of the features of various reform models as well as for consideration of the ways the reform features link to reading outcomes (and learning standards). The comprehensive framework (Figure 3.1) identifies six major components; the framework for reading reforms includes five of these.

The components are listed here:

- *School-wide Features*: The organizational and administrative processes that are used to coordinate the reform with other parts of the school program and governance. (Included for comprehensive reforms, but not always included in reading interventions.)
- *Professional Development Features*: The processes that are used to enable teachers to learn about the reform method.

Figure 3.1 Framework for Comparing Early Reading and Literacy Interventions

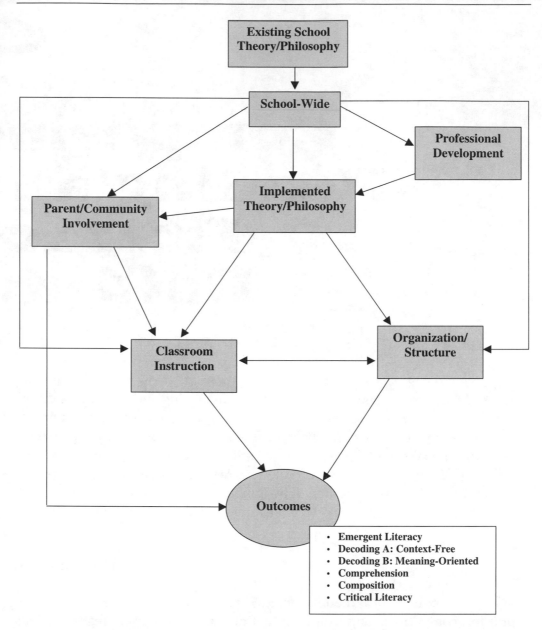

- *Implemented Philosophy*: The values and beliefs about reading skill acquisition that underlie the model's design.
- *Classroom Instruction Features*: The teaching and learning methods that are emphasized in the model implementation process.
- *Organizational/Structural Features*: Curriculum, classroom organization, and other structural features of reforms that provide cohesion in the intervention process.
- *Parent Involvement*: Strategies for involving parents in reading acquisitions that are integral to and provide a system of support for classroom instruction in reading.

Compared to reading reforms, comprehensive reforms place more emphasis on school-wide processes that can have an indirect influence on early reading. These reforms make comprehensive changes in school cultures. Otherwise the types of features related to classroom practices included in both types of reforms are similar, especially features related to early reading instruction. In the models reviewed in this *Guide*, program features are linked together to provide comprehensive strategies for improving acquisition of reading skills by young children (as illustrated in Figure 3.1). The reviews of each model use this framework. Specific program features (e.g., *Pullout Programs* or *Cooperative Learning*) and targeted literacy outcomes are indicated by the use of italicized text. Each program feature is defined in this chapter.

In addition, based on an extensive review of the research on reading acquisition (St. John et al., 1998), the framework identifies six literacy-related outcomes:

- *Emergent Literacy*: Reading readiness and an appreciation of literature that creates an enthusiasm for reading.
- *Decoding A*: Context-free decoding focusing on letter-sound relationships independent of literature.
- *Decoding B*: Meaning-oriented decoding focusing on letter-sound relationships in the context of literature.
- *Comprehension*: The understanding of texts, based on discerning the meaning of written words in context.
- *Composition*: The ability to write stories that communicate ideas, experiences, and themes.
- *Critical Literacy*: The ability to read and analyze texts across the curriculum, as well as to think about the meaning in relation to one's own experience.

Much of the current debate about strategies for early reading focuses on the relative emphasis placed on *decoding A and B* within reading interventions. The National Research Council (Snow et al., 1998) emphasizes context-free rather than meaning-oriented approaches to early reading acquisition, based on laboratory and experimental studies that compared both approaches. However, many of the comprehensive reforms that emphasize phonics, such as Success for All and Four Blocks, place less emphasis on phonics and related approaches than do schools that have not implemented these reforms. In this context, it is important to learn the reforms that have already been implemented. If reforms enable more students to learn to read on grade level, then it is reasonable to expect that funded schools will have improved outcomes, including the following:

- Reductions in special education referral
- Reductions in retention in grade level
- Increases in the percentages of students passing standardized reading tests

The research to date on the Early Intervention Program (formerly referred to as the Early Literacy Intervention Grant Program) indicates that the funded projects have improved these outcomes in Indiana schools and Michigan schools, the two states we have worked with in related evaluation studies. Results of research on specific models are summarized in the chapters that follow.

■ REFORM PROGRAM FEATURES[1]

Each of the reading and comprehensive models reviewed in this *Guide* is distinct, but the models have many common features. To help create a uniform language about reading reforms, this section provides common definitions for the features included in the various reform models examined in this *Guide*.

School-wide Features

Backmapping

Definition: Backmapping is a curriculum development process that begins with a set of specific learning standards and works "backward" to determine what students need to know and be able to do to meet those standards, from which both curriculum and instruction, along with embedded assessments, are designed.

Example: Modern Red Schoolhouse

Buy-In

Definition: Buy-in is a group decision that requires the majority of the personnel in the school to adopt the reform model in question.

Examples: Accelerated Schools, America's Choice, Modern Red Schoolhouse, Success for All

Community Partnership

Definition: The model builds a partnership with local organizations to help schools address students' needs. These features often work to link school achievement to the community.

Examples: America's Choice (High Schools), Modern Red Schoolhouse, School Development Program

Formative Program Evaluation

Definition: This is a periodic evaluation of both program implementation and resultant student outcomes for the explicit purpose of furthering the development of the reform and the school.

Examples: Accelerated Schools, America's Choice, ATLAS, Early Intervention in Reading, First Steps, Lightspan, Modern Red Schoolhouse, School Development Program

Inquiry

Definition: This is a specific process used by groups within the school (i.e., teachers, administrators, possibly parents, and students) to conduct action research in the school and to make recommendations to the school for reform actions to be adopted and implemented. The inquiry groups act as vehicles for directing the reform in the school.

Examples: Accelerated Schools, Reader's and Writer's Workshops, Teacher Inquiry

Instructional Guidance

Definition: This feature provides a common language and understanding among educators in the school about the school's instructional goals, methods, and practices; it is used by the reform model as part of the reform process at the school. The instructional guidance system serves as a directional compass to educators for making decisions about instruction at both the school-wide level and the classroom instruction level.

Examples: Accelerated Schools, America's Choice, ATLAS, First Steps, Modern Red Schoolhouse, School Development Program

Learning Contracts/School

Definition: The school enters a "contract" with students and parents in which each party makes a commitment to take specific action related to the students' education. This is related to Learning Contracts/Parent and Learning Contracts/Student and defines the school's responsibilities in the Contract.

Example: Modern Red Schoolhouse

Looping

Definition: Students stay with the same teacher and student peers for two or more years.

Examples: America's Choice, Modern Red Schoolhouse

Parent/Community Group

Definition: This is a formal group that focuses on parental and/or community involvement in the school; the group often includes school personnel, representative parents, and members of the community.

Examples: ATLAS, School Development Program, Success for All

Reform Team

Definition: This formal group provides leadership in the planning and implementation of the reform model. The group often consists of the principal, on-site facilitator, and representatives of teachers and parents.

Examples: Accelerated Schools, America's Choice, Lightspan, Modern Red Schoolhouse, School Development Program, Success for All

School-Within-a-School

Definition: This middle and high school feature is geared toward breaking down the size and anonymity of the school. Students are divided into smaller groups, often called "families," "academies," or "houses," with typically 120–250 students. Students take core classes together and share the same teachers.

Example: America's Choice

Site-Based Management (SBM)

Definition: The reform model requires implementation of site-based management, a decentralized decision-making structure with less hierarchical leadership.

Examples: Accelerated Schools, ATLAS, Modern Red Schoolhouse, School Development Program

Specialized Courses of Study

Definition: Students choose a course of study based on their interests or career aspirations.

Example: America's Choice

Study Groups/School

Definition: This model is similar to Study Groups/Teachers but includes members of the broader school community (such as parents, noncertified staff, and/or students) in the research about and action planning on reform issues.

Examples: Accelerated Schools, School Development Program

Study Groups/Teachers

Definition: Groups or teams of teachers formed around specific issues conduct research and take actions as specified by the reform model; these groups and their work are integral to the reform process.

Examples: America's Choice, ATLAS, Modern Red Schoolhouse, Teacher Inquiry

Systematic Learning—School-Wide

Definition: The program uses a comprehensive and coordinated structure or set of structures that may allow for some individual flexibility but which ultimately unify and organize the instruction. This program is implemented throughout the school, articulating classroom instruction within and across grade levels and subject areas.

Examples: America's Choice, Early Intervention in Reading, Modern Red Schoolhouse, Success for All

Taking Stock

Definition: Taking stock is a school-wide collection and analysis of data about the school to assess the school's strengths and weaknesses. In essence, taking stock is inventorying the school to understand its current state.

Examples: Accelerated Schools, America's Choice, ATLAS, Modern Red Schoolhouse

Visioning

Definition: A conscious effort is made by members of the school, and sometimes the larger community, to decide how they want the school, instruction, and other elements to look.

Example: Accelerated Schools

Professional Development Features

Certified Specialist

Definition: As part of the intervention, a certified specialist comes to the school to provide support to the school during implementation that may include the training of teachers and other participants.

Examples: Accelerated Schools, America's Choice, Modern Red Schoolhouse, Success for All

Inservice Workshop

Definition: These are teacher-attended workshops provided by a topical expert.

Examples: Accelerated Schools, America's Choice, ATLAS, Lightspan, Modern Red Schoolhouse, School Development Program, Success for All

Modeling With Coaching

Definition: An expert in the intervention (usually a certified or on-site specialist) models specific practices in the classroom; also provides coaching of and follow-up to teachers on how to implement those practices.

Examples: Literacy Collaborative, Reading Recovery, Waterford Early Reading Program

Networking

Definition: Teachers meet with teachers from other schools participating in the same intervention/reform.

Examples: Accelerated Schools, America's Choice, Early Intervention in Reading, First Steps, School Development Program, Success for All

On-Site Facilitator

Definition: The intervention requires a facilitator from the school to attend an extensive training session in the reform model and to work full- or part-time as a school-site facilitator in the reform process. A person from the school or district is trained in the model.

Examples: Accelerate Schools, America's Choice, ATLAS, Lightspan, Early Intervention in Reading, First Steps, Modern Red Schoolhouse, School Development Program

On-Site Specialist

Definition: The intervention places a full- or part-time certified specialist from the model at the school site to assist the school with the implementation of the reform. The on-site specialist is at the school at least once a month.

Examples: Modern Red Schoolhouse, Success for All

Peer Review/Observation

Definition: Teachers have opportunities to observe peers and be observed by colleagues.

Examples: ATLAS, School Development Program, Success for All

School-Site Training

Definition: In this design for training the school in the intervention, a certified specialist comes to the school to train the entire school staff in implementing the reform.

Examples: First Steps, Lightspan, Modern Red Schoolhouse, Success for All

Teacher Collaboration

Definition: Teachers can plan, organize, or teach together in a concentrated effort to improve one another's practice.

Examples: Accelerated Schools, America's Choice, ATLAS, Modern Red Schoolhouse, School Development Program

Teacher Inquiry/Portfolios

Definition: Teachers collect samples of their own and their students' work to be shared, discussed, and analyzed by colleagues; the body of work samples that are collected become a resource to the whole faculty.

Examples: America's Choice, ATLAS, Early Intervention in Reading

Training of Trainers

Definition: In this design for training the school in the intervention, one or more people from the school are sent to be trained in the model; they then provide training to the whole school. The training provided by the reform model acts as a sort of certification process for the trainers who return to the school.

Examples: Accelerated Schools, America's Choice, First Steps, School Development Program

Implemented Theoretical Philosophical Features

Acceleration

Definition: The model advocates believe that enriching techniques and activities are most effective to address basic and higher-order skills.

Examples: Accelerated Schools, America's Choice

Caring Community

Definition: This feature represents a belief that establishing a community of caring adults not only within the school, but also outside the school, will benefit student learning.

Example: School Development Program

Child-Centered/Developmental

Definition: In this theory, the approach is to teach learning through the child's previous understandings and follow the child's natural interests.

Examples: ATLAS, First Steps, Modern Red Schoolhouse, School Development Program

Concept Development

Definition: The emphasis in teaching is on conceptual understanding and using higher-order thinking skills.

Examples: Accelerated Schools, America's Choice, ATLAS, Modern Red Schoolhouse

Constructivist Learning

Definition: This theory is strongly rooted in cognitive psychology, especially that learning is constructed by individuals (students), based on their prior knowledge, interactions with the new learning, and generation of connections to other domains of knowledge.

Examples: Accelerated Schools, ATLAS

Phonological Awareness

Definition: This is a systematic approach to teaching the relationships between oral and written language.

Examples: America's Choice, Early Intervention in Reading, Lightspan, Modern Red Schoolhouse, School Development Program, Success for All

Prescribed Curriculum

Definition: A set curriculum is followed across all grade levels in specified subject areas, and teachers are expected to base all instruction on the curriculum.

Examples: America's Choice, Modern Red Schoolhouse, Success for All

Prescribed Teacher Practices

Definition: Teacher practices are defined in detail (step-by-step) by the program or reform model.

Examples: Early Intervention in Reading, Success for All

Reflective Practice

Definition: Professionals are encouraged to reflect on their daily practices to help them understand which practices are successful and which need improvement. This reflection can be done while in action or in a variety of other ways such as journaling or analyzing conversations.

Examples: Accelerated Schools, America's Choice, ATLAS, First Steps

Self-Extending System

Definition: The program attempts to instill in children the rudiments of a system of learning that each student will adopt and use.

Examples: Early Intervention in Reading, Modern Red Schoolhouse, School Development Program

Standards-Based Instruction

Definition: Instruction should be designed from learning standards, student work should be assessed against standards, and instruction should be revised based on the student work to ensure that students meet standards.

Examples: America's Choice, ATLAS, Lightspan, Modern Red Schoolhouse

Student Empowerment

Definition: Students are encouraged to take charge of their own education in order to foster an enjoyment of learning.

Examples: Accelerated Schools, First Steps, Modern Red Schoolhouse, School Development Program

Teacher Professionalism

Definition: This feature reflects the belief that instructional and reform decisions are best made at the school level by the educators who have the most knowledge about the unique needs of the students at the school, when given the appropriate support/structure/training (related to the specific reform model).

Examples: Accelerated Schools, ATLAS, Modern Red Schoolhouse, School Development Program

Thematic Teaching

Definition: The belief that the curriculum should be organized in a way that allows for integrating lessons and themes across subject areas, in order to increase the relevance of the instruction for the students and deepen their understanding of concepts that are related to multiple domains of learning.

Examples: Accelerated Schools, America's Choice, Success for All

Whole Language

Definition: Whole Language emphasizes that all learning of communication, including written, must be meaningful, and any approach to teaching literacy must be meaning oriented.

Examples: Accelerated Schools, America's Choice, First Steps, Modern Red Schoolhouse, School Development Program, Success for All

Parent/Community Involvement Features

Advocacy

Definition: The program assists parents to act as advocates for their children with teachers or governmental agencies.

Example: School Development Program

Book Distribution

Definition: The program distributes books to households that may have few.

Example: Early Intervention in Reading

Family Literacy

Definition: The program provides literacy instruction to the entire family.

Example: Included in some Accelerated Schools, but not a formal part of the design

Health Care Assistance

Definition: Parents are assisted in providing children with health care

Example: School Development Program

Learning Contracts/Parent

Definition: Each parent is required to enter some type of verbal or written commitment for the child's education.

Examples: America's Choice, Early Intervention in Reading, Lightspan, Modern Red Schoolhouse

Paired Reading/Parent-Child

Definition: The program puts two people together (usually of different abilities) to read. The stronger partner (here, the parent) helps the weaker to read.

Examples: America's Choice, Early Intervention in Reading, First Steps, Success for All

Parent Awareness

Definition: The program keeps the parents informed of program features, reform efforts, and events through outreach efforts from the school.

Examples: Accelerated Schools, America's Choice, ATLAS, Early Intervention in Reading, First Steps, Lightspan, Modern Red Schoolhouse, School Development Program, Success for All

Parent Communication

Definition: Parent newsletters and information about the school events and student homework are conveyed to parents.

Examples: America's Choice, Early Intervention in Reading, First Steps, Lightspan, Modern Red Schoolhouse, School Development Program, Success for All

Parent Participation in Planning Curriculum

Definition: Parents participate in the construction of the curriculum through committee membership.

Example: Accelerated Schools

Parent Participation in Reform Team

Definition: Parent representatives serve on the Reform Team (see under School-wide Features).

Examples: Accelerated Schools, School Development Program, Success for All

Parent Participation in Site-Based Management

Definition: Parents are involved in site-based management (see Site-Based Management in School-wide Features). In participatory Site-Based Management (i.e., everyone participates), parents are invited to play an active role; in representative Site-Based Management, parents select representatives.

Examples: Accelerated Schools, America's Choice, Modern Red Schoolhouse, School Development Program

Parent Reading Instructional Training

Definition: The program trains parents how to read with their children and help their children learn to read.

Examples: First Steps, Lightspan, Success for All

Parent Volunteers

Definition: Parents volunteer their time to participate in programs.

Examples: Accelerated Schools, Early Intervention in Reading, School Development Program, Success for All

Support Services

Definition: Support services are provided to parents.

Examples: ATLAS, School Development Program

Take-Home Literacy Activities

Definition: The program distributes literacy materials and activity tools such as audio- and videocassette tapes and songbooks for home use by children and parents.

Examples: Lightspan Achieve Now, Waterford Early Reading Program

Classroom-Instruction Features

Advanced Writing Mechanics

Definition: This feature comprises activities that not only call attention to the rules and mechanics of writing but also use these skills within the context of planning, drafting, and revising created writing.

Examples: America's Choice, Success for All

Authentic Instruction

Definition: This project-based instruction is related to real issues and situations and allows students to contextualize what they are learning to their own world, giving the instruction relevance. The tasks often arise out of student interest or specific class discussions, providing a "teachable moment" around which the teacher designs the task.

Examples: Accelerated Schools, America's Choice, ATLAS, Modern Red Schoolhouse, School Development Program

Big Books

Definition: With an oversize book, the students read together as a class in a participatory way.

Examples: Early Intervention in Reading, First Steps, Success for All

Collaborative Teams

Definition: Students work in groups toward common and individual goals without much direct guidance from the teacher.

Examples: Accelerated Schools, America's Choice, ATLAS, Early Intervention in Reading, First Steps, Lightspan, Modern Red Schoolhouse, School Development Program, Success for All

Computer as a Tool

Definition: The computer is used as a tool to help students accomplish a learning task.

Examples: Accelerated Schools, America's Choice, ATLAS, Lightspan, Modern Red Schoolhouse

Computer Assisted Instruction

Definition: Computer software is used for instructional delivery.

Example: Lightspan

Cooperative Learning

Definition: In Cooperative Learning, heterogeneously grouped students work together on interdependent tasks in which all students must participate and contribute in order to succeed.

Example: Success for All

Creative Writing

Definition: Students write stories or other imaginative material on their own, sometimes with guidance.

Examples: Accelerated Schools, Early Intervention in Reading, First Steps, Lightspan, School Development Program, Success for All

Cultural Literacy

Definition: Instruction is based on generally accepted "cultural" standards and a defined body of knowledge that every child should know.

Example: Modern Red Schoolhouse

Drama

Definition: Program participants stage a written selection, interacting directly with the text and situating themselves within it.

Examples: Early Intervention in Reading, Success for All

Echo or Choral Reading

Definition: In this variant of pacing oral reading, children also read out loud along with the adult.

Examples: Early Intervention in Reading, Lightspan, School Development Program

Emergent Spelling

Definition: Children are taught basic spelling rules and are encouraged to write using those rules, without worrying about the correctness of the spelling.

Examples: First Steps, Lightspan

Essays

Definition: Students respond in a self-conscious, organized text to a reading problem or situation.

Examples: America's Choice, Early Intervention in Reading, First Steps, Lightspan, School Development Program

Highly Scripted Lessons

Definition: Teachers instruct in a highly prescribed way from a script.

Example: Success for All

Inquiry Learning

Definition: This is an instructional method by which students use a variation of the scientific method of inquiry as a means to study a topic in depth; the goal is both deeper learning about the focus of the inquiry and the processes of inquiry as a learning method.

Examples: Accelerated Schools, ATLAS

Interpreting/Discussion/Reading

Definition: This is a teacher-led class discussion of reading, with emphasis on meaning, interpretation, critical response, critical dialogue, self-expression, and so on.

Examples: Accelerated Schools, ATLAS, Early Intervention in Reading, First Steps, Lightspan, Success for All

Journals

Definition: Students record their thoughts and experiences in regular accounts, usually informal.

Examples: America's Choice, Early Intervention in Reading, First Steps, Lightspan

Learning Contracts/Student

Definition: Individualized, contracted agreements are made with students on what they will accomplish for their education.

Examples: America's Choice, Early Intervention in Reading, Modern Red Schoolhouse

Meaning Context/Predicting

Definition: Children are introduced to the story before they read and are encouraged to predict the outcome or otherwise interact with story structures prior to and separate from the actual narrative experience.

Examples: America's Choice, Early Intervention in Reading, First Steps, Lightspan, Success for All

Multisensory Activity

Definition: This approach emphasizes senses other than seeing and hearing to help students internalize the acts of reading.

Examples: Early Intervention in Reading, Success for All

Pacing Oral Reading

Definition: Adults read to children—one-on-one or in groups—with the children following along (guided perhaps by a finger running under the text as it is read).

Examples: Early Intervention in Reading, Lightspan, School Development Program, Success for All

Paired Reading

Definition: The program puts two people together (usually of different abilities) to read. The stronger partner helps the weaker to read.

Examples: Accelerated Schools, Early Intervention in Reading, Lightspan, School Development Program, Success for All

Pattern Discrimination

Definition: Instructional activities engage students in identifying letter patterns and discerning words that match specified patterns.

Examples: Early Intervention in Reading, Early Steps, Four Blocks, Lightspan Achieve Now, Success for All

Performance Assessment

Definition: Students are given performance tasks to assess learning as a regular part of instruction.

Examples: Accelerated Schools, America's Choice, ATLAS, First Steps, Lightspan, Modern Red Schoolhouse, School Development Program

Phonemic Awareness

Definition: Activities introduce students to and provide them with oral, aural, and visual discrimination of letters and sounds.

Examples: Early Intervention in Reading, Early Steps, First Steps, Four Blocks, Lightspan Achieve Now, Literacy Collaborative, Reading Recovery, Success for All, Waterford Early Reading Program

Phonics Assessment

Definition: The teacher regularly observes and records students' progress on exhibiting specified phonics skills.

Example: Indiana Phonics Toolkit (http:eric.indiana.edu/phonics/)

Problem Solving

Definition: Problem solving is often used as both a rehearsal of skills already learned and an application of newly learned concepts. Typically, the class receives whole class instruction followed by individual or group problem-solving activities to reinforce the instruction.

Examples: Accelerated Schools, America's Choice, ATLAS, Lightspan, Success for All

Project-Based Instruction

Definition: Students are assigned or select a project, as part of formal instruction. Projects generally involve both the in-depth study of a topic and a summary or synthesis of what has been learned in some sort of presentation such as a written report, an oral presentation, or the construction of a representational model.

Examples: Accelerated Schools, America's Choice, ATLAS, Lightspan, Modern Red Schoolhouse

Reading Drills

Definition: The program drills the participants on reading subskills, using specifically targeted, repetitive, and analytic exercises, such as flashcards with the same vowel pattern "ea"—"meat," "heat."

Examples: Early Intervention in Reading, Success for All

Scaffolding

Definition: Teachers model a complex activity to show students how to perform the activity; then the activity is repeated with less and less teacher input as students perform the activity independently.

Examples: ATLAS, First Steps

Self-Selected Reading

Definition: Students, rather than teachers, choose which books they read.

Examples: America's Choice, First Steps

Silent Individual Reading

Definition: Children have time of their own to read silently; these periods are usually scheduled daily.

Examples: Early Intervention in Reading, First Steps, Lightspan, School Development Program, Success for All

Storytelling

Definition: The teacher reads stories out loud to students, usually in a classroom setting rather than in a tutorial setting.

Examples: Early Intervention in Reading, First Steps, Success for All

Worksheets/Workbooks

Definition: Students fill out worksheets.

Examples: Accelerated Schools, America's Choice, School Development Program, Success for All

Writing Mechanics

Definition: This feature comprises activities that call attention to the rules and mechanics of writing.

Examples: Success for All, America's Choice, First Steps, School Development Program

Structural/Organizational Features

Ability Grouping

Definition: Students are clustered on the basis of shared ability, rather than age, grade level, or other factors.
Example: Success for All (Reading)

Basal Readers

Definition: The program uses a series of graded readers or textbooks, usually constructed with controlled vocabulary and syntax.
Examples: Early Intervention Reading, School Development Program, Success for All

Basic Reading Ability Assumed

Definition: The program takes for granted a basic ability to read simple text and is designed to improve and deepen that ability. It also assumes Emergent Literacy or Reading Readiness.
Example: Reading Recovery

Classroom-Based

Definition: The program works with the class as a whole rather than with individuals in tutorial or small-group settings.
Examples: First Steps, Four Blocks, Literacy Collaborative, Waterford Early Reading Program

Cross-Year Portfolios

Definition: Students keep their best work, some selected by teachers and some by students, in an electronic or physical file. Unlike grades, portfolios are student-centered tools.
Examples: America's Choice, ATLAS

Diagnostic Procedures

Definition: The program uses at least a partially explicit set of criteria and/or methods to evaluate individual children's performance and needs prior to participation in the program; this information is used primarily for placement.
Examples: America's Choice, Early Intervention in Reading, First Steps, School Development Program, Success for All

Flexible Grouping

Definition: Teachers use various groupings of students depending upon specific activities planned. Teachers are encouraged to use a range of grouping and instructional strategies and to select those strategies that are most likely to be successful with specific students given a particular lesson.

Examples: ATLAS, Lightspan, Modern Red Schoolhouse

Frequent Assessment

Definition: Students are tested or assessed frequently to monitor academic gains.

Examples: America's Choice, Early Intervention in Reading, First Steps, Lightspan, Modern Red Schoolhouse, Success for All

Grade Limit

Definition: The program excludes certain grades from participating, targeting a specific age group (e.g., Reading Recovery is used only in Grade 1).

Examples: Four Blocks, Full Day Kindergarten, Reading Recovery

Heterogeneous Groups

Definition: Students work in mixed ability groups.

Examples: Accelerated Schools, ATLAS, Success for All (Math)

Individualized Instruction

Definition: Instruction and materials differ depending on individual students' ability and development.

Examples: ATLAS, Lightspan, Modern Red Schoolhouse, School Development Program

Interactive Learning

Definition: During the instruction, students communicate between themselves and with the teacher.

Examples: Accelerated Schools, ATLAS, Early Intervention in Reading, Lightspan, Modern Red Schoolhouse, Success for All.

Literacy-Rich Environment

Definition: The program promotes literacy acquisition by fostering an environment that encourages literate activity.

Examples: America's Choice, First Steps, Success for All

One-on-One Tutoring

Definition: A teacher or a paraprofessional tutors one student.
Examples: America's Choice, ATLAS, Early Intervention in Reading, Lightspan, Success for All

Ongoing Written Observations

Definition: Teachers keep records of and track progress on students' activities, such as books read, on an individual basis.
Examples: America's Choice, Success for All

Peer Tutoring

Definition: Students instruct their peers.
Examples: Accelerated Schools, ATLAS, America's Choice

Pullout Program

Definition: The program identifies a subset of children from the whole class and that subset alone participates in the program. Students are removed from the regular class activity (even if they stay in the classroom) and given alternate instruction.
Examples: Early Intervention in Reading, Lightspan, School Development Program.

Reading Canon

Definition: This is a complete list of books accepted by the program, a list often graduated for difficulty but not necessarily a basal series. Books not on the list are excluded from the program.
Examples: Early Intervention in Reading, School Development Program

Remedial Methodologies

Definition: Instruction is designed primarily to help students who have fallen behind.
Example: Success for All

Small Groups

Definition: Children work together in small groups, led by a teacher, by a paraprofessional, or by the students themselves.
Examples: Accelerated Schools, America's Choice, ATLAS, Early Intervention in Reading, First Steps, Lightspan, Modern Red Schoolhouse, School Development Program, Success for All

Student-Initiated Learning Centers

Definition: Curricular/topical materials are kept in a central area, allowing students to choose the materials that interest them most.

Example: Accelerated Schools

Supplemental Learning

Definition: Students spend extra time engaged in learning, focusing on essentially the same things they are doing in regular classes, but with additional time.

Examples: America's Choice, ATLAS, Lightspan, Modern Red Schoolhouse, School Development Program, Success for All

Systematic Learning

Definition: The program uses a comprehensive and coordinated structure or set of structures that may allow for some individual flexibility but which ultimately unify and organize the instruction.

Examples: Early Intervention in Reading, Four Blocks, Reading Recovery

Thematic Units

Definition: A deeply meaning-oriented approach, this teaches multiple subject areas within the context of a theme, such as oceans, thunderstorms, a piece of literature.

Examples: Accelerated Schools, America's Choice, ATLAS, Lightspan, Modern Red Schoolhouse

Trade Books

Definition: Students read literature-based books, as opposed to books such as basal readers, which are constructed using controlled vocabulary and syntax.

Examples: Accelerated Schools, America's Choice, Early Intervention in Reading, First Steps, School Development Program, Success for All

RELATING FEATURES TO READING STANDARDS ■

Increasingly, schools are expected to address specific state learning standards in their classroom reading instruction. State accountability programs have placed greater emphasis on state tests as a central measure of school performance. Because reading skills are central to how students perform in upper elementary grades and other subject areas, meeting reading standards in Grades 1–5 should be a goal for all schools. Paying attention to reading standards means focusing also on schools' state reading test scores as these tests are usually closely aligned with state reading standards.

Most states have incorporated, or are currently in the process of incorporating, state standards into their state testing programs. This prevents a mismatch between what schools are expected to teach—as specified in the standards—and what is actually covered on the test. Because of the connection between state assessments and state standards, schools can study their students' test results to determine their strengths and weaknesses regarding their reading program. State reading standards (often a component of language arts standards that include writing and oral language) tend to take a balanced approach in early reading skills. Both phonics (*decoding A*) and meaning-oriented (*decoding B*) approaches are included as part of vocabulary development and word fluency. Additionally, reading comprehension strategies include both knowledge of structure (e.g., "concepts in print" and "structural features of text"') and holistic analysis for meaning-getting (e.g., "summarize and raise relevant questions"). Reading standards also focus on building skills for comprehension of informational texts and literature, making distinctions (usually by discrete categories) between skills required to reach *critical literacy* in each type of reading.

The identified reading outcomes used in this *Guide* are directly related to categories of standards and skills that are included in many state standards. Box 3.1 summarizes categories of standards and example standard skills and relates those to specific reading outcomes. The standard categories and examples of skills are drawn from reviews of state standards for California, Indiana, Minnesota, Missouri, Pennsylvania, Texas, and Wisconsin. (See state Web sites for each state's standards).

BOX 3.1 RELATING STANDARDS TO READING OUTCOMES

READING OUTCOME STANDARD CATEGORY AND EXAMPLES

Vocabulary Development, Word Recognition, and Fluency

– Concepts in Print	*Emergent Literacy*
– Phonemic Awareness	*Emergent Literacy*
– Phonics Skills – Decoding	*Decoding A*
– Vocabulary and Word Analysis	*Decoding A/Decoding B*
– Word Fluency/Reading Fluency	*Decoding A/Decoding B/Comprehension*
– Self-Correcting Strategies	*Decoding A/Decoding B/Comprehension*

Reading Comprehension: Informational Texts

– Structural Features of Text	*Comprehension*
– Summarization/Key Ideas (e.g., main idea, supporting details)	*Comprehension*

– Reading for Information and Research   *Comprehension/Critical Literacy*
  (e.g., raise relevant questions, summarize
  information from multiple sources)
– Evaluation and Interpretation   *Critical Literacy*
  (e.g., literal vs. inferential information,
  comparison of multiple sources, applying
  ideas to "students' world" and other
  subject areas)

Reading Comprehension: Literature and Analysis

– Identification and Recall of Key Features   *Comprehension*
  (e.g., main ideas, supporting details, sequence)
– Analysis of Literature   *Comprehension/Critical Literacy*
  (e.g., Inferences, cause/effect relationships,
  generalizations)
– Comparisons Of and Across Genres   *Critical Literacy*
  (e.g., compare techniques across genres:
  character development, plots, style)

Most reading and literacy interventions target a specific set of literacy outcomes but do not address a comprehensive set of reading outcomes identified in these standards. A program targeting basic *comprehension* will likely address directly only those sets of standards linked to comprehension within the standards for Reading Comprehension: Informational Texts and Reading Comprehension: Literature and Analysis. Many reading interventions presume that by building the requisite *comprehension* skills the students will be able to benefit fully from regular classroom instruction. This presumes that the *critical literacy* standards are being addressed in the regular instruction.

When planning for reading reform, teachers and administrators should consider the distinction between *comprehension* and *critical literacy* outcomes along with the standards that are related to both of these outcomes. They should make sure that all are adequately addressed when they choose an intervention model and develop an implementation plan. This is most important when the school selects a reading intervention that is used as the primary language arts curriculum. In this case, if the intervention does not specifically target *critical literacy* outcomes, some of the state learning standards may not be directly addressed through the curriculum. Schools must then develop a plan to incorporate instruction into the program that addresses those specific standard skills. In most cases, the reading program's methods are easily adapted, or built upon, in order to meet those standards not directly covered.

Teachers in elementary grades should study their state's standards in comparison to the selected reading reform's targeted literacy outcomes. The faculty can then identify which standards are automatically addressed through the program, which are indirectly addressed, and which are not targeted. After identifying the gaps between the standards and the outcomes that are the foci of the reform model (see subsequent chapters), the school can plan for curriculum and instruction in ways that address all the state's standards, not just the standards addressed by the selected reform model. Service providers (those providing support for the intervention) may be willing to assist schools in the process of reviewing state standards.

■ GUIDANCE FOR EDUCATORS

In addition to introducing a framework for thinking about and planning for reading reform, this chapter introduced a common language about reading reform. Most reading studies were conducted by advocates for specific reform models or specific approaches to reading. This means that relatively little attention has been given to creating a common language of reading reform. The National Research Council's *Preventing Reading Difficulties in Young Children* contributed to a common language about reading reform by making key distinctions about reading outcomes and process. For example, by distinguishing between phonemic awareness and phonics, the Research Council helped to standardize terms that distinguish between methods of instruction (e.g., phonics) and the early process of learning to decode language (e.g., phonemic awareness). However, their research examined studies conducted by different reform camps (e.g., the proponents of Success for All and Reading Recovery) but did not break down the components of these reform models. In this chapter we have introduced a refined approach to the language of reading reform, developing common definitions of program features. Having a common language should make it easier for teachers to compare reform models and build an understanding of the ways specific reform models might enhance their reading programs.

The remainder of this volume uses the language of reading reform introduced in this chapter. These terms were developed in collaboration with a team of reviewers and are used in a common way to describe the designs of various reform models and approaches in the following chapters. Administrators and teachers can refer to the terms defined in this chapter when they are attempting to understand and compare reform models.

In addition to introducing a common language about reading reform, this book provides guidance to educators about choosing or designing reading reforms. When school districts or schools choose a reform model, they essentially select a "design" for a reading program that is intended to address the learning needs of children with special needs (i.e., targeted reforms) or all children in an elementary school (all other types of reforms). It is crucial that teachers and administrators consider the design concept embedded in the reform models that they choose or develop. Most reform models do not cover every aspect of the reading acquisition process, so by themselves most reforms will not address all reading standards that schools are expected to meet. So teachers need to think about the new design they are choosing—or that was chosen for them—when they adapt their classroom practices to reach the new reading standards.

The fact that states are developing reading standards both encourages reform and complicates the reform process. In this book, we have provided a crosswalk between generic standards and reading outcomes (*emergent literacy, decoding A and B, comprehension, and critical literacy*). These standards are closely aligned with the standards developed in states. We also consider an early writing outcome, *composition*, which is an integral part of the language acquisition process that is overlooked when reading standards are treated as the motivating force for reading reform. By taking this comprehensive view of reading outcomes, we hope to stimulate an informed conversation in schools about the ways students learn to read and about the art of teaching early reading.

Chapters 4–8 provide reviews of five types of reading reforms. For each type of reading and comprehensive reform, we review several models that were being considered or used in the states we have collaborated with in the past few years. However, within each type of reform there are other models and methods that merit consideration. In fact, educational administrators are often contacted by marketing agents who use aggressive marketing tactics to promote their reading models. Reform models are often selected or endorsed by districts and states, which means that teachers often have models imposed on them. At the end of each chapter we provide guidance to educators who are thinking about or who have chosen a reform model of the type reviewed in the chapter.

While we recognize that administrators and teachers must choose reform models in a political, market-driven environment, we think it is important that teachers develop a learning-oriented reform environment and a community-based approach that implements reading reform, fosters student learning, and enables communication among the different stakeholders throughout the reform process. Toward this end, we consider the following issues as part of our guidance to educators in the five review chapters:

- *The Research Base*: While the research base is typically discussed as a body of research that can inform the selection of the reading model, we recognize that most of the research has been written in support of a specific reform method or model. We consider how this extant research base can inform the decision process in schools. We also summarize how our own research can inform these decision processes. Our studies of reading reform and school reform have used the framework and language outlined in this chapter. Rather than report on research that is readily available, we highlight findings that can inform planning and evaluation in schools.
- *Meeting Standards*: There is a high degree of commonality across each type of reform in the ways they go about reforming reading. We provide guidance for educators in schools about the additional steps they will need to take to address the comprehensive nature of reading if they use the approach to reading reforms reviewed in each chapter.
- *Politics of Reform*: Given the strong market forces that can influence the selection of a reading program, it is possible that the new reading reforms will be chosen as a result of a political process. Our aim is to encourage teachers to collaborate in the reading reform process. Whatever reform approach is taken, they must both implement the model and think critically about the limitations of the model because it will not address all of the components of reading. It is important to build on the strength of the

school and of the reform model as well as to overcome the limitations of both. We provide guidance about the political nature of the reform process, based on site visits to a large number of reforming schools.

- *Integrating Inquiry*: In our view, integrating inquiry into the reform process provides a means of overcoming the limitations of commonly chosen reform models. Even a reform model that relies exclusively on inquiry has limitations with respect to the challenges of developing reading programs that address all the components of reading in comprehensive ways. By treating the reform process itself as an experiment that can promote their own learning, teachers can build on the strengths of the schools and of the reform model, in an effort to develop a cohesive reform approach.

- *Building Community*: In our view, the aim of reading reform is to build a community in schools that learns from research, including research by teachers. Thus we view schools as learning communities—communities that focus on children's learning, but also encourage learning among teachers and that also promote parents' involvement in these learning processes. We conclude each chapter with guidance on using reading reform as a means of building learning communities.

NOTE

1. Research associates who contributed to the list of features defined in this section include Glenda Musoba, Kim Manoil, Stacy Jacob, Eric Asker, Margaret Clements, and Osman Cekic. Their contributions are gratefully acknowledged.

4

Targeted Interventions

Most targeted interventions remove children from their regular classrooms for some kind of special instruction, often in a one-on-one setting. Some interventions do not physically remove students from the classroom but pull them aside in individual or small groups for specialized instruction within the classroom setting.

Reading Recovery is the best-known targeted intervention in the United States at present. Early Intervention in Reading (EIR) is a kindergarten through fourth grade intervention that is a *classroom-based pullout program*, in which the teacher works with a small group of students for intensive reading instruction within the classroom. Early Steps is primarily a first-grade intervention that uses trained tutors to deliver one-on-one reading instruction.

While the number of children who participate in the pullout can vary, the proportion is usually between 10 percent and 20 percent of the children in Grade 1 (and Grades 1–3). Careful targeting and diagnosis are critical to ensure that the intervention reaches children who can most benefit from it. Given the low percentages of students reached, it is unreasonable to expect whole classes (not to mention schools) to show significant improvement in test scores. Rather, to evaluate whether a program is successful, schools need to consider improvement among the lowest achieving 20 percent across several indicators, including test scores, referrals to special education, retentions in grade, and attitudes toward reading and school.

Targeted interventions are designed to help the few students who are struggling in regular classrooms. Schools that enjoy success overall with regard to reading and literacy but have a small number of struggling students should strongly consider a targeted intervention. On the other hand, schools with large numbers of students at risk of not learning to read will probably not be able to reach the number of students they need to with this type of intervention. For these schools, a classroom-based intervention or comprehensive school reform program may be more appropriate.

Three specific targeted intervention models are reviewed in this chapter: Early Intervention in Reading (4.1), Early Steps (4.2), and Reading Recovery (4.3). The body of each review describes the features included in these models.

Then additional references and contacts are provided. The chapter concludes with guidance for teachers and other educators who are interested in choosing or developing a targeted intervention model.

■ 4.1. EARLY INTERVENTION IN READING

Reviewed by Stacy Jacob

Early Intervention in Reading is a kindergarten through fourth grade model designed to help children who are struggling to learn to read. Children are placed in *small groups* (5–7 students) within the classroom and are given systematic reading instruction for twenty to thirty minutes each day. The program emphasizes coaching children rather than transmission/reception. Teachers are encouraged to help the children by setting high expectations. The program emphasizes continually asking higher-level questions.

Program Description

EIR is not a school restructuring program but rather a reading intervention that a school could employ within its locally developed comprehensive restructuring program. It could easily be used with other types of instruction or reform models. The reform features included in the EIR model (Figure 4.1) are summarized below.

School-Wide Features

Because EIR is by design a reading intervention program and not a school restructuring reform, school-wide features do not appear. However, the model uses a sophisticated, sequenced set of structures with individual flexibility that is paramount to *systematic learning* for reading instruction. The program for kindergarten is more prescriptive than the one for Grades 1–4. A *formative program evaluation* can be undertaken by individuals from the reform provider at the request of the individual school.

Implemented Theoretical/Philosophical Features

EIR is a program that is built around creating *phonological awareness*. At the heart of the model is the belief that good instruction can instill confidence (through a system of learning) that will allow students to eventually take over the process of learning. Thus, a *self-extending system* is created.

The EIR model has some *prescribed teacher practices* in terms of types and sequence of methods. There is ample room for application of individual creativity in teaching. First-year teachers are urged to follow the process closely and use to EIR materials. As their familiarity with the focus and sophistication of the program grows, teachers are encouraged to adapt the program according to their individual strengths.

Figure 4.1 Early Intervention in Reading Program Features

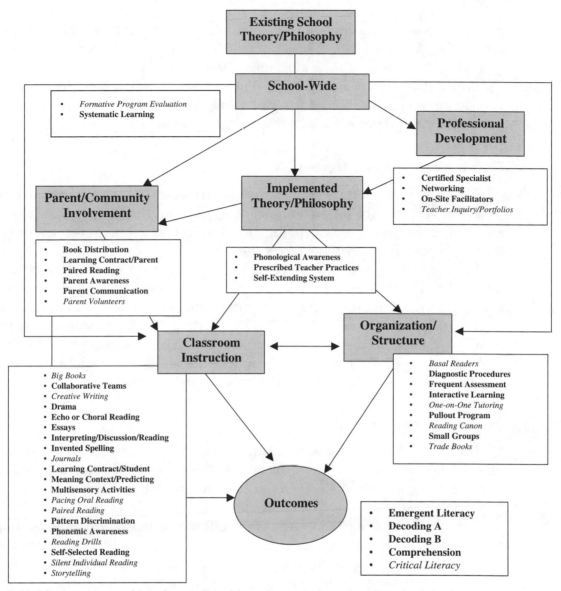

Bolded features are part of the reform; *italicized features* are sometimes adopted by schools implementing the reform.

Professional Development Features

Professional development is important to the EIR model. This development is mainly through various forms of interactive technology (e.g., conference calls, video sharing, the Internet). Teachers can be trained in the EIR model through these interactive methods or, at the request of the school, a *certified specialist* will come to train the teachers. Each EIR site requires two *on-site facilitators*. One facilitator is a technology specialist; the other coordinates the model. EIR offers *networking* and ongoing support through these technologies. In addition, *teacher inquiry/portfolios* are shared and discussed by many EIR teachers through technology.

Parent/Community Involvement Features

Informing parents is an important part of the EIR model. Therefore, both *parent awareness* and *parent communication* take place. Parents of an EIR student enter into a *learning contract/parent* in which they agree to be read to daily by their child. Therefore *paired reading* takes place every day.

Book distribution is a part of the EIR program. Students are lent various books from school and sometimes given little books. *Parent volunteers* may be a part of the EIR program.

Organizational/Structural Features

EIR is a *classroom-based pullout program* that teaches struggling readers in *small groups* within the classroom. *Diagnostic procedures* and *frequent assessments* are used to determine which children need *individualized instruction* and when these children are discontinued from the program.

EIR emphasizes the importance of *interactive learning,* and this can be seen through many of its strategies. For example, *drama* is used quite often, especially in kindergarten. Children in the EIR program read from a variety of sources. This includes both *basal readers* and *trade books* within a *reading canon.* Schools may use their own books; however, they are encouraged to use EIR materials during their first year of implementation as they learn how EIR levels material for children. In addition, *one-on-one tutoring* is used to increase students' success.

Classroom Instruction Features

Because EIR is a systematic approach, classroom instructional features are especially evident. Within this instruction, *multisensory activities* such as *drama* are important, particularly in kindergarten. Students in the EIR program enter into a *learning contract/student,* which requires them to read to their parents daily.

Echo or choral reading is a feature of the EIR program. In addition to reading, children also write *essays* and engage in different guided-writing activities. Children not only read in the program but they also discuss what they read. Therefore, *interpreting/discussion/reading* is an important aspect of the program.

Children in the EIR program read, and they read a great deal. This reading can take the form of *pacing oral reading, paired reading, silent individual reading, storytelling,* and *reading drills.* Students may work on reading alone or as a part of a *collaborative team. Big Books* may be used. When children read along with adults, teachers and volunteers are encouraged to let the child be the leading voice during the reading activity.

Children not only read but are also encouraged to think critically about what they read. Therefore, *meaning context/predicting* is a part of EIR methods. In addition to reading, children in the EIR program also write to ensure literacy acquisition. This writing may be in the form of *journals* or *creative writing.*

Targeted Literacy Outcomes

EIR is a recovery program for students who are struggling to read. The model is aimed at creating *emergent literacy* (reading readiness) in kindergarten, *decoding*

A, and *comprehension*. The coaching approach to reading for understanding focuses on *decoding B* (*meaning oriented*) outcomes. Through this outcome children learn to read. These skills create a base for promoting more advanced skills, such as *composition* and *critical literacy*.

REFERENCES AND CONTACTS:
Early Intervention in Reading

References

Chard, D. (1997). *Final evaluation report.* AY 1996-1997 Early Reading Intervention Project of Springfield Public Schools, Springfield, Massachusetts. Austin: University of Texas.

Northwest Regional Educational Laboratory (NWREL). (1988). *Catalog of school reform models: First edition* [On-line]. Available: www.nwrel.org/scpd/natspec/catalog/

Taylor, B. M. (1995). *The early intervention in reading program: Results and issues spanning six years.* Paper presented at the annual meeting of the American Educational Reading Association, San Francisco.

Taylor, B. M. (1998a). *1997-1998 K-2 literacy initiative evaluation: Executive summary.* Minneapolis: University of Minnesota

Taylor, B. M. (1998b). *Grades 3/4 1997–1998 EIR results in Moundsview.* Unpublished manuscript. Minneapolis: University of Minnesota.

Taylor, B. M. (1999). *EIR 1996–1997 EIR kindergarten results.* Unpublished manuscript. Minneapolis: University of Minnesota.

Taylor, B. M., Frye, B. J., Short, R. A., & Shearer, B. (1992). Classroom teachers prevent reading failure among low-achieving first-grade students. *The Reading Teacher, 45*(8), 592–597.

Taylor, B. M., Hanson, B. E., Justice-Swanson, K., & Watts, S. M. (1997). Helping struggling readers' linking small-group intervention with cross-age tutoring. *The Reading Teacher, 51*(3), 196–208.

Taylor, B. M., Short, R., Shearer, B., & Frye, B. (1995). First grade teachers provide early reading intervention in the classroom. In R. L. Allington & S. A. Walmsley (Eds.), *No quick fix: Rethinking literacy in America's elementary schools.* New York: Teachers College.

Taylor, B. M., Strait, J., & Medo, M. (1994). Early intervention in reading: Supplemental instruction for groups of low-achieving students provided by first-grade teachers. In E. H. Hiebert & B. M. Taylor (Eds.), *Getting reading right from the start: Effective early literacy interventions.* Boston: Allyn & Bacon.

Contact Information

Early Intervention in Reading Program
1517 Goodrich Avenue
St. Paul, MN 55105
Phone: (651) 695-1578
Email: bmtaylor@mr.net
Web Site: www.eireading.com

■ 4.2. EARLY STEPS

Reviewed by Kim Manoil

Early Steps is a systematic one-on-one tutorial reading program designed for at-risk students in Grade 1. Originally developed by Darrell Morris (Morris, Shaw, & Perney, 1990), this reading intervention program has a strong phonological-based component and is similar to Reading Recovery in its emphasis upon reading and re-reading small books and use of strategic writing practices. Daily thirty-minute Early Steps sessions contain four basic components: re-reading familiar books, sentence writing, word study, and reading new books. Though tutoring methods may vary, daily logs must be kept in order to monitor student progress.

Program Description

Program components and features are discussed below and depicted in Figure 4.2.

School-Wide Features

Various assessment instruments are used to provide both summative and *formative program evaluation*. Literacy outcomes for Early Steps can be easily determined for each school in which it is implemented through data obtained from screening instruments. Gains in reading are assessed by examining individual students' results from the "Early Reading Screening Instrument," which is initially used to identify those children at-risk for learning to read, and the "Early Steps End-of-Year Assessment," which is administered at the end of each school year. The instruments, which test the concepts of the alphabet, word recognition, word concepts, spelling, and passage reading, are scored by the examiner and can be analyzed for literacy gains for the individual student or for the entire instructional group. This information is used to guide the school's reading instruction.

Implemented Theory/Philosophy

The Early Steps program is based on the implemented theory/philosophies of *phonological awareness*, *child-centered/developmental*, and *self-extending system*.

The early reading focus emphasizes phonological decoding skills as a prerequisite for building reading *comprehension* skills and incorporates related features. In addition, the Early Steps program emphasizes the notion that children are at different stages within a developmental continuum and that the individual child's position on this continuum should be identified and built on for reading instruction. The program is geared to assist students early on who are not reading at grade level and to make them feel more capable and confident in reading in the classroom through use of the skills they learn through the tutoring sessions.

The Early Steps program is a *self-extending system* that creates in each child a strong foundation of basic skills on which to build in later tutoring sessions

Figure 4.2 Early Steps Program Features

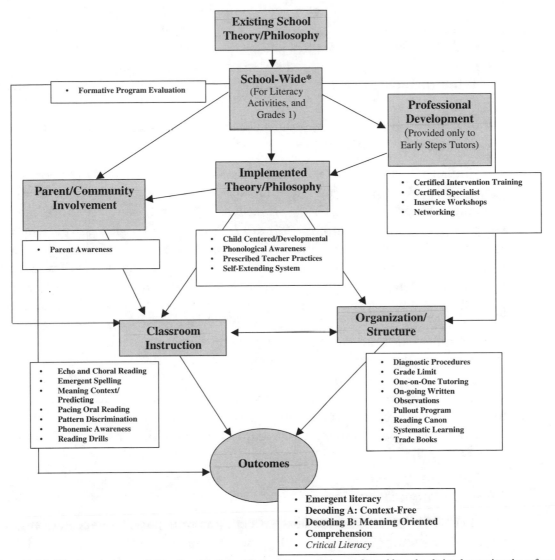

Bolded features are part of the reform; *italicized features* are sometimes adopted by schools implementing the reform.

and classroom experiences. Students develop fluency in reading by re-reading texts. They also strengthen their decoding skills and build *phonemic awareness* through word study and sentence writing.

Professional Development Features

The Early Steps program incorporates professional development as a part of the model. The professional development is primarily made available to the trained tutors. A *certified specialist* provides certified intervention training as well as *in-service workshops* at the beginning of the program's implementation and provides additional *in-service workshops* and ongoing support—including *networking*—throughout program development and implementation.

Parent Involvement Features

Parent involvement is not a core component of the Early Steps Program; however, the program does provide *parent awareness* through information sheets that can be distributed to a child's family. These sheets describe program aspects and offer suggestions on how to promote literacy in the home environment. Information sheets are generally distributed if program resources allow the child to take books home to share with parents.

Organizational/Structural Features

Similar to Reading Recovery, Early Steps is a *pullout, one-on-one tutoring* program for accelerating the reading performance of at-risk students in Grade 1. Although the program's focus is primarily on Grade 1, there are guidelines to support its extension through Grade 2. Like Clay's methods in Reading Recovery (Clay, 1993), the program uses *diagnostic procedures*. Children are identified for Early Steps through observation and an informal individual assessment administered in the first month of Grade 1. Children whose reading level puts them in the lowest 20 percent in their Grade 1 classrooms are placed in the program and receive thirty minutes of one-on-one instruction per day from a trained tutor. The students "graduate" from this program when they are reading at least on the average level for their class (Santa, 1999). Progress during the tutoring sessions is sometimes recorded through *ongoing written observations*.

Each *one-on-one tutoring* session in the Early Steps program follows a systematic organizational structure that provides *systematic learning*. A series of leveled books from a *reading canon* guide the re-reading and introduction of new books. *Trade books* are often used as part of the tutorials.

Classroom Instruction Features

Each Early Steps tutoring session contains four parts: re-reading familiar books, word study, sentence writing, and reading a new book (Santa, 1999). Within these components, *echo or choral reading, emergent spelling, meaning/context/predicting, pacing oral reading,* and *reading drills* are implemented. Each lesson begins with three books the child has already read. The third book read is one that has been introduced the previous day.

In the second part of the lesson, word study, the tutor and child begin *reading drills, phonemic awareness,* and *pattern discrimination*. These activities include instruction on sound and visual discrimination of letters and words. The program places emphasis on pattern instruction versus single-letter word sorting to teach children how to use consistent patterns for reading and spelling words. Students build up to studying word families and progress to short and long vowel patterns. Spelling activities and games reinforce the skills the child has learned.

During the third component of the lesson, sentence writing, the child is encouraged to write a sentence using *emergent spelling*, writing down the sounds that he or she hears. Tutors at the school visited modeled correct spelling after the child had completed and read the sentence. The final part of a tutoring session, reading a new book, is key, for it introduces a child to a novel piece of literature that will be re-read in the upcoming tutoring sessions and, at times, within the regular classroom setting as well.

Targeted Literacy Outcomes

The four components of Early Steps tap both early and intermediary literacy outcomes. In contrast to Reading Recovery, Early Steps includes an explicit, systematic phonological component. Early understanding of the alphabet is developed, *emergent literacy* is targeted as the child progresses, and phonological decoding skills (context-free decoding, or *decoding A*) are targeted in the "word study" and "sentence writing" components of the program. The re-reading and introduction of new books targets a child's meaning-oriented decoding (*decoding B*) as well as *comprehension*. The program uses a variety of strategies including re-reading books to improve early reading skills and also build the child's confidence and motivation in the realm of literacy.

REFERENCES AND CONTACTS:
Early Steps

References

Adams, M. J. (1999). Beginning to read: Thinking and learning about print. In C. Santa (Ed.), *Early Steps: Learning from a reader.* Kalispell, MT: Scott.

Clay, M. M. (1993). *Reading Recovery: A guidebook for teachers for training.* Portsmouth, NH: Heinemann Educational Books.

Morris, D., Shaw, B., & Perney, J. (1990). Helping low readers in grades 2 and 3: An after-school volunteer tutoring program. *Elementary School Journal, 91,* 133–150.

Santa, C. (1999). *Early Steps: Learning from a reader.* Kalispell, MT: Scott.

Santa, C., & Hoien, T. (1999). An assessment of Early Steps: A program for early intervention of reading problems. *Reading Research Quarterly, 34,* 54–78.

Contact Information

Dr. Darrell Morris
Reading Clinic Director
Appalachian State University
Edwin Duncan Hall
Boone, NC 28608
Phone: (828) 262-6054
Email: morrisrd@appstate.edu

or

Scott Publishing
Phone: (800) 375-7645
Email: scottpub@digisys.net

■ 4.3. READING RECOVERY

Reviewed by Jeffrey S. Bardzell

Reading Recovery is a pullout, one-on-one reading intervention for the lowest achieving 20 percent of students in Grade 1. The program is designed to bring those students up to grade level. To do so, the intervention helps children make the difficult transition from decoding to comprehension. The program takes a comprehensive approach to reading acquisition, incorporating carefully structured, sequenced instructional activities adapted for individual students.

Program Description

Program components and features are discussed below and are depicted in Figure 4.3.

School-Wide Features

School-wide features are not a part of the Reading Recovery program.

Implemented Theory/Philosophy

Reading Recovery has a student-centered approach to reading acquisition consistent with the following learning theories: *child-centered/developmental, self-extending system,* and *student empowerment.* The pullout structure of the Reading Recovery program provides for an individualized program that builds on students' existing knowledge (*emergent literacy*). The program tailors instruction to students' interests to foster an enjoyment of reading. The intervention also incorporates strategies for students to continue to teach themselves reading (e.g., figuring out unknown words, using self-correcting strategies) after they complete the intervention.

Reading Recovery is rooted in a balanced literacy approach and incorporates methods consistent with both *whole language* and *phonological awareness* approaches. While the program primarily emphasizes meaning-oriented decoding (*decoding B*) that is built through both reading and writing activities, it also incorporates some *phonemic awareness* (*decoding A*) activities.

Professional Development Features

Because this is a targeted intervention rather than a classroom-based or school-wide program, the professional development features pertain only to those teachers trained as Reading Recovery teachers. The professional development component is one of the most highly praised aspects of the intervention. With its sophisticated theoretical base and its widespread implementation, Reading Recovery poses several challenges to schools attempting to implement it consistently. For these reasons, Reading Recovery builds in a multilevel system of professional development. Teachers go through a *certified intervention training,* which is affiliated with a specified university. After the initial training, teachers participate in ongoing meetings and observation/review sessions with

Figure 4.3 Reading Recovery Program Features

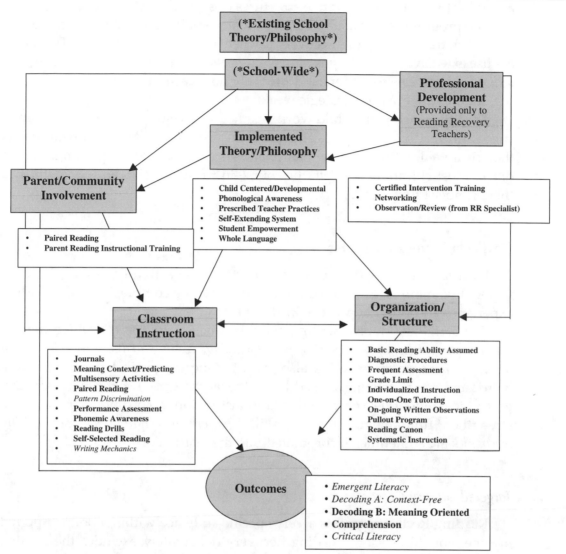

Bolded features are part of the reform; *italicized features* are sometimes adopted by schools implementing the reform.

their trainers and also *network* with other Reading Recovery teachers in other schools.

Parent Involvement Features

The reading activities used in the intervention are replicated in the home. Parents are encouraged to come to school and observe Reading Recovery lessons. The schools provide *parent reading instructional training* so parents can help their children learn to read in ways consistent with the program and engage in *paired reading* with their children at home.

Organizational/Structural Features

Reading Recovery's organizational and structural features reflect its audience and purpose. Limited to first grade (*grade limit*), it assumes that the student has mastered *emergent literacy* skills such as knowledge of letters and the alphabet, and narrative and non-narrative structures (*basic reading ability assumed*).

The program is a *pullout program* in which students leave the classroom to meet with trained Reading Recovery teachers for *one-on-one tutoring*. The teachers use extensive *diagnostic procedures* and *frequent assessments* including *ongoing written observations* to understand precisely how each individual child is reading, identifying areas of strategic weakness.

Then the teacher and child work together to develop a broader spectrum of successful reading strategies. This program provides *systematic instruction*, as there is a well-defined course plan that uses reading materials from a *reading canon*. Most children complete the course in twelve to sixteen weeks, though there is no set time limit.

Classroom Instruction Features

Each lesson is divided into seven parts. These activities, lasting approximately five minutes each, are designed to reflect the complexity of the reading experience and provide practice in all aspects.

The activities involve writing activities such as *journals, meaning context/ predicting, multisensory activities, paired reading, reading drills,* and *self-selected reading. Phonemic awareness* is also taught using magnetic letters to analyze words and create new ones. In addition, the teachers use *performance assessment* to gauge student learning and adapt instruction accordingly. In order to strengthen fundamental reading skills, *pattern discrimination* and *writing mechanics* are sometimes incorporated into the instruction.

Targeted Literacy Outcomes

Reading Recovery targets a very specific audience within a defined period of time. For this reason, Reading Recovery deliberately excludes the reading outcomes that are most affected before and after Grade 1. The result is a program entirely aimed at Grade 1 outcomes of decoding and comprehension. Specifically, the intervention helps children develop strategies to cross the gap between context-free decoding (including phonics) and *comprehension* in the most robust sense of actually understanding full texts.

The program identifies the intermediate reading outcome of *decoding B* as its primary focus, and it is understood as a network of strategies (phonics, semantic, syntactic) used in concert for "meaning-getting." Included in this approach to teaching reading is the integration of emergent writing activities to strengthen students' understanding about symbol-sound relationships within context, and to build facility in transitioning between oral, written, and printed words and sentences. By preventing over-reliance on a limited number of strategies, the intervention improves reading *comprehension* even as it motivates children to read more.

REFERENCES AND CONTACTS:
Reading Recovery

References

Askew, B. J., & Frasier, D. F. (1994). Sustained effects of Reading Recovery intervention on the cognitive behaviors of second grade children and the perceptions of their teachers. *Literacy, Teaching, and Learning, 1*(1), 87–107.

Center, Y., Wheldhall, K., Freeman, L., Outhred, L., & McNaught, N. (1995). An evaluation of Reading Recovery. *Reading Research Quarterly, 30*(2), 240–263.

Iverson, S., & Tunmer, W. E. (1993). Phonological processing skills and the Reading Recovery program. *Journal of Educational Psychology, 85*(1), 112–126.

Pinnell, G. S., Deford, D. E., & Lyons, C. A. (1988). *Reading Recovery: Early intervention for at-risk first graders.* Arlington, VA: Educational Research Service.

Rowe, K. J. (1997). Factors affecting students' progress in reading: Key findings from a longitudinal study. In S. Swartz & A. Klein (Eds.), *Research in Reading Recovery* (pp. 53–101). Portsmouth, NH: Heinemann.

Contact Information

Indiana Reading Recovery Program
Purdue University
1442 Liberal Arts and Education Building
West Lafayette, IN 47907-1442
Phone: (317) 494-9750

The Ohio State University
Reading Recovery Program
200 Ramseyer Hall
29 West Woodruff Avenue
Columbus, OH 43210

GUIDANCE FOR EDUCATORS ■

It is crucial for educators to understand that targeted reforms work best either in schools that are already successful with teaching most children to read, or in schools with a comprehensive approach to reading that is aligned with the targeted approach being used in the school. Both these limitations of target reforms merit modest elaboration before we consider specific areas of guidance.

Targeted reforms work best in schools that are already successful in early reading. This assumption is implicit in the design of these reforms. For example, the literature of Reading Recovery consistently argues that the reform should be targeted at the 20 percent of children who are having trouble learning to read, an argument that assumes other children are not having trouble. If a reform model targets only a few children who are having trouble learning to read, it is reasonable to expect that even when these programs are successful with the children served, they will have little influence on school-wide indicators (e.g., test scores and retention rates).

The long-standing limitations of Title I (Wong, in press) are related to this design problem. Early in the history of Title I, schools moved toward a pullout intervention method and many state agencies favored this approach. This method of reform made it easier for school districts to account for the use of Title I funds. However, the pullout process did not always work well in schools receiving Title I money because they were usually schools with high poverty rates and substantial need for reform. The more recent effort to promote school-wide reform through Title I provides an opportunity to overcome this inherent design limitation.

Further, the need to align the methods used for students in the pullout pro-gram with the methods used in the regular classroom can hardly be overem-phasized. If the pullout process introduces students to new skills, such as phonemic awareness and other *emergent literacy* skills often overlooked in early reading programs, these students need to reenter a classroom where reading is taught in a way that supports and reinforces these skills. When classroom teachers focus on decoding, especially when they focus on direct approaches to teaching letter-sound relationships in words, they might not be able to sup-port students who lack some of these skills or who are still trying to grasp these skills. Consequently, the pullout process works best when children in targeted programs can reenter classrooms where reading and language are taught in ways that support and enhance the skills emphasized in the pullout process.

The Research Base

Targeted approaches have a long history in the United States, so there is also a long history of research on reading reforms that use these methods. Historically the debates in reading education centered on teaching that empha-sizes whole words versus teaching that focuses on letter-sound relationships (Chall, 1967). The research then (Chall, 1967), as now (Snow, Burns, & Griffin, 1998), confirms that it is crucial to used a balanced approach integrating an emphasis on *phonemic awareness*. The three interventions reviewed in this chap-ter have this emphasis, as do many other reform models.

Research by Model Providers

The National Research Council's report was critical of Reading Recovery because it did not place an explicit emphasis on letter-sound relationships (Snow et al., 1998). These conclusions were influenced by research that had integrated a direct phonics approach (*decoding B*) into Reading Recovery (e.g., Iverson & Tunmer, 1993). There is a strong body of research demonstrating that the methods used by Reading Recovery are associated with improvement in student reading acquisition and reductions in special education referrals and retention in first grade (Askew & Frasier, 1994; Pinnell, DeFord, & Lyons, 1988. Thus, while the intervention program remains controversial, there are compelling reasons to consider the model; this is addressed in the review of the Policy Center's research in the next section. While Reading Recovery has many strengths, one of which is the strong integrated literature base that links to a developmental approach to reading, it has a design limitation: it overlooks *emergent literacy* (and *decoding A*), essentially assuming students will enter with a foundation in literacy.

The other two methods reviewed here have not been widely studied by neutral researchers. Early Interventions in Reading has an exceptionally strong research base, mostly from Barbara Taylor and her colleagues who developed the method. Their research shows consistent patterns of success when fully implemented (Taylor, 1995; Taylor, Strait, & Medo, 1994). There are also published studies that support the Early Steps approach (Morris, Shaw, & Perny, 1990; Santa, 1999), although it has not been as extensively studied, and it is supported by a textbook publisher. However, both these models share a major strength not evident in Reading Recovery: they emphasize *emergent literacy* as well as *decoding (A & B)*. Thus, they provide a balanced approach and do not assume children already have emergent reading skills.

The Policy Center's Studies

The Indiana Education Policy Center has conducted studies of early reading interventions for several years, using the conceptual framework (see Chapters 2 and 3) as a base. Reading Recovery was widely used in Indiana during the four years of our research, and Early Steps has been used in several schools in the past few years. No school that we studied was using Early Interventions in Reading, so we can reach no conclusions about this intervention method. Three of the findings from this research provide further information for schools making choices about the reform.

First, thus far we have been able to consider only one year of school effects using the "effects size" method to consider pass rates on standardized reading achievement tests offered in the third grade. It was necessary for students served in the first grade to reach the third grade in order to use this widely accepted method. In these analyses, we found that schools with Reading Recovery did not have significant effects, especially when analyses controlled for poverty (Manset, St. John, Chung, & Simmons, 2000).

Second, in using regression analysis to assess the effects of different interventions on student outcomes for the first three years of state funding, we found that having teachers trained for Reading Recovery was significantly associated with subsequent lower grade-level retention rates in elementary grades (St. John, Manset, Chung, & Worthington, 2001). The analyses found that the impact of Reading Recovery was more evident when there was a strong pattern of ongoing professional development that included *certified training* and *certified specialists*. The supplemental training provided by Reading Recovery helped explain why this program was associated with lower retention. Also, it is clear from the review earlier in this chapter that Reading Recovery intends to keep more children learning at grade level. Reductions in retention would be a clear indicator of program effect.

Finally, a descriptive fourth-year evaluation study (St. John, Michael, et al., 2001) found that schools with Reading Recovery had high compatibility between the program features included in these models (i.e., the program designs reviewed above) and the practices of classroom teachers in Grades 1–5. These schools also had lower retention and higher ISTEP+ (Indiana Statewide Testing for Educational Progress) rates than did comparison schools. However, an effect size analysis had not yet been conducted to test statistical significance.

Thus, the Policy Center's research is generally confirmatory and explanatory of the general research. It confirms that targeted reforms have limited effects on school-wide outcomes largely because they serve low numbers of students. The findings also indicate that alignment of classroom practices and intervention methods might enhance the overall effects of these interventions, but further research is needed to confirm this initial finding.

Meeting Standards

Targeted interventions can help schools keep children in the educational mainstream, but they do not have much effect on school-wide outcomes. Further, targeted interventions do not help schools organize curriculum to meet generally accepted standards in early reading. There generally is a strong alignment between the feature of targeted interventions, the outcomes they target, and the standards that are related to these outcomes, but only the pullout intervention itself meets the standards. For classrooms to meet these standards, it is necessary for reading programs in classrooms to change in ways that align the intervention and classroom practices.

Politics of Reform

Historically, choices about curriculum have been made in school district offices but have been influenced by state policy, a practice that is consistent with the tradition of local control of schools. From the perspective of teachers, for curriculum choices to be made outside the school can be problematic. State and local policies have had an especially strong influence on reading specialists in high-poverty schools since 1965 as a consequence of the elaborate procedures used to administer the Title I program. Often, district polices about pullout have extended to reading assistance in schools regardless of whether this assistance is funded by Title I.

In this context, decisions about the selection of methods for targeted reading reforms frequently involve district administrators. It is important that these decisions be made in collaboration with schools, however, since the targeted assistance strategy a school uses should be coordinated with the reading curriculum and instruction in the schools. District offices should encourage collaboration within schools between reading specialists and teachers, both in the selection of reading reforms and in the coordination of targeted assistance processes and the coordination of school curriculum. Collaboration on these choices offers the most workable approach to solving the serious problems facing reading programs in many elementary schools.

Integrating Inquiry

When schools have a targeted assistance program, a crucial element is for regular classroom teachers and reading specialists to collaborate in a school-wide reform process. Having a skilled reading specialist in a school can contribute to the improvement in reading outcomes in two ways:

- Having a direct impact on skill acquisition by children who are having the most trouble learning to read.
- Fostering collaboration in the school on refinement of the reading program in Grades 1–5. This helps teachers develop the skills they need to help children learn to read.

Maximizing the success of targeted reading programs necessarily involves both these functions. Teachers should work together to create a cohesive, coherent, and comprehensive reading program in the school as a whole.

Building Community

The goal of reading reform is to enable all children to learn how to read by the end of third grade. Targeted reforms can help schools toward this end if they are implemented in schools that already have strong reading programs but need targeted interventions to enable children who are struggling to get back on grade level. A number of proven methods can be used for the pullout process. However, the challenge for schools that rely on the pullout method is to align their regular classroom reading programs with the targeted intervention. To achieve this goal, it is essential that reading specialists and classroom teachers collaborate in ways that build learning bridges for children:

- Children who receive pullout instruction need a bridge back into the classroom (e.g., an aligned curriculum).
- There should be congruity across grade levels to support the building of reading skills.

Thus, the best environment for targeted interventions is a collaborative school community, one that engages classroom teachers and reading specialists in designing a curriculum that is aligned, coherent, and cohesive. This means that teachers need to organize so they can learn together.

Unfortunately, the legacy of three decades of urban school reform is that most with high concentrations of low-income students have fragmented programs in early reading. Schools that are challenged by having large numbers of children who have trouble learning to read should consider alternative methods. The following chapters present a range of alternatives for schools to consider.

5

Classroom-Based Interventions

Classroom-based interventions are reading and literacy programs designed for use in regular classrooms, as opposed to the more targeted pullout interventions. As such, they are not usually tailored specifically to the needs of students in at-risk situations; rather, they are usually fairly comprehensive and balanced programs grounded in integrated theories designed to enable all students to succeed. The program features are heavily concentrated at the instructional and organizational levels, with comparatively fewer program features involving parents, professional development, theory, and teacher inquiry.

At the traditional level of programming, teachers have an abundant selection of choices. Indeed, most basal series can be considered classroom-based reading programs. However, several comprehensive classroom-based reading and literacy interventions have been developed more recently, including the four reviewed here.

All children in the class are served by these interventions, though children in other classes might participate in another program. However, children participate in them only as long as these interventions last, which can vary from one year (typically first grade) to all elementary grades.

The classroom-wide interventions are all designed to work for all children. The interventions discussed below are all distinguishable by a highly comprehensive and varied set of features and activities, which should be especially useful resources for schools with highly diverse student populations.

This chapter reviews four classroom-based interventions that are in use in many states: First Steps (5.1), Four Blocks (5.2), Literacy Collaborative (5.3), and Waterford Early Reading Program (5.4). These reviews provide an overview of the program features included in the reform model and then provide references and contacts. We conclude by providing guidance for educators considering classroom-based interventions.

■ 5.1. FIRST STEPS

Reviewed by Kim Manoil

First Steps is a classroom-based professional development model focusing on language development. The model serves as a teacher resource for closing the loop between diagnostic observation of child development and classroom instruction. At the center of the model (and the process) are developmental continua for reading, writing, spelling, and oral language. These continua list hundreds of behaviors and attitudes, grouped into several stages of development. The model provides understanding about the developmental nature of reading acquisition and more complex reading skills. The model includes teaching strategies, specific outcomes, and parent involvement ideas for each stage of development.

These continua—and the suggested material associated with them—were designed to enable an iterative process. This includes careful observation of child behavior, assessment of this behavior in comparison to the developmental continua, adoption of methods intended to build on strengths and improve areas of weakness, and a return to observation to repeat the cycle.

Program Description

The program is designed to meet the needs of all students regardless of age or range of abilities. In First Steps, the progress of all students is monitored, a procedure that enables them to progress based on their individual stages of development. The program features included in First Steps (Figure 5.1) are summarized below.

School-Wide Processes

First Steps is concerned with "linking assessment, teaching, and learning" at both the classroom and the school-wide level. A *formative program evaluation* is used to assess the school's progress in addressing students' language development needs and to identify possible areas for additional professional development.

Implemented Theoretical/Philosophical Features

The First Steps model emphasizes the importance of a child-centered/developmental curriculum in a whole language environment. Supporting the developmental approach is student empowerment that allows students' interests and experiences to help dictate the direction of some of the instruction.

Reflective practice is emphasized in the model through the continual loop of assessing student work on the developmental continua and revising instructional plans based on that student work.

Professional Development Features

First Steps provides *school-site training* at the beginning of a school's implementation of the program. Simultaneously, designated *on-site facilitators* go through a *training of trainers* to prepare educators to become users, presenters,

Figure 5.1 First Steps Program Features

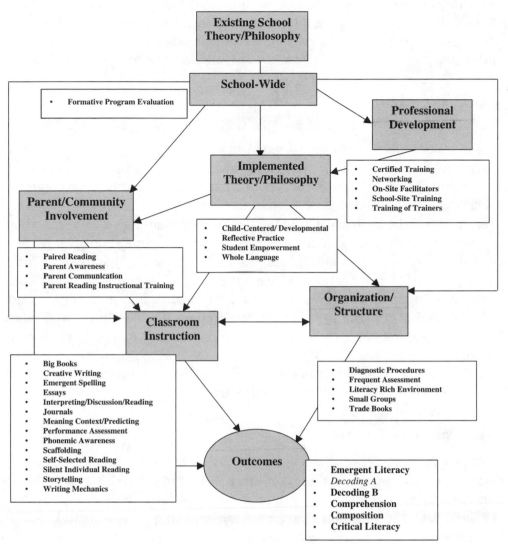

Bolded features are part of the reform; *italicized features* are sometimes adopted by schools implementing the reform.

and support providers for First Steps teachers within their district. Future First Steps trainings are provided by the on-site facilitators.

The increasing reliance on the *on-site facilitator* to assist the school in moving forward with the reform through years one and beyond makes *networking* key to the professional development, by providing ongoing support to both *on-site facilitators* and schools. Each component of First Steps (reading, writing, spelling, and oral language) has its own developmental continuum and teaching strategies. This makes it important for classroom teachers to be trained in each of the components through school-based courses.

Parent/Community Involvement Features

Parents learn about the First Steps program through *parent awareness* and are involved in the language development process through *parent communication*.

Through this communication teachers include parents in the assessment and monitoring process of First Steps by asking them for observations they have made of their child at home. In addition, parents are also provided with ideas that suggest ways they can support their children's development at home; this includes *paired reading* and *parent reading instructional training*.

Organizational/Structural Features

First Steps is a reading program that is based on *diagnostic procedures* and *frequent assessment*. Because of its extended developmental continuum, used to help students in their literacy acquisition, First Steps functions best as a school-wide program. Used throughout the school, it can provide continuity in language instruction across grade levels.

Teachers use the individual developmental continua to guide their evaluation of what their students can do as well as to inform their planning for further development. Although continua are used, they are not intended to be a sequential order of progression. Instead, the program emphasizes that each student's developmental pathway is unique, and students may exhibit behaviors that are indicative of various phases of development. The continua are used to reflect a developmental view of learning and teaching to guide classroom instruction.

The First Steps program emphasizes the need for a *literacy-rich environment* with the use of *trade books* and *small group* activities.

Classroom Instruction Features

Primary to First Steps is the use of *performance assessment* to gauge student development. Accordingly, the instructional features used in First Steps depend on the developmental phase of the student. The strategies across the continua reflect the program's emphasis on meaning. These include *storytelling, interpreting/discussion,* and *meaning context/predicting. Student empowerment* and love of reading are encouraged through *Big Books, self-selected reading,* and *silent individual reading*. First Steps blends reading and writing development through features such as *creative writing, essays,* and *journals.* Other teaching strategies include *phonemic awareness, writing mechanics,* and *emergent spelling.*

Targeted Literacy Outcomes

First Steps provides a comprehensive set of developmental continua for reading, writing, spelling, and oral language. Specific teaching strategies are emphasized at each of the stages of development along these continua. The program addresses students at all stages of reading development and consequently influences all reading outcomes. At the classroom level, specific outcomes that are targeted depend on the child's stage or "phase" of development.

First Steps emphasizes developmental, meaning-oriented reading instruction. As a result, *emergent literacy, decoding B, comprehension,* and *critical literacy* are the outcomes emphasized by the reading curriculum of the First Steps program. Throughout the stages of development, the program emphasizes strategies that foster students' independence and enjoyment of reading.

REFERENCES AND CONTACTS:
First Steps

References

Au, K. H. (1994a). *Oral language developmental continuum.* Portsmouth, NH: Heinemann.

Au, K. H. (1994b). *Reading resource book.* Portsmouth, NH: Heinemann.

Au, K. H. (1994c). *Spelling developmental continuum.* Portsmouth, NH: Heinemann.

Au, K. H. (1994d). *Writing developmental continuum.* Portsmouth, NH: Heinemann.

Australian Council for Educational Research. (1993a). *The impact of First Steps on the reading and writing ability of western Australian year 5 school students.* An interim report to the Curriculum Development Branch Western Australian Ministry of Education.

Australian Council for Educational Research. (1993b). *The impact of First Steps on schools and teachers.* An interim report to the Curriculum Development Branch Western Australian Ministry of Education.

Deschamp, P. (n.d.). *The development and implementation of the First Steps Project in Western Australia.* Perth, Western Australia: Precision Information Pty., Ltd.

Deschamp, P. (1995). *Case studies of the implementation of the First Steps Project in twelve schools.* Western Australia Education Department, Perth. (ERIC Document Reproduction Service No. ED419425)

First Steps. (2000). Welcome to the world of First Steps [On-line]. Available: www.heinemann.com/firststeps/

Freidus, H., & Grose, C. (1998). *Implementing curriculum change: Lessons from the field.* Paper presented at the annual meeting of the American Educational Reading Association, San Francisco.

Northwest Regional Educational Laboratory (NWREL). (1988). *Catalog of school reform models: First edition* [On-line]. Available: www.nwrel.org/scpd/natspec/catalog

Contact Information

First Steps
361 Hanover Street
Portsmouth, NH 03801-3912
Phone: (800) 541-2086 ext. 281
Email: firststeps@heinemann.com
Web Site: www.heinemann.com/firststeps

■ 5.2. FOUR BLOCKS

Reviewed by Kim Manoil and Jeffrey S. Bardzell

Multilevel, multimethod instruction, commonly referred to as the Four Blocks method, is a framework that provides an organized, systematic structure for providing early literacy instruction. The program is used primarily in Grade 1, but it has also been applied to other early grade levels, especially when it is used as a basis for comprehensive reform.

Program Description

The Four Blocks framework is designed for children with a wide range of abilities. Its design implements a wide variety of highly adaptable literacy instruction techniques that allow teachers to avoid *ability grouping* altogether. These techniques fit into an overall framework comprising Four Blocks: Guided Reading, Self-Selected Reading, Writing, and Working With Words. The program features are described below and are depicted in Figure 5.2.

School-Wide Features

The Four Blocks intervention focuses on first-grade classes and sometimes other early grades but is not implemented school-wide (across all subject areas or all grades).

Implemented Theory and Philosophy

The Four Blocks method has a balanced literacy approach and draws on the theories of both *phonological awareness* and *whole language*. Thus, the program incorporates explicit phonics instruction as well as meaning-oriented activities. The intervention is also rooted in *student empowerment* and emphasizes nurturing a love for reading through incorporating features for pursuing and expressing individual interests (e.g., self-selection of reading materials and expressive writing activities).

Professional Development Features

There is no standard professional development component for the Four Blocks method. The model assumes that professional development and training will take on various forms depending on the school and availability of professionals knowledgeable of the program. Books, videos, and Internet news groups are available for training purposes. Some teachers also use *study groups*.

Parent Involvement Features

The Four Blocks method does not include a specified parent involvement program.

Figure 5.2 Four Blocks Program Features

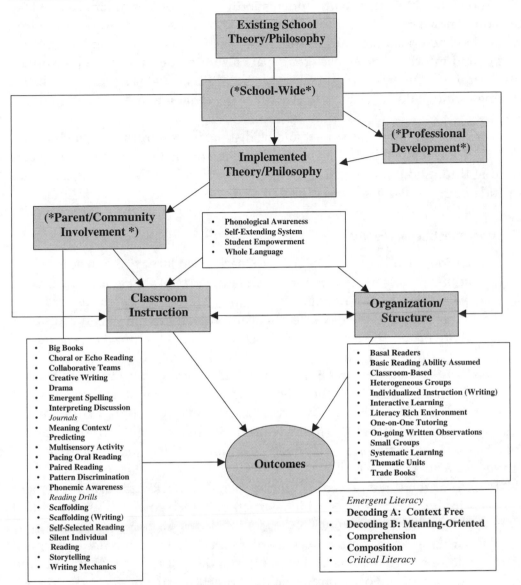

Bolded features are part of the reform; *italicized features* are sometimes adopted by schools implementing the reform.

Organizational/Structural Features

The Four Blocks method's wide range of organizational and structural features enables it to reach *heterogeneous groups* of children with a variety of ability levels and learning styles. The program provides a framework for *systematic learning* through its *classroom-based* language arts instruction. The language arts instructional time is divided into four 30- to 40-minute blocks that are performed daily: Guided Reading, Self-Selected Reading, Writing, and Working With Words. The intervention uses a *grade limit*—that is, only students in designated grades (usually Grade 1)—participate, and *basic reading ability is assumed* (*emergent literacy*).

Diagnostic procedures such as *ongoing written observation* are used within the classroom. Teachers meet with students individually on a regular basis to take anecdotal notes on their reading. Individual conferences are held with children to discuss the books they are reading in the self-selected reading block. *Small groups* and informal *one-on-one tutoring* are also provided for students who are not reading at their instructional level. In addition, *individualized instruction* during writing allows teachers to customize instruction to meet specific student needs.

The Four Blocks classroom should be distinct in its atmosphere, including a *literacy-rich environment* and *interactive learning* and incorporating reading and writing throughout subject areas through *thematic units*. The reading materials include both leveled *basal readers* and *trade books*.

Classroom Instruction Features

The Guided Reading Block begins as a teacher-led large group reading time, including *interpreting/discussion* and *meaning context/predicting*, and eventually shifts to *paired reading* or *silent individual reading*. Although *basal readers* have traditionally been used in the block, teachers also use other materials such as *trade books* and *Big Books*. The activities may include *echo or choral reading, pacing oral reading, storytelling,* and *drama*.

The Self-Selected Reading Block involves children reading *trade books* alone or with partners. As a part of this block, children take turns sharing their books with the whole class. The Writing Block usually involves a brief (10 minutes) mini-lesson for the entire class followed by individual student writing and editing. The writing instruction may include *creative writing, journal writing,* and *writing mechanics*.

In each of the three preceding blocks, there is a back-and-forth movement between individual and class-wide instruction, which fosters both individual skills and a literate community.

The Working With Words Block involves teacher-led and *collaborative team* activities to reinforce reading and an understanding of *phonemic awareness* and *pattern discrimination*. For example, children practice learning to read and spell words posted on the word wall through chanting, clapping, writing, and *emergent spelling* activities. Children also manipulate letters to make words called out by their teacher in the "making words" activity. These *multisensory activities* may include *scaffolding* of instruction.

Targeted Literacy Outcomes

The Four Blocks method focuses on three intermediary literacy outcomes: *decoding A* (context-free), *decoding B* (meaning-oriented), and *comprehension*. This focus provides a balanced, intermediary literacy instructional framework that develops basic reading skills including *comprehension* and *composition*.

Although many aspects of Four Blocks assume that children have acquired *emergent literacy* skills (knowledge of letters and the alphabet, narrative and nonnarrative structures), some of its techniques target instruction in these areas. These include "pretend reading" (telling the story of a familiar book without actually reading the words) and "picture reading" (talking about the pictures in a book).

The Four Blocks framework does not explicitly target *critical literacy* skills, although the program may foster such development as a result of the intermediary reading foundation skills it provides and the variety of instructional techniques included in the program.

REFERENCES AND CONTACTS:
Four Blocks

References

Cunningham, P. M. (1991). Research directions: Multimethod, multilevel literacy instruction in first grade. *Language Arts, 68,* 578–584.

Cunningham, P. M., Hall, D. P., & Defee, M. (1991). Non-ability-grouped, multilevel instruction: A year in a first-grade classroom. *The Reading Teacher, 44*(8), 556–571.

Cunningham, P. M., Hall, D. P., & Defee, M. (1998). Non-ability-grouped, multilevel instruction: Eight years later. *The Reading Teacher, 51*(8), 652–664.

Contact Information

Patricia M. Cunningham
Wake Forest University
P.O. Box 7266
Winston-Salem, NC 27109
Email: cunningh@wfu.edu
Web Site: www.wfu.edu/~cunningh/fourblocks/

5.3. LITERACY COLLABORATIVE   ■

Reviewed by Jeffrey S. Bardzell

The Literacy Collaborative is a school-wide language arts restructuring model that focuses on *classroom-based* instruction and includes Reading Recovery as a "safety net" for those students still not succeeding. A significant element of the Literacy Collaborative is its literacy framework, which includes eight elements—four each for reading and writing. It was originally developed to respond to the problem of successfully discharged Reading Recovery students not receiving appropriate support in the classrooms when they returned.

Program Description

Self-described as a professional development program, the intervention involves the whole school—especially teachers and families—in a comprehensive

Figure 5.3 Literacy Collaborative Program Features

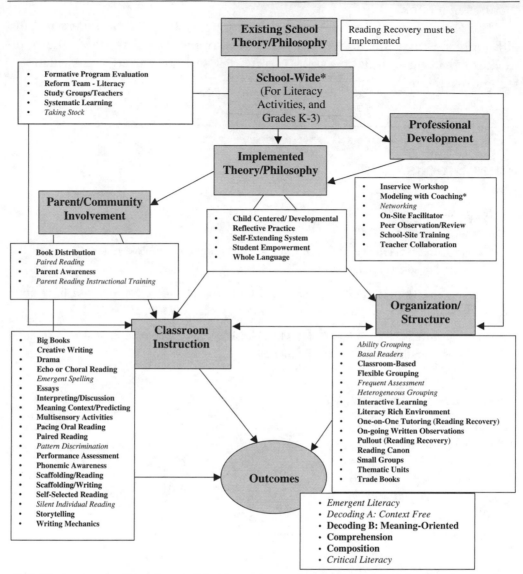

Bolded features are part of the reform; *italicized features* are sometimes adopted by schools implementing the reform.

and reflective approach to literacy instruction appropriate for all children. The components and features of the program are described below and depicted in Figure 5.3.

School-Wide Features

The Literacy Collaborative intervention involves a *reform team* consisting of the *on-site facilitator*, an administrator, teachers, and possibly parents who in turn engage the entire school in developing and implementing the reform. The school often is involved in *taking stock* of literacy practices, materials, and student performance. Over time, this information is revisited through *formative program evaluations*.

The Literacy Collaborative framework provides school-wide *systematic learning* that flows across grade levels resulting in a school-wide program that has an articulated and coordinated set of instructional activities and expectations. *Study groups* of teachers focus on literacy instruction and student performance in order to strengthen cohesiveness of the school-wide program.

Implemented Theory/Philosophy

The Literacy Collaborative program is a student-centered approach to literacy acquisition geared to increasing reading skills and encouraging the development of dispositions and behaviors (e.g., "a love of reading") that are indicative of self-motivated, self-directed learners. The program is *child-centered/developmental* and allows for tailoring instructional activities to individual needs. The model is rooted in *whole language* and *student empowerment* approaches; most instructional activities are meaning-getting and involve student choice. The program also addresses metacognitive skills, such as self-correction, consistent with *self-extending system* approaches.

The Literacy Collaborative's emphasis on *reflective practice* as a means for improved student outcomes is evidenced by professional development and school-wide features that encourage teacher interaction and reflective study. Individually and in groups, teachers study their own practice in relation to student performance.

Professional Development Features

Literacy Collaborative schools designate an *on-site facilitator* (the literacy coordinator) who is trained by an affiliated university and who maintains a connection to the university. The facilitator may assist in the *school-site training* through which the faculty are trained in implementing the program. *Inservice workshops* provide additional training for teachers.

The intervention encourages *teacher collaboration* (in teacher study groups) and *modeling with coaching* by the *on-site facilitator* to support teacher reflection and professional growth.

Parent Involvement Features

Parent involvement is considered important to the success of the program. *Parent awareness* activities include encouraging parents to come into the school to see how their children are learning. This participation may include hands-on *parent reading instructional training* to help parents learn to assist their children in learning to read.

Book distribution provides parents with inexpensive "keep" books that parents are encouraged to use for *paired reading* with their child.

Organizational/Structural Features

The Literacy Collaborative provides several features to encourage student engagement and increase instructional effectiveness. The model provides *interactive learning* through the use of *flexible grouping* such as *small groups*, and *ability groups*, *heterogeneous groups* and *one-on-one tutoring* (Reading Recovery). To increase student interest, the model recommends *thematic units* to integrate lessons across the curriculum. To ensure student success, *ongoing written observations* and *frequent assessments* are used by teachers to monitor student progress, provide evidence of program effectiveness, and indicate instructional refinements that might be needed in the program.

The classroom's *literacy-rich environment* reflects the centrality of the meaning orientation in the intervention. So, too, does the high reliance on *trade books*. *Trade books* permit greater self-selection than do traditional *basal readers*. To ensure that the self-selection of reading materials does not allow students to read only one genre of books or to select only "easy" books, the Literacy Collaborative provides a master list of *trade books* for a *reading canon*; in this list, books are graded and leveled by difficulty. In addition, the intervention also makes use of *basal readers*.

Classroom Instruction Features

As with other school-wide and classroom-based interventions, the Literacy Collaborative uses a wide variety of instructional features in concert to reach every child. Most of the features—*Big Books*, *echo or choral reading*, *creative writing*, *drama*, *essays*, *paired reading*, *storytelling*, and *silent individual reading*—are consistent with the meaning orientation of the intervention and affect meaning-oriented decoding (*decoding B*) and *comprehension*. Guided reading approaches such as *interpreting/discussion* and *meaning context/predicting* help students extend and internalize reading processes that are prerequisite for *critical literacy*.

While the intervention emphasizes meaning-oriented approaches, several features such as *phonemic awareness*, *scaffolding*, *multisensory activities*, *writing mechanics*, and sometimes *emergent spelling* and *pattern discrimination* are incorporated through both reading and writing to strengthen *decoding A* (context free) skills.

Targeted Literacy Outcomes

The comprehensive Literacy Collaborative model was designed to influence all reading outcomes. However, consistent with Reading Recovery, the Literacy Collaborative emphasizes meaning-oriented decoding (or *decoding B*), *comprehension*, and *composition*. It would be false, however, to say that the other three outcomes are not substantially targeted. Several elements emphasize *emergent literacy*, context-free decoding (*decoding A*), and *critical literacy*. These outcomes are targeted, but they are done so in a way that makes them consistent with—and yet subordinate to—the two main outcomes. *Emergent literacy* is targeted in meaning-oriented ways; context-free decoding takes place in the writing component; and *critical literacy* is the intended result of the meaning-driven activities.

REFERENCES AND CONTACTS:
Literacy Collaborative

References

Ohio State University. (1998). *Literacy Collaborative*. (Informational package on Literacy Collaborative offered by program directors.) Columbus, OH: Author.

Contact Information:

Indiana Reading Recovery Program
Purdue University
1442 Liberal Arts and Education Building
West Lafayette, IN 47907-1442
Phone: (317) 494-9750

The Ohio State University
Reading Recovery Program
200 Ramseyer Hall
29 West Woodruff Avenue
Columbus, OH 43210

5.4. WATERFORD EARLY READING PROGRAM ■

Reviewed by Siri Ann Loescher

The Waterford Early Reading Program is a technology-based, supplemental reading program for kindergarten through Grade 2 that provides students with daily, *individualized instruction* in literacy acquisition. The model is designed to ensure that all students, regardless of their literacy skills and experiences prior to entering school, acquire and maintain grade-level reading skills. The instructional program is divided into three levels: Level One (primarily *emergent literacy* and *decoding A* skills), Level Two (*decoding A and B* skills and some *comprehension* skills), and Level Three (*comprehension* and *composition* skills). The model was designed by a nonprofit research organization (the Waterford Foundation) that maintains its independence from the organization that markets the electronic program. A licensing agreement between the two entities provides the finances to continue researching, developing, and piloting the instructional programs.

Program Description

Unique to this model is the sophisticated use of technology to deliver instruction that integrates pre-reading skills, *comprehension* skills, and writing activities in ways that are multisensory, interactive, and comprehensive (Figure 5.4). Rather than merely using the medium to deliver traditional instruction in a more interesting manner (e.g., use of graphics and positive reinforcements in the program in lessons similar to traditional reading/question/answer exercises), the model integrates researched-based methods that are delivered through the technology. This includes continual assessment of student performance that includes assignment of on- and off-line materials, allowing teachers to focus on areas of weakness and build on students' strengths. Instead of having a limited set of exercises related to specific skills that students are to master before moving on, the technology links a multitude of related instructional activities that are branched and assigned according to the previous day's activities. So even if a student has seemingly mastered a skill one day (e.g., scored an 80% mastery on a skill set), if in a later assignment that skill is not repeated, the program would select new materials to review and reincorporate instruction on that skill.

The reading program is designed to be used by each student daily (suggested fifteen to thirty minutes), and the teacher is provided with numerous off-line materials to complement the program; however, the program designers advocate using the reading program to supplement the school's curriculum rather than to replace it. Indeed, the automated computer program itself is designed to be self-managing so that it does not disrupt the flow of the regular classroom instruction. Thus, rather than experiencing a disruption or pullout, students move on and off the computer stations that are housed in the classroom and return to the primary classroom instruction in a seamless fashion.

School-Wide Features

The Waterford Program may be used as a component of a school's whole-school restructuring effort, but it does not provide a process for whole-school change. Instead it provides a classroom-based, comprehensive approach ensuring successful literacy acquisition for all students. Thus, school-wide features are not a focus of this model. One school-wide feature, however, plays an important role in the intervention. *Formative program evaluation*, conducted by the *certified specialist*, is used to help the school plan for implementation in the following school year, including specifying any professional development needs that are related to the instructional program.

Implemented Theory/Philosophy

Child-centered/developmental learning is the intervention's primary philosophy. Language acquisition is believed to be developmental. Effective instruction should be individualized to each student's current skill level. Thus, while the program is divided into three separate levels, students progress through those levels according to development rather than age or grade. It is possible for a kindergarten student to be in a more advanced level (rather than Level One) and for a second grade student to be working on earlier level skills (rather than Level Three). Furthermore the intervention is designed to ensure that even if

Figure 5.4 Waterford Early Reading Program Features

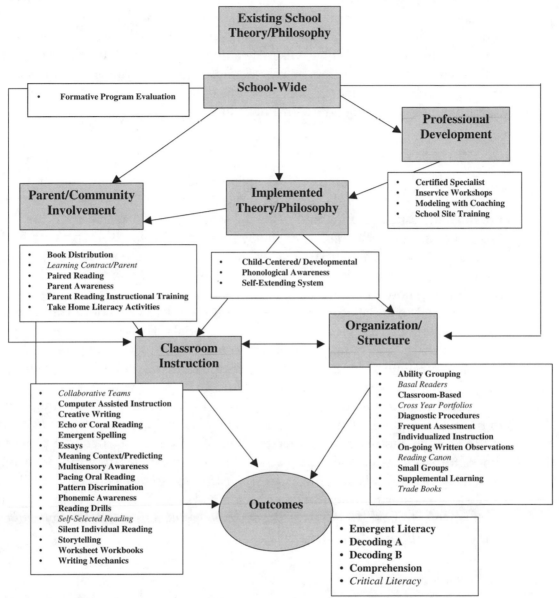

Bolded features are part of the reform; *italicized features* are sometimes adopted by schools implementing the reform.

students enter school with weak or nonexistent pre-literacy skills, they will acquire those skills, will catch up, and will successfully advance through all three levels of the program.

Reading as a *self-extending system* is promoted through the many available activities combined with the self-management instructional system. The program is geared toward fostering student independence in learning and encouraging students to learn how to strengthen their own reading skills. By Level Three, students are taught specific *comprehension* skills in a metacognitive approach and are expected to apply these skills when reading across the curriculum in all subject areas.

The Waterford Early Reading Program's philosophy toward early reading acquisition is clearly in the *phonological awareness* tradition. Building *phonemic awareness (decoding A)* and understanding about print concepts precedes all other instruction and is the primary focus in Level One. Once these skills are mastered, the intervention weaves in meaning-oriented decoding, reading *comprehension*, and the building of *composition* skills. So while the model does encourage meaning-oriented decoding, this emphasis comes sequentially after intensive instruction in context-free decoding.

Professional Development Features

The model provides support for implementation of the intervention through professional development. The school works directly with a *certified specialist* who provides the initial training and visits the school several times during the year. The initial training is a *school-site training* provided in a small setting with six to eight teachers at a time. These sessions are small to promote interaction between the teachers and the trainer, among teachers, and with the technology. Teachers are trained in how to use the technology-based program and in how the off-line supplemental materials can be integrated into regular classroom instruction as well as how to use the parent involvement materials. The intervention also provides the school with ongoing support resources such as on-line tutorials and videotaped training sessions, both related to the use of the technology system, and technical support for the hardware setup and maintenance.

Throughout the year, the *certified specialist* makes several visits to the school to provide one-on-one coaching to teachers. This includes *modeling with coaching* to deepen the teachers' understanding of how the instructional program works for students and to help teachers improve their classroom implementation. The specialist also conducts several *inservice workshops* on using available Waterford teacher resources and reviewing end-of-the-year reports on student performance (related to the *formative program evaluation*). Schools may request (for a fee) additional trainings.

Parent Involvement

Promoting involvement in literacy activities at home is the focus of the Waterford Program's parent involvement component. *Parent awareness* about Waterford involves providing parents with information about the program and about their child's progress. The awareness activities include newsletters and conferences.

Parents receive *parent reading instructional training* through "family literacy nights" at the school and through instructional take-home videos. During this training parents learn how to best support their child's reading acquisition through activities such as *paired reading*. The intervention promotes these home activities and encourages the development of literacy-rich home environments through *book distribution* and *take-home literacy activities* that include videos, CDs, and sing-along cassettes. Some of these materials are available in Spanish as well as English. To encourage regular parent-child literacy interaction, some schools may institute *learning contracts/parents* in which parents agree to read with their child for a specified amount of time (e.g., twenty minutes a day).

Organization/Structure

The Waterford Program is *classroom-based* and is organized as a *supplemental learning* program that provides self-managing *individualized instruction* to students throughout the school day. The model lends itself well to *ability grouping,* as students work through the different levels of the program. In addition the model provides teachers with materials and instructional classroom activities that involve *small groups.*

The technology component links performance/assessment/assignment in a continual cycle. Thus, embedded in the instruction are both *diagnostic procedures* and *frequent assessment.* In addition, teachers can generate regular student progress reports that can be used for *ongoing written observations.* Teachers can use these reports to adjust the regular classroom instruction and/or to tailor the materials and activities students receive for take-home literacy activities. The technology component allows for easy collection of samples of student work that demonstrate growth in literacy acquisition over time. Some schools will use this aspect of the program for the development of *cross-year portfolios.*

The Waterford Early Reading Program is recommended as a complement to rather than as a replacement for the existing reading curriculum used by the school. Therefore schools using Waterford may utilize *basal readers, trade books,* or a *reading canon* as part of the language arts program.

Classroom Instruction

The *computer-assisted instruction* provided by the Waterford Early Reading Program is designed to be interactive and multisensory. For example, a reviewed lesson teaching recognition of a specific letter included repetition and echo response (aural and oral), movement and practice with writing the letter (kinesthetic), and rhyme and visual clues. The Waterford Early Reading Program incorporates numerous instructional features through the technology program, supplemented by off-line teaching activities. Features related to *emergent literacy* acquisition include *phonemic awareness, multisensory activities, pattern discrimination,* and *reading drills.* Simultaneously students are engaged in the act of reading through *echo or choral reading* and *pacing oral reading.* Teachers often supplement this work through classroom activities including *storytelling, worksheet/workbooks,* and *emergent spelling.*

As students advance to meaning-oriented decoding and *comprehension,* additional instructional strategies are incorporated into the program including *meaning context/predicting, creative writing,* and *essays.* Some teachers may use *collaborative teams* in some of this work. Additionally "concepts about print" and understanding structures about text are reinforced through *writing mechanics.*

Students gain independence in reading through *silent individual reading,* and in some classes through *self-selected reading.* By the completion of Level Three, students have learned how to improve their own reading skills and begin to apply those while reading in other curricular areas.

Targeted Literacy Outcomes

The Waterford Early Literacy Program provides a supplemental instructional program that provides delivery of *individualized instruction* to students in an interesting and interactive way that incorporates recitation, *multisensory activities*, writing, and *comprehension* and critical thinking. The intervention is particularly strong in building *emergent literacy* and *decoding A* at the earliest level. A number of preliminary studies and evaluation reports have been conducted and reviewed, and these suggest positive results for participating students and schools. However, most of this early confirmatory research has been conducted on the *emergent literacy* acquisition (Level One) program. Less has been written about the development and maintenance of the literacy skills targeted in Levels Two and Three.

The primary focus on context-free decoding lessens with an increased focus on meaning-oriented decoding (*decoding B*) and *comprehension* during the Level Two program. By Level Three, *comprehension* is fostered through a metacognitive approach and through a stronger focus on *composition*. The model, which is usually implemented at the kindergarten through second grade level, builds the skills that are prerequisite for *critical literacy*, suggesting that students who complete this program will be more successful in later grades in acquiring *critical literacy* skills.

REFERENCES AND CONTACTS:
Waterford Early Reading Program

References

References marked with an asterisk indicate studies included in a research review (Tracey, 2000).

*Albritton, G. (1999). *Evaluation of the Waterford Early Reading Program.* Tampa, FL: Hillsborough County Public School, Division of Instruction.

Brown, A. (2001). *Waterford Early Reading Program.* Unpublished manuscript.

*Duncanville I.S.D. (n.d.). *Waterford Early Reading Program Implementation Results 1996–1997.* Duncanville, TX: Author.

Electronic Education. (n.d.). *Waterford Early Reading Program training cycle.* Scottsdale, AZ: Author.

Electronic Education. (n.d.). *Waterford Early Reading Program: Keyboarding to read and write.* [Brochure]. Scottsdale, AZ: Author.

Electronic Education. (n.d.). *Waterford Early Reading Program: Level one.* [Brochure]. Scottsdale, AZ: Author.

Electronic Education. (n.d.). *Waterford Early Reading Program: Level two.* [Brochure]. Scottsdale, AZ: Author.

Electronic Education. (n.d.). *Waterford Early Reading Program: Level three.* [Brochure]. Scottsdale, AZ: Author.

Electronic Education. (n.d.). *Waterford Early Reading Program: Nine components of comprehensive school reform and the Waterford Early Reading Program.* [Brochure]. Scottsdale, AZ: Author.

Electronic Education. (2001). *Correlation, Indiana Academic Standards 2000 English language arts K-2, Waterford Early Reading Program Level 2 – Level 2 – Level 3.* Scottsdale, AZ: Author.

*Research, Assessment and Measurement, Inc. (n.d.). *Evaluation of Waterford Early Reading Program, Collins Garden and Nelson Elementary Schools, San Antonio, TX, School Year 1997–98.* San Antonio, TX: San Antonio Independent School District.

*Research, Assessment and Measurement, Inc. (n.d.). *Evaluation of Waterford Early Reading Program, Hacienda La Puente Unified School District, Whittier School District, Los Angeles County, CA, program year 1997–1998.* Los Angeles, CA: Technology for Results in Elementary Education.

Tracey, D.H. (2000). *The Waterford Early Reading Program: Research orientation, studies and findings.* Scottsdale, AZ: Electronic Education.

*Ward-Murray, M. (1999). *El Centrito interim grant report for the period of July 1, 1998 to December 30, 1998.* (Report no. 107). Thousand Oaks, CA: California Lutheran University, Educational Research and Leadership Institute.

Waterford Early Reading Program. [On-line]. Available: www. electroniceducation.com.

*Waterford Institute. (n.d.). *Evaluation of the Waterford Early Reading Program Level 1, Norwalk Public Schools, Norwalk, CT 1998–1999 School Year.* Sandy, UT: Author.

*Waterford Institute. (n.d.). *Preliminary research data on the effect of the Waterford Early Reading Program based on daily use of computer materials for 15 minutes.* Sandy, UT: Author.

*Waterford Institute. (n.d.). *Preliminary results from elementary schools in the Dallas ISC on the effectiveness of the Waterford Early Reading Program.* Sandy, UT: Author.

*Young, J.W., & Tracey, D.H. (n.d.). *An evaluation of the Waterford Early Reading Program, Newark, New Jersey 1997–98 School Year.* Scottsdale, AZ: Electronic Education.

Contact Information

Electronic Education
6710 East Camelback Road
Scottsdale, AZ 85251
Phone: (888) 977-9700
Web Site: www.electroniceducation.com

Indiana Contact:
Michael Miller
Phone: (317) 773-7632

GUIDANCE FOR EDUCATORS ■

Classroom-based reading reforms provide an alternative for schools that wish to make a concerted effort to improve school-wide reading programs in Grades 1–5. Classroom reforms work best when they are used across the grade levels in schools, enabling students to experience a congruent, seamless learning process in reading and literacy as they progress across grade levels. Classroom-based reading reforms can be adopted as part of a school-wide process that focuses explicitly on early reading or as a component of a process-oriented reform. Several states have encouraged schools to use classroom-based reading models as an integral part of Comprehensive School Reform.

The Research Base

The classroom-based reading reforms reviewed in this chapter were not as widely investigated by researchers as either targeted reforms or comprehensive reforms. However, the model providers generally based their model designs on an understanding of the research on reading. Thus, these reforms are based on research, even if many of these models do not have strong confirmatory research bases.

Research by Model Providers

Model providers typically conduct the first generation of confirmatory research on their reading reforms. Over time, as the models are more widely disseminated, there is a greater chance that external evaluators and policy researchers will assess the effects of these models in practice. Below, we summarize key elements of the research on the reforms included in this chapter.

First Steps is a relatively mature classroom-based method with a substantial body of supporting texts (e.g., Au, 1994a, 1994b) but limited confirmatory research, conducted mostly in Australia where the model originated. Most of the Australia studies were descriptive (Australian Council for Educational Research, 1993a, 1993b; Dechamp, 1995) and do not include the controls typically used in U.S. research on reading reform. State and federal studies should further assess the effects of this intervention method in the U.S. context.

Four Blocks provides a classroom method that integrates literature-based methods with phonics and writing, providing an integrated approach that is consonant with the research literature (Snow et al., 1998). Most of the early research was largely descriptive and was conducted by Patricia Cunningham and her colleagues (Cunningham, 1991; Cunningham, Hall, & Defee, 1991). The model is widely disseminated in some states. In Indiana, for example, the state has provided training in the method and encourages schools to use ongoing professional development and teacher collaboration in the implementation process, an approach that potentially overcomes some of the limitations of this model.

Our review of the Literacy Collaborative used an informational package provided by the Ohio State University Reading Recovery project. While both Ohio State and Purdue University have conducted pilot studies of this project, these results have not been widely disseminated.

The Waterford Early Reading Program has an extensive set of in-house studies that are noted in the review. However, while this research can be accessed on the Web and by request, it has not been widely disseminated. (This evaluation literature was discussed in review 5.4.)

Further policy-oriented and evaluation research is needed on these and other classroom-based reading models. As the national efforts to promote "research-based" reform continue, it is crucial that research on various methods be published and widely disseminated.

The Policy Center's Studies

The Policy Center's studies of early reading programs in Indiana have examined a number of schools using Four Blocks and Literacy Collaborative, but research on other classroom methods is not yet available. We summarize key findings.

First, the effects size analyses indicate that both Four Blocks and Literacy Collaborative were associated with high pass rates on Indiana's ISTEP+ reading and language arts tests (Manset, St. John, Chung, & Simmons, 2000). When schools with early literacy programs were compared with control schools, Literacy Collaborative and those with Four Blocks demonstrated significant gains in passing rates compared to control schools. When high-poverty schools were examined, schools using both methods showed improvement compared to control schools. When low-poverty schools were compared, the effects were more moderate, but still significant.

Second, the analyses using regression models with more statistical controls provided additional insights into the effects of First Steps, Literacy Collaborative, and Four Blocks (St. John, Manset, Chung, & Worthington, 2001). The results provided compelling evidence for the effectiveness of First Steps and Literacy Collaborative, but not Four Blocks.

First Steps was consistently associated with lower special education referral, but not with changes on student reading achievement or retention rates (St. John, Manset, et al., 2001). The finding that First Steps was associated with lower referral would seem to confirm that the systematic tracing of progress and intervening to promote learning enables more children to learn on grade level. It appears to keep more children in the educational mainstream because it provides a method of targeting special needs while enabling teachers to work with all students.

Literacy Collaborative was significantly associated with higher pass rates on standardized tests, lower special education referrals, and lower retention in grade level in analyses that controlled for poverty, other district and school characteristics, and classroom practices (St. John, Manset, et al., 2001). The findings concerning the effects of the Literacy Collaborative on standardized pass rates indicated that these were related to the use of *book distribution*, a method for involving parents in reading with their children, a unique aspect of this literature-based reform method. The effects on lower retention rates were explained in part by the professional development activities (ongoing professional development and specialists).

Four Blocks was associated with higher special education referral rates. It was not associated with other outcomes (St. John, Manset, et al., 2001), a troublesome finding.

Third, these analyses also included factor analyses of classroom practices. The findings on two of the factors (St. John, Manset, et al., 2001) merit review:

- *The Connected-Text Approaches* factor includes independent reading, cooperative learning, creative writing, emergent spelling, paired reading (student-to-student), and reading aloud. Schools that used these methods combined techniques that engage students in the learning process.
- *The Direct/Explicit Approaches* factor combines basal readers, phonics instruction, reading drills, and workshops/workbooks. Schools that used these approaches emphasized systematic approaches to teaching the components of language and reading. (p. 11)

The analyses found that text-connected approaches were significantly associated with lower retention rates, whereas direct/explicit approaches were associated with higher retention levels (St. John, Manset, et al., 2001). This provides compelling evidence that literature-rich methods are needed to engage more students in learning to reading, to create interest in reading. On the other hand, overemphasizing systematic approaches can cause problems relative to student engagement.

Meeting Standards

By creating standards for reading programs in Grades 1–5, states are focusing explicitly on all the components of reading, encouraging schools to take a comprehensive, coherent approach. The classroom-based intervention methods provide a workable way to engage teachers in collaboration on reading reform while they provide the tools to use in addressing this challenge. The research is incomplete and ongoing, but extant studies provide clear evidence that classroom-based methods can help schools address standards and improve reading outcomes.

There is a clear link between reading outcomes (*emergent literacy, decoding A and B, comprehensive,* and *critical literacy*), state standards for reading (see Chapter 3), and student outcomes. Making standards explicit can encourage teachers and reading specialists to coordinate their efforts to develop coherent, cohesive early reading programs that introduce students to phonics, create phonemic awareness skills, and engage students in learning. We advocate coordination between program design and assessment so that (student) learning and (the education community's) assessment are strongly related. Having literature-rich approaches is essential for creating engaging learning environments, but no single method seems complete. Teachers and specialists must work together to create engaging learning environments.

Politics of Reform

Reading reform has become exceedingly political. The federal government has made early reading the central component of the reauthorization of the ESEA, bringing reading reform into the debate about school reform at all levels of policy. This attention has many consequences for teachers and schools. The increased attention means that more policy bodies—school boards, state boards, standards boards—will try to influence educational practice through their decisions. While this can create a compliance nightmare for educators—principals, reading specialists, and classroom teachers—it can also create a climate that is supportive of reform that engages teachers. To avoid difficulties with compliance, every possible effort should be made to create a supportive climate. We advocate collaboration on the selection of reform models precisely because the selection process helps teachers build a shared understanding of the challenge and alerts them to the need to work together on implementing early reading programs.

Classroom-based reading reforms are necessary in schools that are lagging behind in their efforts to enable all children to learn to read, but they can be helpful in schools that have a successful record. Indeed, the focus on whole class reading and literacy is a key to improving the quality of elementary schools. These schools should be judged on their ability to enable children to attain grade level, not just on achievement tests. Focusing exclusively on reading tests provides a subtle encouragement for schools to hold students back if they are not learning to read rather than reworking their reading programs to address the reading challenge in a more coherent way.

Integrating Inquiry

In spite of the politics of school reform, schools need to create a climate that supports collaboration in schools. Teachers and reading specialists must work together to evolve a school practice that

- Provides support for children who are having trouble learning to read based entirely on the curriculum and instruction provided in the regular classroom.
- Provides alignment between targeted interventions and regular classroom practices in the reading and language arts program.
- Provides a coherent set of reading practices that enable students to progress across grade levels, with skills building across grade levels, until students develop the capacity to read critically in all areas of the curriculum.

Having a coherent, cohesive, and comprehensive approach to classroom reading programs in Grades 1–5 is crucial. The reforms reviewed in this chapter provide a resource for teachers and specialists, allowing them to review different programs and to assess how their current practices match up with all the learning standards for reading. Schools that fall short in their efforts to address any of these challenges should use the inquiry-based method outlined in Chapter 2 to review their current practices, set new directions, and take the steps toward a more coherent approach through deliberate collaboration.

Building Community

The overarching challenge facing elementary schools that are confronted by the new realities of research-based reform is clear: to build a community of practitioners who can increase the number of children reading by Grade 3 and reading critically across diverse texts by the end of Grade 5. Too often, school communities have been fragmented, with upper- and lower-grade teachers blaming each other for the school's failure. If schools have certified reading specialists, these teachers have often been isolated in pullout classrooms. As a consequence there has been little congruity between the targeted reading instruction and the regular classroom where children are expected to work after they complete the pullout process.

Creating a sense of community in the school as a whole can help educators address this overarching challenge. Taking a cohesive and coherent approach to the reading program—that is, evolving a coordinated approach to reading and literacy across grade levels—is central to success. Involving parents in the early reading process also helps, as the Policy Center's research on Literacy Collaborative illustrates. Engaging parents in reading with their children and supporting parents in this process extends the commitment. The new comprehensive reform models provide a way for schools to engage in this community-building process and merit consideration as an alternative to focusing exclusively on reading reform.

6

Teacher Inquiry Models

Teacher inquiry models are programs that set up systematic, structured processes of inquiry. Inquiry is an iterative process that involves taking stock of the existing situation, conducting relevant research, collectively proposing and approving changes, implementing new practices, critically assessing their effects, making adjustments, and returning to the beginning of the cycle. In these models, teachers are professionals and equals, taking accountability for and charge of their schools.

Teacher inquiry is focused primarily on the teachers rather than the students; while it affects all students in a school, it typically does so indirectly. However, it is possible to treat early reading and literacy as the main focus of teacher inquiry teams in Grades 1–5.

This chapter includes reviews of two models: Reader's and Writer's Workshops (6.1) and Teacher Inquiry (6.2). These interventions provide systematic processes for engaging teachers in inquiry on reading and writing initiatives.

Teacher inquiry is designed to help schools learn about and implement new ideas. For this reason, a school undergoing any type of change—in population, in curriculum, by adopting an intervention—could benefit from teacher inquiry.

In addition, the Accelerated Schools Project, a process-oriented restructuring model (see review 7.1), is also based on teacher inquiry as central to the reform process. This chapter concludes with guidance on integrating teacher inquiry into reform in early reading and literacy.

6.1. READER'S AND WRITER'S WORKSHOPS ■

Reviewed by Amy Flint

Reader's and writer's workshops are process- and strategy-oriented approaches that build on a *whole language* philosophy of stressing social interactions with peers and meaningful texts. Students engage in varied reading and *composition* activities. At the heart of the workshop is the premise that children learn to read and write by reading and writing authentic and meaningful texts.

During writer's workshop, children compose individual and collaborative pieces in a structure that allows them to work with others, experiment with texts, and explore various options in their writing. Reader's workshops focus on children's efforts to use strategies to make sense of and think about texts. In both workshop approaches, activities are chosen and led by students, supplemented with mini-lessons and one-on-one or small group interaction with the teacher.

Program Description

Reader's and writer's workshops are flexible approaches that strongly emphasize child empowerment and interest (see Figure 6.1). Robust, disciplined self-expression characterizes many of the activities. The activities that demand and develop these capacities are highly varied, in both instructional technique and structural organization. The coherent implementation of these variable features is supported by a strong set of implemented philosophies, which are themselves often supported by an ongoing professional development program.

Organizational/Structural Features

A key organizational feature of reader's and writer's workshop approaches is flexibility. The materials used, space for learning and teaching, time spent in various activities, and the grouping patterns of students are dependent on the identified needs of students. Self-selected reading and writing is a key instructional feature, and several organizational features support it, including a literacy-rich environment, a strong and varied classroom library, and many varieties of materials, including writing instruments and kinds of paper. A large sustained silent reading block is a part of each week's activities.

Collaborating and conferencing with peers and teachers enable workshop participants to share their experiences and understandings. Students are often paired and assembled in *small groups* to address a common problem area with a targeted mini-lesson. In addition, children are also encouraged to collaborate with each other on specific projects and activities.

The workshop approach also includes ongoing alternative assessment, such as portfolios, anecdotal records, checklists, tape recordings, and field notes. These assessment methods are intended to provide more holistic feedback than conventional measures.

Classroom Instruction Features

Classroom instruction features are intended to open multiple and flexible paths to rich and holistic literacy experiences. Many classes alternate between brief mini-lessons (in which a skill is taught and/or modeled using direct instruction) and conferencing, in which children—alone, in pairs, or in

Figure 6.1 Reader's and Writer's Workshop Program Features

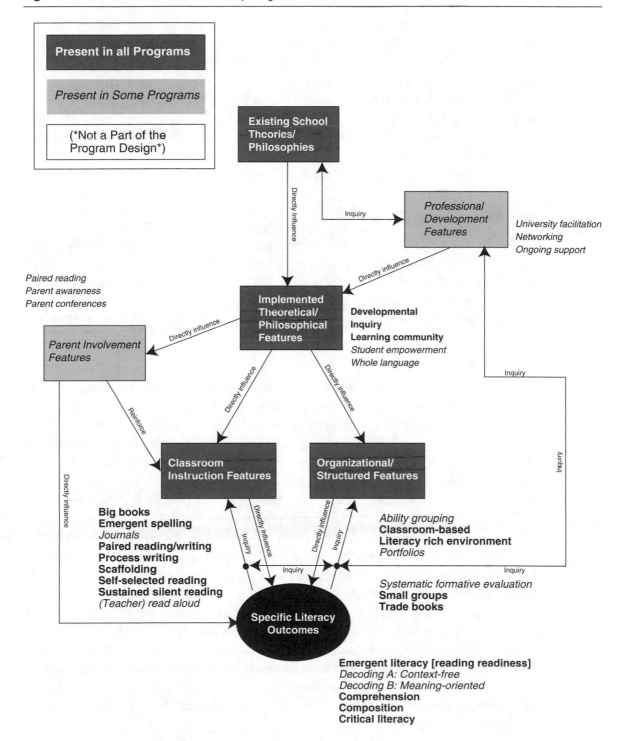

groups—work on reading or writing projects with teachers moving about the room assisting the children. In these conferences, children interact with both texts and other people, using many features—*Big Books, trade books, journal writing,* interpretive discussion—in combination to access meaning and understand its relevance in the class community.

Professional Development Features

Professional development is in concert with the National Writing Project. This model of professional development is based on the idea of teachers teaching teachers. Teachers come together during summer institutes to discuss exemplary practices and strategies, teaching, and the complexities of writing.

Teachers then assume consultant/mentoring roles in their schools over the course of the school year. In addition to sharing successes and tensions with teaching writing, the teachers also write on a range of topics and in various forms, going through editing and revision processes together. In addition, teachers read, discuss, and write about significant research in the field.

Parental Involvement Features

While the workshops do not explicitly specify a formal parent involvement component, schools generally ask parents to read with their children (a variant of *paired reading*), often from the same books covered at school. Teachers often send home samples of writing for parents to read and respond to. In parent conferences, held regularly, students' portfolios for reading and writing are shared.

Targeted Literacy Outcomes

Because of the inherent flexibility of an approach that provides interactions with classmates and texts, outcomes will vary. Reader's and writer's workshops are implemented in elementary grades through high school.

Comprehension and *critical literacy* are the focus in many reader's workshop classrooms. Children are encouraged to reflect on and respond to various aspects of the texts. Book talks and discussions support children's understandings and connections made to other texts. *Composition* is highly developed through writer's workshop. The workshop encourages children to use a process approach for writing (i.e., a broad range of strategies that encourage extended time spent on drafting, multiple revisions, and reflection and further revision). To the degree that writing is a form of expression representing one among many possible perspectives and intentions, *critical literacy* is also fostered.

In addition to these three outcomes—*composition, comprehension,* and *critical literacy*, around which the program is designed—reader's and writer's workshops also affect the other major outcomes: *emergent literacy* and *decoding A and B*. Targeted *emergent literacy* behaviors include concepts of print, story structure, and book awareness. Phonemic awareness is targeted through an emergent-spelling component. *Decoding A and B* are developed through instruction in multiple cueing systems.

Research Base

Writer's and reader's workshop approaches have a solid and diverse research base, including both quantitative and qualitative studies. Quantitative studies have found that students in classrooms with reader's and writer's workshops perform at least as well as those in the skills-oriented classrooms they were compared to, exceeding students in skills-based classrooms in certain skills, such as spelling. Studies also showed that the use of invented spelling helped develop phonemic awareness.

One key finding from the research was that affective results were more significant than cognitive behaviors. One study revealed that literacy development was accomplished in both the whole-language and skills-based classrooms, but children in the *whole language* classrooms were able to assume literacy behaviors, including reflecting, explaining, responding, and valuing while the skills-based children remained on literacy skills, such as letter recognition, *phonemic awareness*, and decoding.

The confidence and self-monitoring abilities of the students in the reader's and writer's workshops also increased significantly. Qualitative studies revealed that young writers in these approaches use writing to position themselves in relation to their peers and the social contexts in which they live.

Reader's and writer's workshops are good examples of how *whole language* philosophies can be implemented in balanced classroom practice. The approach makes use of direct instruction of specific skills without compromising the emphasis on meaning-making, critical reflection, and purposive self-expression. Structurally, the program's flexibility provides the necessary conditions for teachers to create a constructive iterative cycle between meaningful activities and projects and close observation, or "kid watching." That the program is backed by a solid theoretical grounding and often ongoing professional development also helps ensure the coherence of this iterative process.

Writer's and reader's workshops are also fine examples of converting Vygotskian developmental theory into classroom practice. The program takes full advantage of the Vygotskian principle that children can often do things as a part of groups that they cannot do alone. The multi-tiered social organization—which includes voluntary pairing and *small groups*, brief sessions of *ability grouping*, and one-on-one interaction with a teacher—should promote the emergence of sophisticated interpretive and expressive capabilities, in addition to the improved attitudes toward literacy found in the research.

An inherent potentially negative consequence of any program that does not prescribe a curriculum or a specific teaching sequence (e.g., Success for All and Reading Recovery, respectively) is that the program becomes more dependent on factors external to program design, such as teacher quality, class size, and book availability. Writer's and reader's workshops rely heavily on teacher judgment, which itself in this program should be based on both a solid understanding of the *whole language* theories that inform it and careful observation of the children. The quality and consistency of implementation of these workshops may depend in large part on the extent that the theories are available to and understood by teachers, as well as the extent of relevant professional development available in support of these theories.

Similarly, the lack of a standard parent involvement component also represents a potential problem area. While it is evident that many schools involve parents, the lack of a specific component within the design itself puts the responsibility on schools to design an appropriate parent involvement component.

Finally, even if schools ensure solid ongoing professional development (such as through participation in the National Writing Project) and a parent participation component, the open-endedness of the design could result in varied results for different schools.

REFERENCES AND CONTACTS:
Reader's and Writer's Workshops

References

Atwell, N. (1986). *In the middle: Writing, reading, and learning with adolescents.* Portsmouth, NH: Heinemann.

Clarke, L. (1988). Invented versus traditional spelling in first graders' writings: Effects on learning to spell and read. *Research in the Teaching of English, 22,* 281–309.

Dahl, K., & Freepon, P. (1995). A comparison of inner city interpretations of reading and writing instruction in the early grades in skills based and whole language classrooms. *Reading Research Quarterly, 30,* 50–74.

Graves, D. (1983). *Writing: Teachers and children at work.* Portsmouth, NH: Heinemann.

Hansen, J. (1987). *When writers read.* Portsmouth, NH: Heinemann.

Richgels, D. (1995). Invented spelling ability and printed word learning in kindergarten. *Reading Research Quarterly, 30,* 96–109.

Roller, C. (1996). *Variability, not disability.* Newark, DE: International Reading Association.

Sipe, L. (1996). Transitions to the conventional: An examination of a first grader's composing process. *Journal of Literacy Research, 30,* 357–388.

Contact Information

Amy Flint
Language Education Department
201 North Rose Ave.
W.W. Wright School of Education
Indiana University
Bloomington, IN 47405

■ 6.2. TEACHER INQUIRY

Reviewed by Mitzi Lewison

Teacher inquiry is not a single program but a broad, generally agreed-on set of insider research practices that encourage teachers to take a close, critical look at their teaching and the academic and social development of their students. The goal of teacher inquiry is to build teachers' and schools' capacities to understand and solve problems of teaching and learning.

Although known by many names—teacher research, action research, practitioner research, insider research—teacher inquiry involves classroom teachers in a cycle of inquiry, reflection, and action. In this cycle, teachers question common practice, approach problems from new perspectives, consider research and evidence to propose new solutions, implement these solutions, and evaluate the results, starting the cycle anew.

Program Description

Teacher inquiry is essentially a professional development model that does not in itself specify classroom activity (see Figure 6.2). As such, it is somewhat different from many of the other models in this review, and therefore the application of our framework needs minor adjustment. Thus, rather than focusing exclusively on what is embedded formally in the model, this review describes program features that are typically found in schools that implement teacher inquiry, as reported in the studies.

Organizational/Structural Features

Despite the tremendous variability in teacher inquiry studies, there is overwhelmingly common agreement on a set of structural features that underlie this form of teacher research. In classroom inquiry, teachers systematically study individual children, a specific curriculum component, or their own teaching. All classroom inquiry starts with teachers posing questions about one of these three areas. The process involves close observation, data collection, data analysis, reflection, and some type of action. Teachers are involved in a continuing cycle of inquiry, which includes planning, implementing, and evaluating literacy interventions.

The specific tools of teacher inquiry are varied and include interviews, oral histories, surveys, questionnaires, observation checklists, rating scales, observation *journals*, student artifacts, audiotape recordings, transcripts of student dialogue, and photographs. Data analysis is usually qualitative, although this analysis is often supplemented with quantitative data, and can be used in either ongoing informal analysis or formal analysis in published reports.

Classroom Instruction Features

Even though there is wide variability in teacher inquiry studies, three classroom components were present in nearly all the investigations. First, reader's and/or writer's workshops were extremely prevalent features of these classrooms. Second, there was also a strong focus on teacher demonstrations, modeling, or direct instruction related to the focus of the inquiry (i.e., demonstrations on how students organize content they've learned from reading, student misconceptions, keeping portfolios, conducting literature discussions, and goal setting for reading and writing). Third, skills were almost exclusively taught in the context of authentic literacy activities.

In some of the studies there were daily read-aloud times (often more than once during the day), the use of a variety of texts beyond *basal readers* or children's literature, and explicit extra support for struggling readers.

Figure 6.2 Teacher Inquiry Program Features

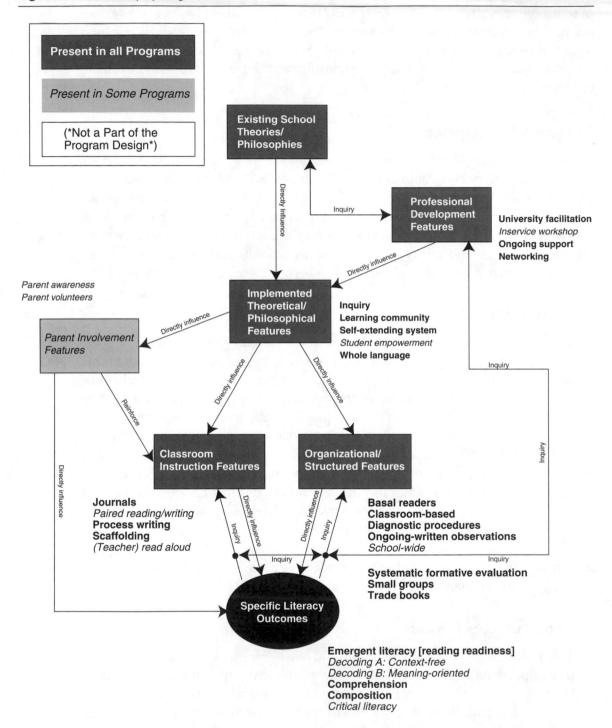

Professional Development Features

Teacher inquiry programs are founded on the belief that the most effective teacher inquiry takes place when teachers regularly meet with other teacher researchers and create a community of practice. In some cases, individual teachers have read professional articles and books that have served as new lenses through which to question and research their practice; but in general, working with other teachers and a facilitator is preferable. Most commonly, teachers meet with a consultant, teacher leader, or professor on a regular basis to share their classroom inquiries and to learn more about data collection, analysis, and conducting research. These meetings can take the form of teacher study groups, support groups, or even university classes.

Parental Involvement Features

Although not necessarily a part of teacher inquiry, over half the studies included parent components. Parents volunteered at the request of teachers, were involved in classroom activities with their children, helped out at home on specific assignments, or completed surveys to assist classroom teachers in better understanding how to work with their children.

Targeted Literacy Outcomes

Teacher inquiry emphasizes *emergent literacy, comprehension,* and *composition*. The theoretical underpinnings of this model focus on classroom features and outcomes that focus on more holistic, child-centered literacy interventions. There are also some instances of *decoding B* and *critical literacy* outcomes in the research studies.

In addition to these outcomes, there is also an emphasis on experimenting with strategies that increase student motivation to read and write. That is, teacher inquirers also seek to improve affective outcomes—attitudes toward reading, motivation, and lifelong habitual reading.

Research Base

The research base for teacher inquiry is made up of studies that are generally qualitative or ethnographic in nature. This type of research does not try to make claims that are generalizable or based on objective, context-independent research methods. Instead, teacher inquiry is directed at the subjective, lived experience of teachers and students. The goal for teacher inquiry is the generation of useful information that, first, informs teachers of more effective ways to work with their students, and second, contributes to the professional knowledge base.

Thus, one of the greatest contributions of this research is its thick description of classroom environments, children's literacy development, specific interventions, and the teacher's role—all of which can be of great assistance to schools and classroom teachers concerned about student achievement in reading and writing. Teacher inquiry allows us to see classrooms, teachers, and students in real-world, genuine ways. The elaborate descriptions of teacher inquiry projects have the potential to provide a rich source of information that may be even more helpful to a teacher with struggling readers and writers than statistical data gleaned from large groups of children.

In summary, the strength of this program is clearly the combination of teachers, research, reflection, evaluation, and experimentation taking place as a structured community effort. Teachers are not only viewed as professionals in the model, but they are also given the opportunity to use that professionalism for the betterment of their schools. There are several positive consequences: teachers become better teachers, they are better informed about best practices and also more attuned to their individual children, and they both become more focused on and have more effective strategies for helping struggling learners.

In this way, nationally significant research and best practices to improve schools can be accessed by the people who know their children, strengths, and problem areas best: local teachers. This is possible because of the iterative nature of teacher inquiry, which ensures that research and nationally (and even internationally) constructed intervention packages actually make sense and are successful in individual schools. Teachers critique these packages, evaluating how well the packages fit into their individual schools, and they identify the children not succeeding within the packages and try to find other means of reaching those children. In other words, all national packages have an inherent "one size fits all" aspect to them; teacher inquiry enables schools to overcome this limitation and optimize instruction to fit the school.

As with all intervention models, this one has certain limitations. Professional development does not directly affect learning outcomes but does so by changing implemented school philosophy, classroom practices, and other important elements. Where it appears to be strongest, in terms of outcomes, is in its improvement of literacy attitudes and motivation. It would be unreasonable to expect that standardized test scores will jump the year after teacher inquiry is adopted. Not only does it affect outcomes indirectly, but it becomes more effective over time, as teachers have an opportunity to turn research into changes in practice, a process that needs continual evaluation and adjustment.

Also, since teacher inquiry does not specify any particular literacy curriculum or classroom organization, schools needing or desiring large-scale changes/reforms will have to look elsewhere for models.

REFERENCES AND CONTACTS:
Teacher Inquiry

References

Border, K., & Tanski, M. (1997). The effects of reading aloud vs. sustained silent reading on student comprehension. In D. Snodgrass & J. Salzman (Eds.), *Action research monograph* (pp. 36–55). Ohio Department of Education. (ERIC Document Reproduction Service No. ED421454)

Jewell, T. A., & Pratt, D. (1999). Literature discussions in the primary grades: Children's thoughtful discourse about books and what teachers can do to make it happen. *The Reading Teacher, 52*(8), 842–850.

Lewison, M. (1995). Taking the lead from teachers: Seeking a new model of staff development. In J. Lemlech (Ed.), *Teachers and principals at work: Becoming a professional leader* (pp. 76–113). New York: Scholastic.

Santa, C. M., Isaacon, L., & Manning, G. (1987). Changing content instruction through action research. *The Reading Teacher, 40,* 434–438.

Swift, K. (1993). Try reading workshop in your classroom. *The Reading Teacher, 46*(5), 366–371.

Contact Information

Mitzi Lewison
Language Education Department
201 North Rose Ave.
W.W. Wright School of Education
Indiana University
Bloomington, IN 47405

GUIDANCE FOR EDUCATORS ■

These reviews of teacher inquiry and workshop methods of reform provide a more complete foundation for thinking about reading reform than is typically included in the current discourse about early reading and literacy reform. Yet these reviews point to the need to integrate an emphasis on writing and teacher collaboration in the reform process that can be overlooked in the current market-oriented reform environment. To extend the foundations for thinking about the research base, we review some key findings from the Policy Center's research on comprehensive school reform, then consider the implications of this broader view for meeting standards and reading reform in general.

The Research Base

The two reviews in this chapter included a summary of the research on which the rationales for these inquiry reform strategies are based. While these reform strategies are consonant with a long tradition of research on language and literacy education, these studies are generally outside the domain of research on literacy. One of the Policy Center's recent studies relates to the general understandings evident in these reviews.

The Policy Center has recently completed a study of classroom teachers in schools involved in Michigan's Comprehensive School Reform (CSR) program (St. John, Musoba, et al., 2002). This study used a generalized version of the survey instrument included in this text that asked about classroom practices related to reading and other types of reforms. As part of the study, we conducted factor analyses of responses to questions about classroom practices and professional development. Both sets of findings are summarized below, as they related to their role in teacher inquiry.

Focusing on Improvement in Classroom Practices

Three factors related to classroom practices frequently used by teachers were significantly associated with classroom outcomes in the Michigan CSR study (St. John, Musoba, et al., 2002):

- *Writing-Based Approaches*—combining frequent use of essays/creative writing, *journals*, meaning/context predicting, writing mechanics, and study/test-taking skills—were associated with reductions in retention. This suggests that frequent use of writing, integrating this practice into the curriculum, enables more children to achieve on grade level.
- *Individualized-Diagnostic Approaches*—combining frequent use of ability grouping, diagnostic procedures, individualized instruction, and one-on-one tutoring—were associated with reductions in special educational referrals. This reinforces the finding in the analysis of First Steps that diagnostic procedures reduce special education referrals and keep more children in the educational mainstream.
- *Performance-Based Approaches*—including frequent use of performance assessment—were also associated with reductions in special education referrals.

In combination, these findings provide insight about curriculum, especially relative to the integration of writing across subjects, and the role of diagnosis and testing in the inquiry process. If teacher classroom inquiry can use assessment tools, it can increase performance and reduce failure.

Focusing Teacher Inquiry on Classroom Practices

In addition, the Policy Center study of CSR schools in Michigan included a more complete set of questions related to professional development than were included in the classroom survey in Chapter 3. One of the factors had a significant (above a .5 level) association with improvement in classroom outcomes. *Collaboration on Classroom Practices*—a factor that combined frequent collaboration on student achievement and needs, district/state/school initiatives, curriculum/subject matter, lives outside school, school routines, and extracurricular activities—was associated with reductions in grade-level retention (St. John, Musoba, et al., 2002). This finding reinforces the argument that teacher inquiry focusing on classroom instruction, in reading or other curricular areas, can promote improvement in student outcomes.

Meeting Standards

The inquiry-based approaches reviewed in this chapter provide a broader framework for examining literacy outcomes than is routinely emphasized in the literature on research-based reading reform. These reviews broaden the definition of reading and language arts to include *composition*, as a complement to the focus on *comprehension* and *critical literacy*. Indeed, in the reviews above, Flint and Lewison argue that *composition* is a critical link between *comprehension* and *critical literacy*, that students need a deeper connection with language to read critically and understand the array of subjects included in the curriculum.

The analysis of comprehensive reforms in Michigan, a study that extends the logical model and framework developed in Chapter 3 to take a broader view of curriculum reform (St. John, Musoba, et al., 2002), supports this reconstructed rationale. Building an emphasis on writing into the entire curriculum was associated with reductions in retention across grade levels in Michigan's CSR schools. This finding strongly suggests that to meet the intent of state standards for literacy reform, which focused on building *critical literacy* skills, schools need to emphasize writing as an integral part of reform in reading and language arts.

Thus, there are clear limitations to a standards-driven reform, especially if the standards are the sole criteria for deciding on a reform strategy. A broader and more complete approach to language education may be needed. Indeed, to achieve success with the student learning outcomes associated with higher-level reading standards (i.e., those associated with *critical literacy*), it may be necessary to integrate writing into the school's overall curriculum approach.

Politics of Reform

With the new emphasis on early reading in elementary schools it is possible to push writing out of the language arts curriculum by overlooking its role. These reviews of inquiry-based methods emphasize the importance of integrating *composition* into a more complete language arts strategy, a view supported in the school reform research. Using teacher inquiry to focus on a more comprehensive approach to literacy helps build the bridge between the early skills-based aspects of reading and the later and more critical aspects of literacy that students will need in upper elementary grades, middle school, and high school.

This means that teachers need to work together to building writing-based approaches into the entire curriculum. Writing and context predicting skills are needed to make the transition from recognizing words through building *comprehension* skills to understanding meaning across content areas. If these skills are overlooked because of an emphasis on direct instruction and testing, children who learn only to recognize letters and read words may fail when they are required to construct meanings about more complicated concepts in upper elementary grades.

This emphasis runs counter to the prevailing politics of reform. The following research-based argument has had extensive influence on the politics of school reform:

> Controlling for differences in age, ethnicity, and verbal IQ, we found that children in the direct code (DC) approach improved in word reading at a faster rate and had higher word recognition skills than . . . children receiving the implicit code (IC) approach (either research-based IC or district's standard IC). More importantly, children in all instructional groups with higher phonological processing scores in the beginning of the year demonstrated improvement across the year. (Foorman, Fletcher, Francis, & Schatschneider, 2000, p. 29)

Based on this and related research-supported rationales, several states—including Texas, Washington, California, New York, and Wisconsin—have required direct phonics instruction (Allington & Woodside-Jiron, 1999). Our purpose is not to dispute the importance of teaching direct code or of phonological awareness, but rather to emphasize the broader context of reform in reading and language arts. The emphasis on literature and writing fosters student engagement and more advanced literacy skills that are increasingly important as students progress across the grade levels.

In the midst of the politics about reading standards and reform, teachers must be given the opportunity to integrate writing into the curriculum as well as to use literature-based approaches that engage students and create interest in content and willingness to predict meaning and think critically. This broader sense of language arts is essential. Over twenty years of standards-driven education reform, the percentage of children who graduate from high school has steadily declined (St. John, in press). Using a broader, more balanced approach to language arts education—one that integrates a focus on phonological awareness and direct code with emphases on meaning, writing, and context prediction—is crucial to creating schools that enable more children to learn on grade level.

Integrating Inquiry

Teacher inquiry, as outlined here, is logically connected to a more complete view of literacy that is fostered in the current political debates about reading. The infusion of a standards-driven approach can lead to an overemphasis on direct instruction that supports rapid development of word recognition skills, but can limit the development of more advanced skills, unless teachers take an integrated approach to language arts.

Many reading reforms, even some of the classroom-based reforms reviewed in Chapter 5, take a narrow view of reading that does not place sufficient emphasis on writing and context predicting. It is crucial that teachers expand their inquiry about language arts education, adopting a framework that includes these components of literacy. An inquiry-based approach to language education can be used to foster integration of language arts into the entire learning model used in elementary schools. Such an approach has merit. As teams of teachers gain experience with collaboration on classroom practices and inquiry into new methods of teaching, they can achieve a more integrative approach to language arts education.

Building Community

Standards-driven reform can lead to a deconstruction of the curriculum into decontextualized chunks of information, clouding the linkages between basic skills and more advanced ways of reading and thinking. The increased emphasis on testing and standards-driven reform has contributed to the erosion of high school graduation rates over the past two decades (Jacob, 2001; Manset-Williamson & Washburn, in press; St. John, in press), leading some to question whether school reform has failed (Miron & St. John, in press). However, the new emphasis on research-based reform in reading provides one potential way of overcoming this limitation. By enabling schools to select and develop reform strategies that enhance their reading programs, this latest wave of reform can redress the failure of earlier reform efforts.

For this latest wave of reform to succeed, teachers must work together in schools to build an understanding of the challenges they face. A major component of the challenge is to construct a cohesive, coherent, and comprehensive reading program that enables children to develop basic reading skills and progress through the stages of reading to acquire critical thinking and literacy skills. This developmental pathway requires that students be engaged in learning. It also means that curriculum will need to integrate an emphasis on writing and context predicting that helps children build the link between basic reading skills (i.e., letter and word recognition) and the more advanced skills needed to learn in upper elementary grades and beyond.

This broader view of language arts education is more complete than the one offered by reading standards because it treats language in a more comprehensive way that is implicit in the new, research-based paradigm of reading reform. To achieve a broader understanding of the use of language in reading reform in schools, the entire school community must engage in creating a challenging and engaging curriculum, a conclusion reinforced by the Michigan CSR study (St. John, Musoba, et al., 2002). In this context, more schools may wish to consider the option of collaborating on a comprehensive school reform strategy, one that focuses on a broader definition of language arts as being integral to learning across the curriculum.

7

Process-Oriented Comprehensive Reforms

Process-oriented comprehensive reforms are school restructuring programs designed to improve educational outcomes for all students. They are often implemented in schools with large populations of students in at-risk situations. These models are aimed at comprehensively restructuring the educational program of the school, encouraging changes that may include classroom configurations, modes of professional development, and delivery of instruction. These reforms prescribe a set of processes that are time-consuming and require a great commitment from staff. By working through the processes, the school determines and directs the reform activities and tailors specific changes at the classroom level to the needs of the student body.

There is a growing number of process-oriented reforms, each with a different theory of reform (why students are failing to succeed), and thus a unique approach to school reform. The Accelerated Schools model (7.1) promotes an inquiry-based approach for school improvement tied to participatory school governance and changing instructional approaches. The ATLAS Communities reform (7.2) also addresses standards, but it focuses on the need for multiple assessments and reflective practice. The Modern Red Schoolhouse (7.3) assumes school failure to be a lack of a comprehensive, standards-based curriculum and has reform processes related to developing a standards-based curriculum. Yet another approach is available in the School Development Program (7.4), which seeks to develop a caring learning community that develops reforms based on the holistic developmental needs of students.

All students in the school are served by these reforms. Because the reforms are designed to create change over time, students continue to benefit from the program as they progress through the grades in the school.

These reforms are designed to create sustainable improvements throughout the school, and could be used by any school. Schools that are serving substantial numbers of students at risk of school failure and that are seeking to improve all areas of academic achievement for all students would be well suited for process-oriented reforms. These models require a great deal of participation in decision making at the school level and often increase the level of accountability for school improvement. Schools that have experience with site-based management and have strong leadership on the faculty are likely to be interested in these types of reforms. However, because of the time-intensive approach requiring extensive collaboration and professional development, not all schools will want or need to make this level of investment in school improvement.

Four widely used process-oriented reform models are reviewed in this chapter: Accelerated Schools Project (7.1), ATLAS Communities (7.2), Modern Red Schoolhouse (7.3), and School Development Program (7.4). The chapter concludes with guidance for educators who are interested in integrating an emphasis on early reading and literacy into process-oriented comprehensive reforms.

7.1. ACCELERATED SCHOOLS PROJECT ■

Reviewed by Siri Ann Loescher and Kim Manoil

The Accelerated Schools Project (ASP) is a process-oriented comprehensive school reform, involving the whole school staff (certified and noncertified), parents, students, and members of the community. The model was developed for underperforming schools that serve high proportions of students in at-risk situations. To change the school culture, all stakeholders (faculty, administration, parents, students, and community members) work together to restructure the school while embracing three principles: unity of purpose, empowerment coupled with responsibility, and building on strengths. The model advocates using instructional techniques traditionally associated with gifted and talented instruction to provide accelerated rather than remediated learning. The ASP emphasizes providing all students with "powerful learning" experiences that translate into increased student learning outcomes.

Program Description

The ASP model does not specify a curriculum or instructional method. Instead the model focuses on professional development based on inquiry and reflective practice, along with structures and processes that take a focused approach to determining what changes work best for all the students in the school. Thus, while some features should look similar for all Accelerated Schools (e.g., school-wide application, professional development, and implemented theories), each school's reform activities will evolve uniquely, resulting in the adoption of specific classroom instruction, organization/structure, and parent involvement features.

The ASP does not have a specific model for reading instruction and does not advocate any specific features. Instead, a process—carried out by school communities and shaped by Accelerated Schools Project principles—determines

Figure 7.1 Accelerated Schools Project Program Features

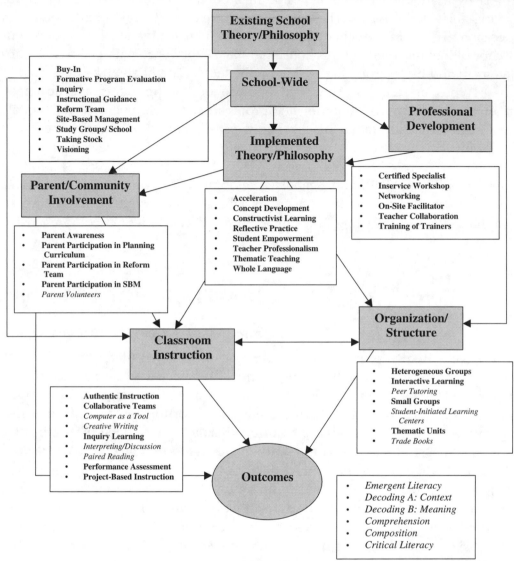

Bolded features are part of the reform; *italicized features* are sometimes adopted by schools implementing the reform.

program features. Nonetheless, some features of Accelerated Schools suggest an approach to early reading and language education. To a large extent, evidence supporting these speculations can be found in the Accelerated Schools research, in which descriptions provide some indication of which literacy-related features schools used. Specific program features related to literacy programs within Accelerated Schools are shown in Figure 7.1.

School-Wide Processes

The Accelerated Schools Project requires school *buy-in*. The reform model uses *site-based management* for shared decision making in the school. During the first year, a *reform team* is established that includes representation from each stakeholder group. In this year, the school works through two processes— *taking stock* and *visioning*—in order to compare current performance with where the school would like to be. Both the processes and the products of these features are important to the ASP reform. The processes build community among stakeholders, provide a deep knowledge base and consensus about the school, and engage the entire school in determining what specific reform efforts (e.g., adoption of specific curricular materials or developing a new parent program) will be implemented by the school. The *vision* provides the school with *instructional guidance* that informs the school's reform activities as well as shapes individual instructional decisions within each classroom.

After the reform agenda (areas for study) for the school has been set, the school establishes *study groups/schools,* called cadres, that conduct in-depth *inquiry* on the priority areas, including the formation of hypotheses, collection and analysis of data, and pilot testing of programs. The *inquiry* process often involves studying classrooms and student work, conducting surveys, and exploring available resources in order to develop, refine, and implement specific reform activities.

At the end of each school year, the model requires an annual *formative program evaluation,* used to refine the school's reform. Schools use an ASP tool kit to gather information across the school year that includes rubrics to assess implementation of the reform model and student performance data. Based on these evaluations, all areas for inquiry are identified as the focus for the school's ongoing school improvement efforts.

Implemented Theories/Philosophies

The Accelerated Schools Project philosophies about learning are related to the belief that all students benefit from teaching strategies used for the gifted and talented. The ASP reform advocates *acceleration*—as opposed to remediation methods—to ensure that students acquire the basic skills and apply those skills in more sophisticated work. The ASP reform promotes *constructivist learning,* characterized as "Powerful Learning." This approach to learning, rooted in cognitive psychology, is related to five instructional components that are linked to research; they are described as authentic, interactive, inclusive, learner-centered, and continuous. The focus on *constructivist learning* and *student empowerment* (incorporating student choice into instructional activities) suggests that instruction in ASP schools should vary greatly from traditional lecture or workbook/skill review methods.

ASP also promotes *concept development* to encourage the development of higher order thinking skills, and *thematic teaching* to increase the relevance of classroom instruction and strengthen the cognitive connections between subject areas. Consistent with these approaches, the model recommends reading approaches that are related to *whole language,* or meaning-oriented approaches to reading acquisition.

The ASP model's theories of school reform center around *teacher professionalism* and *reflective practice.* The model asserts that a school that employs the three principles, embraces the teaching philosophies, and engages in inquiry and action research will be able to direct, implement, and sustain changes at the core level of the schools.

Professional Development Reform Features

The Accelerated Schools Project requires schools to designate an *on-site facilitator* to act as the Accelerated School's coach, and it uses a *training of trainers* design to provide for school training in the reform process. To support the school in implementing the model, each school has a *certified specialist* affiliated with the Accelerated Schools Project through a regional mentoring center.[1] Through *inservice workshops* the school learns about implementing the reform and receives specific training in Powerful Learning. Additional professional development is determined and conducted at the school level, and, where appropriate, is led by teachers from the school. *Teacher collaboration*, in and across grade levels or subject areas, is used to reinforce professional development activities.

Networking opportunities include regional and national conferences. Accelerated Schools also send several faculty members a year to a regional Powerful Learning Laboratory (PLL) that concentrates on delivering Powerful Learning through classroom instruction. The PLL also focuses on using Powerful Learning to address state standards.

Parent/Community Involvement Reform Features

The model encourages strengthening parent-school connections. *Parent awareness* about the school's reform efforts includes involving parents in *buy-in*, and soliciting parent input and participation during *taking stock* and *visioning*. Parent representatives are involved in the school governance through *parent participation in reform team*, and *parent participation in site-based management*. Parent participation in school inquiry-study groups creates *parent participation in planning curriculum*. The ASP model also urges active parent involvement related to classrooms through parent conferencing and use of *parent volunteers*.

Participation of the larger community includes soliciting of feedback during *taking stock* and *visioning*. Additionally, *taking stock* study groups and inquiry groups are encouraged to look to the community when compiling information about existing resources and potential partnerships.

Organizational/Structural Features

Accelerated Schools' organizational and structural features clearly reflect the program's focus on Powerful Learning to make learning dynamic and relevant. Its purpose is school-wide reform accomplished through an enriched curriculum and constructivist instruction. For example, ASP teachers collaborate to develop and use content-rich *thematic units*. *Interactive learning* activities engage students and often include the use of *small group* activities, including cross-age and *heterogeneous groups*.

The model encourages the adoption of features to foster both interdependent thinking and independent learning. Thus, ASP schools often adopt features such as *student-initiated learning centers* and *peer tutoring*. Some studies also make reference to the use of *trade books* rather than "decodable" and/or basal books.

Classroom Instruction Features

The ASP model focuses on *authentic instruction* and *collaborative teams* to create relevant, high-interest learning experiences. Consistent with the focus on implementing more enriched teaching techniques, the model encourages the use of instructional features that emphasize student strengths, language development across subjects, *problem solving*, and higher order thinking skills such as *inquiry learning* and *project-based instruction*. The model also encourages developing language skills through *creative writing* along with other methods that emphasize the teaching of concepts in meaningful contexts rather than in abstraction. Some schools adopt the use of *computer as a tool, interpreting/discussion,* and *paired reading* to develop meaning-centered reading skills.

ASP teachers incorporate *reflective practice* into the classroom through *performance assessment*. Teachers have the flexibility to adapt instruction based on these assessments to ensure student learning.

Targeted Literacy Outcomes

While there is no specific literacy approach denoted by the Accelerated Schools Project, the ASP is based on a strong inquiry model in which individual schools evaluate their own needs and make changes accordingly. As every school has a unique community of students, teachers, and parents, Accelerated Schools usually have distinctive reading and literacy programs. For this reason, the program in itself does not specifically target any of the literacy outcomes. Instead, the process of identifying and targeting reading and literacy outcomes is left to the individual schools. Targeted literacy outcomes are based on each school's process of *taking stock, visioning,* and *inquiry*. Schools can use the ASP process to focus on the learning outcomes for reading and language arts—*emergent literacy, decoding A* (context free), *decoding B* (meaning oriented), *comprehension, composition,* and *critical literacy*—but emphasis on these outcomes remains dependent on the school's reform plan, according to the model design.

REFERENCES AND CONTACTS:
Accelerated Schools Project

References

Accelerated Schools Project [ASP]. (1997). *Powerful learning: Conceptual foundations.* Stanford, CA: National Center for the Accelerated Schools Project, Stanford University.

Finnan, C., St. John, E. P., Slovacek, S. P., & McCarthy, J. (Eds.). (1996). *Accelerated Schools in action: Lessons from the field.* Thousand Oaks, CA: Corwin Press.

Hopfenberg, W. S., Levin, H. M., & Associates. (1993). *Accelerated Schools resource guide.* San Francisco: Jossey-Bass.

Kim, L., & Zitzer, M. (1999). *Powerful learning framework for teachers.* (ERIC Document Reproduction Service No. ED431069)

Knight, S. L., & Stallings, J. A. (1995). The implementation of the Accelerated School model in an urban elementary school. In R. L. Allington & S. A. Walmsley (Eds.), *No quick fix: Rethinking literacy programs in America's elementary schools* (pp. 236–251). New York: Teachers College Press.

Marble, K., & Wagner, S. (1998). *Accelerated Schools Newsletter*, (7), 2.

McCarthy, J., & Still, S. (1993). Hollibrook Accelerated Elementary School. In J. Murphy & P. Hallinger (Eds.), *Restructuring schooling: Learning from on-going efforts* (pp. 63–83). Newbury Park, CA: Corwin Press.

National Center for the Accelerated Schools Project. (1998). *Powerful learning: Conceptual frameworks* [On-line]. Available: www.stanford.edu/group/ASP/pl_conceptfdns.html

Northwest Regional Educational Laboratory (NWREL). (1988). *Catalog of school reform models: First edition* [On-line]. Available: www.nwrel.org/scpd/natspec/catalog/

Contact Information

University of Connecticut
Neag School of Education
National Center for Accelerated Schools
2131 Hillside Road, Unit 3224
Storrs, CT 06269-3224
Phone: (860) 486-6330
Email: info@acceleratedschools.et
Web Site: www.acceleratedschools.net

■ 7.2. ATLAS COMMUNITIES

Reviewed by Siri Ann Loescher and Stacy Jacob

The ATLAS (Authentic Teaching, Learning and Assessment for all Students) Communities is a process-oriented school reform model designed as a collaboration between four school reform organizations: the Coalition for Essential Schools, the School Development Program, Project Zero, and the Education Development Center.[2] The ATLAS design places emphasis on two areas: (1) the development of an educational pathway of schools from elementary through high school that work in conjunction with one another to articulate standards, assessments, and educational reform efforts throughout the pathway; and (2) changing classroom practices with an emphasis on "Teaching for Understanding"—focusing on fewer topics in much greater depth—and the use of constructivist teaching methods and authentic, performance-based assessment.

Program Description

The model promotes building teachers' capacities for implementing classroom innovations through professional development supported primarily through *study group/teachers, teacher collaboration,* and *reflective practice.* The model also posits that for this reform to be successful specific organizational structures must be created within the schools and the pathway. The design requires *site-based management*, emphasizes district coordination (to support the K–12 pathway), and encourages schools to involve the greater school community in the reform process. The ATLAS design is firmly rooted in *teacher professionalism*, asserting that for change to be meaningful and sustainable, it must be designed and implemented by the school itself.

ATLAS is ambitious in scope. For each of the many reform activities, the ATLAS design asserts that schools are responsible for charting their own path (e.g., schools design their own system of assessments and instruction rather than adopting a *prescribed curriculum*). This is a time-intensive process. A lengthy timeline is expected for schools to fully implement the model (typically three years). The model also strives for a balance between an externally designed model for reform and an internally (at the school) designed path and set of reform activities. It allows some flexibility in the implementation of the model, including the sequence and shape of some of the reform activities. Because of this flexibility it is less clear than with some of the other process-oriented models which program components are required versus recommended parts of the reform process.

ATLAS Communities' approach toward improving reading instruction is embedded in its overall reform model. The design allows schools to create their own solutions to literacy, develop strong language arts skills through action research, develop and link learning standards and assessments, and incorporate teaching methods consistent with Teaching for Understanding. The schools use state reading standards as a part of this process. ATLAS is also concerned with creating a community of involved teachers, administrators, and parents who develop strategies to help children learn to read. The model relies on *reflective practice* and teacher research as means of improving the teaching of reading and thus student reading outcomes. In upper grades, the approach suggests that ATLAS schools would encourage reading development throughout all curricular areas. The model's program features are depicted in Figure 7.2.

School-Wide Features

Before agreeing to work with a school, the ATLAS design team requires a commitment from the school district to provide support to the school in its reform efforts, including providing a district employee to serve as an ATLAS liaison. The liaison works with each of the pathway schools, as well as a committee of representatives from each school, to coordinate the pathway's reform efforts. In addition, the district agrees to devolve autonomy to the school with regard to decision making in areas such as resource allocation and staffing so as to give the school more latitude in developing, implementing, and evaluating various reform efforts. The schools, in turn, agree to use a form of participatory *site-based management*.

The *site-based management* body is called a School Planning and Management Team (SPMT); it is composed of representative teachers and

Figure 7.2 ATLAS Communities Program Features

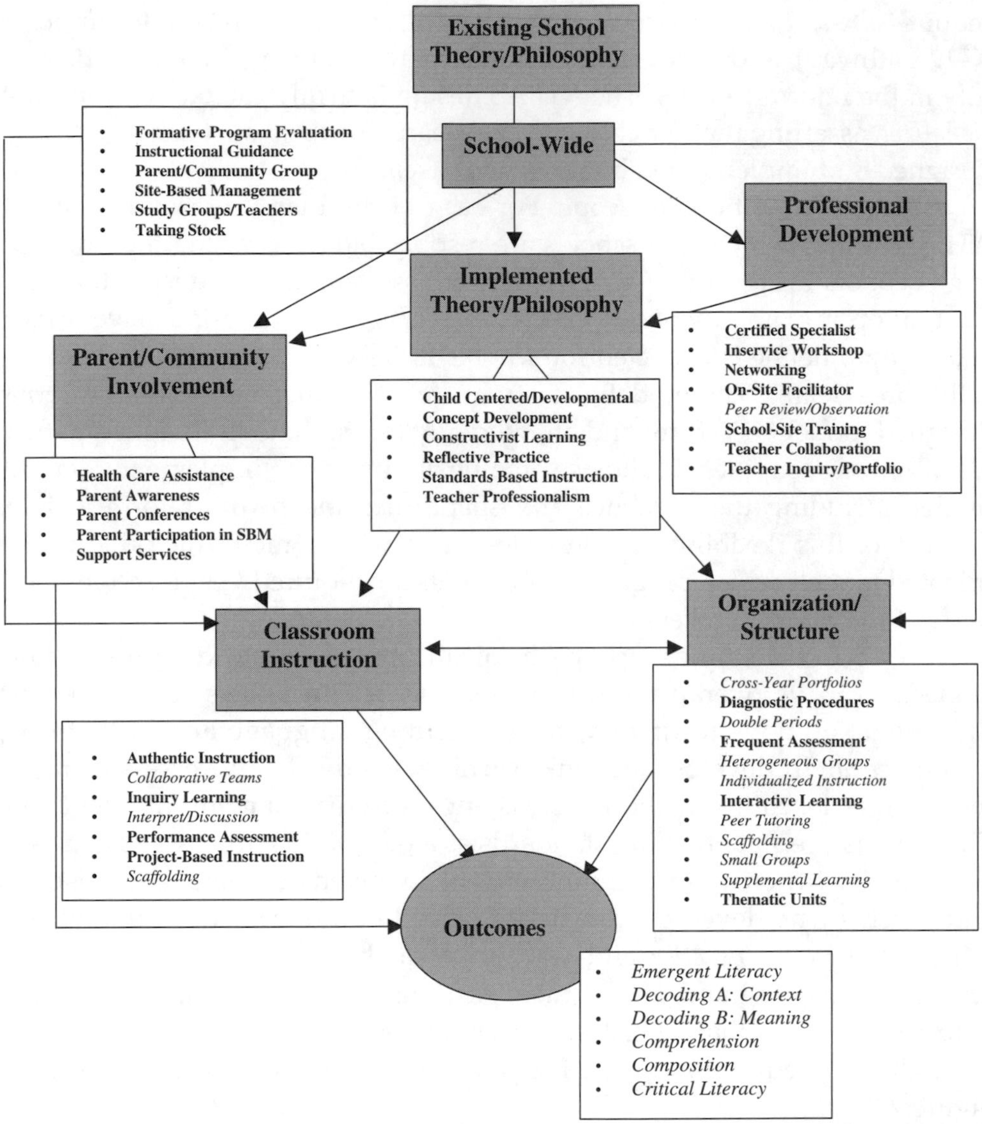

Existing School Theory/Philosophy

School-Wide

- Formative Program Evaluation
- Instructional Guidance
- Parent/Community Group
- Site-Based Management
- Study Groups/Teachers
- Taking Stock

Professional Development

- Certified Specialist
- Inservice Workshop
- Networking
- On-Site Facilitator
- *Peer Review/Observation*
- School-Site Training
- Teacher Collaboration
- Teacher Inquiry/Portfolio

Implemented Theory/Philosophy

- Child Centered/Developmental
- Concept Development
- Constructivist Learning
- Reflective Practice
- Standards Based Instruction
- Teacher Professionalism

Parent/Community Involvement

- Health Care Assistance
- Parent Awareness
- Parent Conferences
- Parent Participation in SBM
- Support Services

Classroom Instruction

- Authentic Instruction
- *Collaborative Teams*
- Inquiry Learning
- *Interpret/Discussion*
- Performance Assessment
- Project-Based Instruction
- *Scaffolding*

Organization/ Structure

- *Cross-Year Portfolios*
- Diagnostic Procedures
- *Double Periods*
- Frequent Assessment
- *Heterogeneous Groups*
- *Individualized Instruction*
- Interactive Learning
- *Peer Tutoring*
- *Scaffolding*
- *Small Groups*
- *Supplemental Learning*
- Thematic Units

Outcomes

- *Emergent Literacy*
- *Decoding A: Context*
- *Decoding B: Meaning*
- *Comprehension*
- *Composition*
- *Critical Literacy*

Bolded features are part of the reform; *italicized features* are sometimes adopted by schools implementing the reform.

administrators and may include parent and community representatives. The SPMT facilitates the reform activities conducted by *study group/teachers,* and along with the ATLAS coordinators, guides the school through the ATLAS implementation process. In addition to the SPMT, the model requires the establishment of a representative group for the entire pathway of schools. Representatives from ATLAS pathway schools coordinate reform activities in order to extend the curriculum and assessment across the K–12 pathway.

The ATLAS model requires several school-wide processes, though not in a specific sequential order or dictated form, for which the *study group/teachers* are responsible. The roles of the study groups vary depending on the task, but most often they work in one of the following capacities: to conduct and analyze research, to develop "solutions" to address identified needs, to design learning standards and aligned assessments, and to provide teachers with ongoing professional development through collaborative action research and *reflective practice*. The study groups meet regularly to conduct this work.

ATLAS schools use the baseline data from *taking stock* as well as data from ongoing *formative program evaluations* to guide their reform efforts. The school analyzes this information to determine areas to be addressed by study groups. These activities reflect key aspects of the reform that are true for student learning as well as for the reform process itself: the model asserts that assessment is vital to guiding learning (and reform); that data need to be continually gathered and reviewed in order to adjust teaching (and reform efforts); and that multiple sources of authentic data should be sought in order to give the teacher (or school) more accurate information to guide the decisions about teaching (and the reform activities).

The ATLAS school establishes *instructional guidance* through the development of learning standards and assessments that are integral to the model. Clearly articulated standards—understood by the learner—are considered essential for successful student achievement. Authentic assessment tools that are directly aligned with the standards give teachers and students a better understanding of what has and has not been learned. This guides the instruction to be adapted accordingly and increases the likelihood that students will meet learning standards. *Study groups/teachers* conduct research, analyze student work, and collaborate to develop these learning standards and assessment tools.

The ATLAS designers envision a learning community that extends beyond the school. Thus many ATLAS schools will establish a *parent/community group* to steer this part of the reform.

Implemented Theories/Philosophies

The ATLAS model's theories of learning are rooted in the philosophy of Teaching for Understanding, and promote both *concept development* and *constructivist learning*. The approach centers around teaching that focuses on understanding and uses higher order thinking skills as a means for acquiring knowledge. This approach emphasizes the ability to use knowledge (or facts) in complex tasks that demonstrate both concrete and abstract comprehension rather than the ability to retain and recite facts as an instructional end. The model views the learning process itself as *constructivist learning*—in which new learning is constructed by building cognitive connections between a student's existing understanding and the new information in an interactive process.

The ATLAS reform creates a balance between two potentially conflicting learning theories/approaches: *child-centered/developmental* and *standards-based instruction*. With the first, the *child-centered/developmental* approach, attention is given at both the classroom and the school-wide level to the developmental appropriateness of instruction and methods, and to individual students' development. This suggests allowing flexibility at both the classroom level (allowing differences between how teachers teach specific materials based on the individual class) and the student level (allowing some degree of individualization of instruction for students). The second theory, *standards-based instruction*, places an emphasis on establishing very clear learning objectives for all students and designing both instruction and assessments that are directly related to those standards. Thus, while the model suggests a key role for standards, it also asserts that students may reach the same standards by slightly different paths.

The ATLAS reform is rooted in *teacher professionalism,* based on the belief that reform actions developed at the school will be implemented with greater investment and willingness to challenge and change traditional beliefs and practices at the school than will reforms imposed externally. ATLAS adheres to this so strongly that some leverage in applying the model to the school is given away from the model's designers to the school. This allows for greater flexibility for the school, but results in less consistency in implementation of the model.

The model also subscribes to *reflective practice* as a primary model of improving teaching and sustaining professional development. Change in instructional practice is assumed to happen through ongoing discussions about practice, study of student and teacher work, and collaborative planning and teaching.

Professional Development Features

The ATLAS reform initially trains the school through a *school-site training.* Both the initial training and all aspects of program implementation are supported by a *certified specialist* and an *on-site facilitator. Inservice workshops* are used to provide additional training. The model also promotes continued training and growth in understanding the model through a coordinated set of site visits that connect new schools (those beginning implementation of the model) to more mature ATLAS schools. The "new school" sends teams of teachers to the mature school for observations and discussions about the ATLAS reform and methods. Later, the ties between the schools form a "critical friends" support system, where the more mature school provides feedback, ideas, and support to the new school.

The ATLAS reform delivers additional professional development through various *networking* opportunities, including several in-depth training institutes for teachers and administrators. These institutes mirror a *training of trainers* method. Those who attend are expected to provide training to the rest of the faculty at their school.

ATLAS emphasizes the role of *study group/teachers* in professional development. The schools' professional development activities are determined by needs identified by the study groups rather than by externally prescribed directives (e.g., a district mandate on science education). Additionally, the study groups themselves are considered to be primary vehicles for sustaining professional development through *teacher collaboration* and action research conducted through *teacher inquiry portfolios* and sometimes through *peer review/observation.*

Parent/Community Involvement Features

Parent involvement in the ATLAS reform efforts is valued at all levels and phases of the reform. The model posits that the reform process engages parents and the community in order to create a cohesive community effort to improve the students' educational outcomes. The model encourages schools to reach out, but it leaves the specifics of how to do so up to the school.

ATLAS promotes incorporating several specific parent involvement features into schools' reform activities. *Parent awareness* efforts are encouraged to inform parents of the school's activities. *Parent participation in site-based management* is advocated by the model. Parent conferences are also encouraged to serve as points to bring parents more actively into their children's education.

ATLAS also promotes a proactive role for the school in meeting the needs of children, which sometimes include areas beyond the traditional scope of schools. As such, both *health care assistance* and *support services* may be implemented by ATLAS schools.

Organizational/Structural Features

Because ATLAS is a process-oriented reform, organizational/structural features are not prevalent. Assessment is central. Both *diagnostic procedures* and *frequent assessment* are essential in the classroom. Portfolios are another way that children's learning is assessed and demonstrated. This may include the use of *cross-year portfolios* to demonstrate student growth across grade levels.

Depending on a school's improvement plan, several other features may be a part of the instructional program based on their consistency with the model's implemented theories. These features include, but are not limited to, *interactive learning, thematic units, individualized instruction, heterogeneous grouping*, and *small groups*.

ATLAS schools are encouraged to consider programmatic means of addressing the needs of students who are struggling to meet academic standards. Accordingly, some ATLAS schools may implement the following strategies: *supplemental learning, peer tutoring*, and *double periods* (double reading time) of English (at the middle or high school level).

Classroom Instructional Features

As earlier stated, ATLAS is process oriented and thus, while a type of teaching is suggested through the focus on Teaching for Understanding, it is not prescribed. However, several methods associated with reading instruction—related to creating meaning-oriented instruction—are important to the model. These include *authentic instruction, inquiry learning*, and *project-based instruction*. In addition, *performance assessment* helps measure a child's success in the classroom and suggests areas of emphasis to the teacher. Other features that fit well with the philosophy of the model and that may be present in a particular school's implementation are *interpreting/discussion, scaffolding*, and use of *collaborative teams*.

Targeted Literacy Outcomes

Because the ATLAS model is process oriented, each school's implementation of the model emerges differently and is unique to that school. Therefore, the links to specific reading outcomes are weak. However, several aspects of the model suggest there is such a linkage. First, the model requires schools to establish clear learning standards and assessments to guide the instructional program of the school, and the schools incorporate state standards as a part of this process. Thus, the resulting curricular program will be associated with those standards. Schools using the ATLAS model will target specific literary outcomes (e.g., *emergent literacy, decoding A*, and so forth) to the extent that state standards emphasize these outcomes. Second, the creation of a *caring community* of adults who are committed to each child's education can be highly effective in mobilizing resources and efforts in order to create effective readers.

REFERENCES AND CONTACTS:
ATLAS Communities

References

Gardner, H. (1999). A disciplined approach to school reform. *Peabody Journal of Education, 74*(1), 166–174.

Glazer, N. (1999). ATLAS and curriculum. *Peabody Journal of Education, 74*(1), 174–182

Janet, W. (1999). Curriculum in ATLAS. *Peabody Journal of Education, 74*(1), 146–154.

McDonald, J. P., Hatch, T., Kirby, E., Ames, N., Haynes, N. M., & Joyner, E. T. (1999). *School reform behind the scenes: How ATLAS is shaping the future of education.* New York: Teachers College Press.

Muncey, D. E., Payne, J., & White, N. S. (1999). Making curriculum and instructional reform happen: A case study. *Peabody Journal of Education, 74*(1), 68–110.

Orrell, C. J. (1996). ATLAS Communities: Authentic teaching, learning and assessment. In S. Stringfield, S. Ross, & L. Smith (Eds.), *Bold plans for school restructuring: New American School designs* (pp. 53–74). Hillsdale, NJ: Erlbaum.

Rogers, B. (1999). Conflicting approaches to curriculum: Recognizing how fundamental beliefs can sustain or sabotage school reform. *Peabody Journal of Education, 74*(1), 29–67.

Squires, D. A. (1999). Changing curriculum and school's structure: Commentary on ATLAS. *Peabody Journal of Education, 74*(1), 154–160.

Squires, D. A., & Kranyik, R. D. (1999). Connecting school-based management and instructional improvement: A case study of two ATLAS schools. *Journal of Education for Students Placed at Risk, 4*(3), 241–258.

Contact Information

ATLAS Communities
55 Chapel Street
Newton, MA 02458
Phone: (617) 618-2401
Fax: (617) 969-3440
Email: ATLAS@edc.org
Web Site: www.edc.org/ATLAS/

7.3. MODERN RED SCHOOLHOUSE ■

Reviewed by Siri Ann Loescher and Stacy Jacob

Modern Red Schoolhouse (MRSh) is a process-oriented, standards-driven school reform process that can be used in elementary, middle, and high schools. The design places emphasis on the development of a learning community to find and implement effective ways to teach. Originally the project developed a set of rigorous content standards and "Hudson Units" (a curriculum) with related assessments based on those standards from which schools would work. The major premises of Modern Red Schoolhouse are that all instruction should be carefully and intentionally designed to meet rigorous learning standards, should use varying methods of instruction, and should foster greater independence to—and give increasing responsibility for—students in the learning process. Since most states have developed learning standards to which schools are held accountable through public reporting and accreditation processes, Modern Red Schoolhouse adapted their reform design to use the schools' state standards in place of the MRSh standards and materials, which are used instead as resources. Thus, the schools develop and implement a standards-based curriculum that is based on their state standards.

Program Description

Because the reading program for each MRSh school is locally developed and based on local state standards, the reading program will look different from school to school. The model is more than a design to develop a curriculum. Various program components such as professional development and parent involvement are structured to maximize the impact of the school's program on student learning. For example, during the process of developing the reading curriculum, teachers study the state reading standards, do research on methods and assessments that are appropriate for the curriculum, and acquire professional development in those methods. Therefore, the MRSh program identifies primarily process-oriented features and leaves most instructional and organizational features to the school. The program features associated with the MRSh reform design are depicted in Figure 7.3.

School-Wide Features

After a *buy-in* process the school *takes stock,* gathering both student data, to determine how the school is currently performing, and information about resources used by and available to the school. The school uses the results of the *taking stock* as baseline information that, along with the state standards, guides a *backmapping* process for the development of a curriculum framework, instruction units, and assessments.

The *backmapping* process and the resulting curricular units are the primary vehicles for change at the school. *Study groups/teacher* work though the process across the school year; the goal is to develop a fully articulated curriculum that has been tested by classroom teachers during the design process and is ready to

Figure 7.3 Modern Red Schoolhouse Program Features

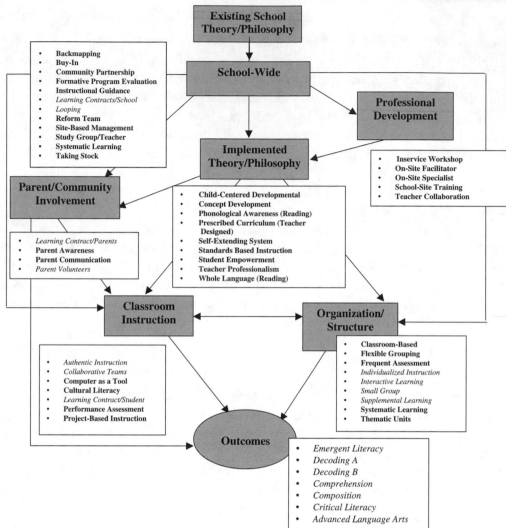

Bolded features are part of the reform; *italicized features* are sometimes adopted by schools implementing the reform.

be implemented school-wide. The state standards, through the *backmapping* process, provide *instructional guidance* to the school by creating the framework that guides the school's reform activities. The teacher-designed curriculum includes specifically sequenced instructional activities and assessments that create school-wide *systematic learning*.

Several school-wide features are related to classrooms' instruction and organization. First is the broadening of classrooms at the elementary level from strict grade levels to looser groupings of several grades (e.g., first through third) in multi-age classrooms; it may include *looping*. By freeing the adherence to *grade limit*, this feature provides teachers with greater latitude to teach developmentally, to use a variety of strategies, such as *flexible grouping* (see organization/structure), and to adapt instruction to individual students' needs. The second feature is technology requirements for the school—the investment in technology prior to implementation. Schools are expected to utilize technology to enhance learning and expand the number of available learning resources.

Technology is used for direct instruction, as a tool for instruction (such as regular viewing and analysis of cable news), and as a means for communication among individuals within a school, between school sites, and with the MRSh specialists. Finally, schools are encouraged to develop *learning contracts/school* based on students' Individual Education Compacts (IEC), in which the school, the student, and the parents each agree to specific activities and responsibilities related to the student's IEC (see classroom instructional features).

The model places value on decisions about the reform being made at the school site (rather than at the district) and on broad participation in the making of those decisions. The school designates a *reform team* to work with MRSh specialists to plan, coordinate, and facilitate reform activities. In addition, Modern Red Schoolhouse uses *site-based management* to relegate more decision-making autonomy from the district to the school, and to involve teachers in shared decision making.

Participation in the reform is sought beyond the school through *community partnerships*. Schools are encouraged to seek different kinds of partnerships from all sectors of the community in three different types of initiatives: developing a preschool consortium, a school-to-work initiative (generally at the high school level), and issues related to school climate.

An annual *formative program evaluation* is conducted by the Modern Red Schoolhouse specialists. Data are collected electronically throughout the year to give feedback to the school and the model providers about implementation, student performance, school performance, and needs of the school. This evaluation is used by the MRSh specialists to determine how best to serve the school and is returned to the school to assist the school in ongoing reform efforts.

Implemented Theory/Philosophy

The Modern Red Schoolhouse subscribes to a set of philosophies about learning that suggests the general direction of the academic program likely to evolve in a MRSh school. The model subscribes to a *child-centered/developmental* theory of learning, building on the strengths of a child in a developmentally appropriate manner rather than prescribing sets of lessons determined by grade or age. Consistent with the developmental approach to learning, MRSh advocates a balanced literacy program that draws from both *phonological awareness* and *whole language*.

Modern Red Schoolhouse emphasizes *concept development* in instruction. The model uses the term "spiraling curriculum" to focus on the nature of an articulated curriculum (K–12) that grows not only in scope of knowledge but also in complexity and sophistication of academic work; conceptual understanding is needed at every level of the curriculum so that students may build on those understandings at more advanced levels. The model views the curriculum as building toward a *self-extending system*; this gives students the skills and responsibility to take on increasing independence in their learning and studies and encourages *student empowerment*.

The Modern Red Schoolhouse theories on reform are strongly interrelated. The model adheres to *teacher professionalism*, in which reform is believed to be most effective and efficacious when planned and implemented at the school site using the expertise of the faculty. The model also posits that reforming the *what* and *how* of teaching in schools should be based on *standards-based instruction*. The standards should drive the selection of content and should suggest the instructional methods and related embedded *performance assessments*. To ensure that all students attending the school receive the same *standards-based instruction*, there should be a *prescribed curriculum* developed by the teachers, which is based on the standards.

Professional Development

Modern Red Schoolhouse uses an *on-site specialist* to provide the initial *school-site training* in the reform process. The school designates a leadership team whose members receive additional training from Modern Red Schoolhouse and serve as *on-site facilitators*. The leadership team coordinates additional school-site professional development efforts and provides support to the faculty during implementation.

The reform relies heavily on professional development and recommends that teachers attend twenty days of training across the school year. The extensive professional development includes training in the reform process and in specific instructional and assessment methods. This professional development assists teachers in the *backmapping* process and in the classroom implementation of the teacher-developed, standards-based units. The configuration of the training is set by the school and district in terms of setting aside the time for training that often includes *inservice workshops*, release time, after-school activities, and/or summer institutes. During the *taking stock* and *backmapping* processes, the *reform team*, along with the *on-site specialist*, determines the professional development needs of the faculty and plans the training activities accordingly.

Along with professional development, teacher improvement is supported through *teacher collaboration* in planning of instruction. Teachers are encouraged to share their expertise, to test new teaching methods, and to share the results of those trials during the implementation of the reform. To support these efforts, the model recommends that schools find ways to provide opportunities for collaboration. Teacher improvement is also supported by the model's electronic instructional management system that provides teachers with the means to record, analyze, and manage student performance data. These data are also aggregated at the school level as part of the ongoing formative evaluation process.

Parent/Community Involvement Features

Modern Red Schoolhouse advocates parent involvement. *Parent communication* is fostered through regular communication between teachers and parents through direct contact, parent conferences, and technology. *Parent awareness* activities inform parents about all aspects of the MRSh reform process including *buy-in* and *taking stock*.

Parents are also expected to play an active role in their children's education. MRSh suggests that schools develop *learning contracts/parent*, related to students' Individual Education Compact, in which the parents agree to certain activities to assist students in reaching the goals specified in the IEC. The model encourages the use of *parent volunteers*.

Organizational/Structural Features

Modern Red Schoolhouse is a reform organized as a school-wide learning community. The building of this community is important in the first year of the program. In and of itself, Modern Red Schoolhouse is not a systematic reading reform; however, the curriculum developed through the learning community could provide *systematic learning*. That is to say, the extent to which Modern Red Schoolhouse is systematic is entirely dependent on the curriculum created by teachers in the community. While the model allows flexibility in the organizational structures, it strongly advocates that several features be incorporated. MRSh encourages schools to develop programs that foster *interactive learning*. *Thematic units* are often used to organize course content. *Frequent assessments* are to be used to gauge student learning and allow for adapting instruction accordingly. The model recommends using *flexible grouping* so that teachers can consider students and projects and decide what type of grouping would be best suited to a given project, such as *small groups* or *individualized instruction*.

The model encourages schools to develop strategies to ensure that all students achieve academically. This includes creating strategies and programs for students struggling with literacy acquisition. Thus schools are likely to implement program features such as *supplemental learning*.

Classroom Instructional Features

At the classroom/instructional level, very few features are intrinsically part of the reform. This is due to the Modern Red Schoolhouse philosophy that the reform should be developed based on the individual school. However, the reform—through *backmapping*—requires the incorporation of *performance assessments* into the standards-based units. The model also requires the use of *computer as a tool* to simultaneously strengthen skills and build technological literacy. MRSh recommends *project-based instruction* as a means for developing content-rich, relevant instruction. Related methods that are encouraged by the model include *authentic instruction* and use of *collaborative teams*. To individualize the program, some MRSh schools develop individual education compacts for each student, which serve as *learning contracts/student* and specify the learning goals and responsibilities of the student, school, and parent.

An interesting required part of this reform is that foreign language instruction must occur in every grade, along with a focus on *cultural literacy*. This is a type of literacy that we have not seen in other reforms.

Targeted Literacy Outcomes

Because there are no standard classroom features in this model, it is difficult to claim that there are specific literacy outcomes for students. Outcomes will be related to the standards on which the *backmapping* is based and the types of professional development sought by the school. Based on this approach, the reform suggests that students will experience achievement in reading. Whether the implementation of classroom practices links to literacy outcomes *(emergent literacy, decoding A and B, comprehension, composition,* and *critical literacy)* depends on the strategies teachers implement.

REFERENCES AND CONTACTS:
Modern Red Schoolhouse

References

Heady, R., & Kilgore, S. B. (1996). The Modern Red Schoolhouse. In S. Stringfield, S. M. Ross, & L. Smith (Eds.), *Bold plans for school restructuring: The New American Schools designs* (pp. 139–178). Hillsdale, NJ: Erlbaum.

Kilgore, S. B. (Ed.). (1997). *Designing schools for the 21st century: Essential elements of a Modern Red Schoolhouse version 2.1.* Alexandria, VA: New American Schools.

New American Schools Development Corporation. (1995a). *A parent's guide to academic standards in the Modern Red Schoolhouse: Primary, intermediate, and upper.* Alexandria, VA: Author

New American Schools Development Corporation. (1995b). *The Modern Red Schoolhouse design document: Version 1.1.* Alexandria, VA: Author.

New American Schools. (1999). *Working toward excellence: Examining the effectiveness of New American Schools designs.* Alexandria, VA: Author.

Contact Information

Pam Randall
Modern Red Schoolhouse Institute
208 23rd Avenue North
Nashville, TN 37203

or

Brian Spears
Vice-President for Development
Phone: (888) 234-8073
(615) 320-5366
(888) ASK-MRSH (275-6774), Extension 17
Email: jlyles@mrsh.org
Prandall@mrsh.org
Web Site: www.mrsh.org

7.4. SCHOOL DEVELOPMENT PROGRAM

Reviewed by Siri Ann Loescher and Stacy Jacob

The School Development Program was initiated in 1968 and first implemented in the schools of New Haven, Connecticut, by James Comer and his colleagues at Yale University. The model addresses the concern that schools, especially those serving disadvantaged youth, do not meet all the developmental needs of students; thus those students are less likely to succeed in school. To address this concern, the model considers the range of developmental needs and broadens the schools' resource base to include the entire community in meeting these needs. The reform model focuses on community mental health and a holistic approach to child development as well as on curriculum reform. Over time, the School Development Program has evolved into a national reform that balances community development, through outreach and mental health, with educational reform for urban schools. The School Development Program remains distinctive among the reforms reviewed here because of the role given to the community and its focus on well-balanced child development.

Program Description

The School Development Program (SDP) is a process-oriented, school-wide reform that emphasizes child, adolescent, and adult development through *teacher professionalism* and community building. Students' holistic development and academic success are the primary goals of the program. To achieve this, the SDP process mobilizes parents, teachers, administrators, counselors, nonteaching staff, and community members.

The model posits that many students in inner-city schools enter school without the personal, social, and moral development necessary for academic success. If students' basic needs are met and they are challenged enough to do their best, these students have the potential for success. The reform design builds on the existing school programs to address six "developmental pathways": physical, psychological, language, social, ethical, and cognitive. The six developmental pathways are viewed as a whole, with each given equal importance in a child's development. The model advocates a balanced approach toward child development, and overemphasis on one area at the expense of the others is considered to be potentially detrimental to a student's success in school. The model is a process-oriented reform that provides a structure and a philosophical framework for school restructuring.

While the SDP design does not include a specific reading program, the overall approach suggests an emphasis on tailoring reading instruction to meet students' needs and monitoring student performance. The SDP model is based on the idea that all students can achieve high levels of academic success. The specific reform activities of the school, including instructional focus, are guided by a Comprehensive School Plan and are developed with a holistic eye, balancing academic and social needs. The model suggests that schools adjust the language arts program to balance between meeting state standards and ensuring that instruction is engaging and developmentally appropriate. To help schools meet this objective, the model provides training to schools in developing a "balanced curriculum."

To ensure that all students are building the strong literacy skills needed to be successful in school, the model has recently developed a targeted literacy intervention for struggling students. The program, called "The SDP Essentials of Literacy Process," includes pulling students out for enriched literacy instruction. The program features associated with the School Development Program are depicted in Figure 7.4.

Figure 7.4 School Development Program Features

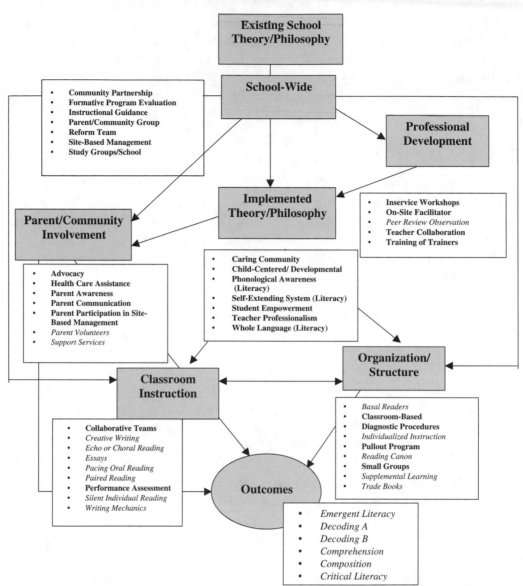

Bolded features are part of the reform; *italicized features* are sometimes adopted by schools implementing the reform.

School-Wide Features

The design requires a school and district "entry process" that includes extensive exploration of the School Development Program process and concludes with making specific time and resource commitments to the program. To ensure that new schools will receive adequate support from both SDP training centers and from the local school district, new schools are accepted only from districts that already have SDP schools or are part of a cluster of new SDP schools within a district.

The school establishes a *reform team* consisting of a district facilitator and the school principal, and may include teachers or parents. The *reform team* supports the initial reform implementation, including establishing a specific form of *site-based management*.

The SDP design provides an SBM structure that incorporates three separate bodies that function together to develop and implement the reform activities at the school: the School Planning and Management Team (hereafter "Management Team"), the Student and Staff Support Team (hereafter "Support Team"), and a Parent Team. The Management Team has the primary responsibility for activities that drive the school's reform efforts. The other groups, along with *study groups/school,* provide information and feedback to the Management Team and initiate plans to implement reform activities defined by the Management Team. The Support Team is primarily concerned with the school's social climate and prevention issues, and at times it manages individual student cases. The Support Team is also charged with paying particular attention to the developmental pathways and how each area is addressed in all reform activities. This group is composed of school faculty with child development and mental health backgrounds. The Parent Team is a *parent community/group* that includes parent representatives and is primarily concerned with parental involvement in all aspects of the school. This group ensures that parent perspectives are included in the Comprehensive School Plan.

The Management Team is responsible for developing and enacting the comprehensive school plan, which directs the school's improvement efforts and is designed to address each of the following areas: student performance, curriculum and instruction, assessment, school climate, and parent and community involvement. The comprehensive school plan provides *instructional guidance* to the school. The SDP model provides training for schools on how to develop a "Balanced Curriculum," in which schools study and take into account state standards when developing the comprehensive school plan, specific curricula, and professional development.

In addition to tasks related to the comprehensive school plan, the Management Team creates a Staff Development Plan that identifies and initiates professional development activities based on the comprehensive school plan. The Management Team also has the task of conducting the ongoing *formative program evaluation,* which is used by the study groups to adapt the school's reform activities.

The SDP model seeks broad community involvement including *community partnerships* in the reform activities of the school. Adults in both the school and the greater community are considered resources for providing holistic, developmentally rich programs to ensure the academic success of students.

Implemented Theoretical/Philosophical Features

The School Development Model is strongly rooted in *child centered/ developmental* learning theories. The model's embedded theory of reform is that many students arrive at school at a different level of development from what is assumed by traditional schools. Traditional school programs may not adequately address all the developmental needs of the students; thus students will be more likely to experience academic failure. Great attention is given to the six developmental pathways in program development, review of curriculum and instruction, and professional development. Also important to the model are the implemented philosophies of *student empowerment* to encourage a love of learning and the *self-extending system* to develop independent learning skills. The model intends to create schools where students' developmental needs are met and where students flourish as directors of their own learning.

The activities of the Essentials for Literacy program, which targets students who are struggling in the acquisition of literacy skills, reflect an emphasis on *whole language*. This emphasis on learning reading through meaning and development of conceptual understanding is consistent with the developmental approach of the model.

The School Development Program's reform theories are rooted in *teacher professionalism*; the school is given tools and a framework through the SDP model by which to analyze and direct the progress and reform activities of the school. Like other process-oriented reforms, in recent years the model has increased its emphasis on specific strategies, including aligning the school's curriculum with state standards and incorporating methods to address literacy skills. However, the model, even in these efforts, relies on *teacher professionalism*. Because sustainable change in the classroom is assumed to evolve from collegiality and collaboration rather than to be imposed externally, schools are given the latitude to adapt existing materials and specify their own professional development plans. Change in classrooms is more sustainable when it is internally defined (from collegiality and collaboration) than when it is externally imposed.

The School Development Program also strongly adheres to a theory of *caring community*. Combining the emphasis on holistic child development and on building a community-based support system for the schools' and students' academic success creates an environment in which students are valued, respected, and nurtured. The model encourages schools to extend this view to the larger community in terms of providing services to meet family and community mental health needs.

Professional Development Features

Professional development features are highly important to the SDP Process, a characteristic of process-oriented models. Part of the school district's commitment to the SDP program is the designation of a district person to be trained and to serve as an *on-site facilitator* for the district SDP schools. The School Development Program offers a *training of trainers* program to provide training for the entire faculty. Each school is associated with a regional training center that provides guidance and support to the school. In addition, professional development is provided throughout the year via *in-service workshops* that are identified in the Comprehensive School Plan in order to build teacher capacity to implement classroom reform activities.

Teacher collaboration is considered vital to the process of improving student outcomes. The model supports these efforts by providing opportunities to collaborate and a specific reform process: "Teachers Helping Teachers." This process is designed to establish norms, attitudes, and procedures to encourage trust, reflection on practice and student work, and classroom improvement through collaboration. The process includes *peer review/observation*.

Parent/Community Involvement Features

Parent involvement features are important to SDP. Parents are active in the development of the comprehensive school plan through *parent participation in site-based management.* In SDP schools, increased communication is the key to parent involvement; thus the model utilizes both *parent awareness* and *parent communication.* Direct involvement in the school is encouraged through *parent volunteers.* Indeed, this involvement is meant not only to include parents but also to extend to the community surrounding the school. Since the model is based on theories of child development, *advocacy, health care assistance,* and *support services* are usually part of any SDP school.

Organizational/Structural Features

SDP does not provide a specific literacy model except for students who fall behind. If identified through *diagnostic procedures,* children go into a *pullout program* called the Essentials of Literacy Process, which features a classroom set up as a "Comer Reading Room." Within this program, students work in *small groups* at developmental workstations addressing different literacy skills. The school utilizes whatever reading materials it has, so these children could be working with *basal readers, reading canon books,* or *trade books,* depending on the school's resources. In addition to the Essentials of Literacy Process, SDP schools may provide *supplemental learning* for students needing extra instruction.

Classroom Instructional Features

Again, because of the process-oriented approach of SDP, there is no set of classroom features that epitomizes its language arts instruction. However, the SDP Essentials of Literacy Process is a specialized program for students with weak literacy skills. This program uses an enrichment approach that includes *echo or choral reading,* and encourages fostering writing skills through *essays, creative writing,* and *writing mechanics.*

While an SDP school's reading program is not specified by the model, the model's approach to literacy acquisition in the Essentials of Literacy Process together with its focus on child development give an indication of the types of reading program features a school using the model might adopt. *Performance assessment* is encouraged as a means for measuring student learning as opposed to a sole reliance on standardized tests. The model's approach to *student empowerment* suggests the use of any number of reading techniques within the program. *Collaborative teams* might use *pacing oral reading, paired reading,* or *silent individual reading* as they build reading skills. Within these *small groups, echo or choral reading* is a technique that may be used to help the students learn to read.

Targeted Literacy Outcomes

Because there is no specific reading/language arts curriculum in the School Development Program, literacy outcomes are difficult to evaluate. However, the Essentials of Literacy Process does identify and recommend methods related to early literacy outcomes (specifically *emergent literacy, decoding A and B,* and *comprehension*). However, these this will only address students who participate in the pullout intervention in those schools that adopt the Essentials of Literacy Process.

SDP is a process-oriented model that mobilizes the home, school, and community to evaluate and address student needs and assess whether there is success in meeting these needs. This mobilization can be powerful. The attention to academic needs and performance and to creating a balanced curriculum suggests a strong linkage to the literacy/language arts outcome. However, the degree of linkage (tight or loose) will depend on local classroom practices and enhancement by SDP.

REFERENCES AND CONTACTS:
School Development Program

References

Comer, J. P. (Ed.). (1996). *Rallying the whole village: The Comer process for reforming education.* New York: Teachers College Press.

Comer, J. P., Ben-Avie, M., Haynes, N. M., & Joyner, E. T. (Eds.). (1999). *Child by child: The Comer process for change in education.* New York: Teachers College Press.

Northwest Regional Educational Laboratory (NWREL). (1988). *Catalog of school reform models: First edition* [On-line]. Available: www.nwrel.org/scpd/natspec/catalog/

School Development Program. (1999a). *Applying the principles of child and adolescent development.* New Haven, CT: School Development Program at the Yale Child Study Center.

School Development Program. (1999b). *The SDP essentials of literacy process.* New Haven, CT: School Development Program at the Yale Child Study Center.

Contact Information

School Development Program
Yale Child Study Center
53 College Street
New Haven, CT 06510
Phone: (203) 737-1020
Email: beverly.crowther@yale.edu
Web Site: http:/info.med.yale.edu/comer

■ GUIDANCE FOR EDUCATORS

Process-oriented comprehensive reforms allow schools to engage in structured processes that foster inquiry about the school in ways that accelerate student learning. These reform models generally do not include specific content in reading instruction but encourage teachers to develop and revise their reading programs. They also allow teachers to engage in professional development that builds the community of learning. However, process reforms can take longer to fully implement than more structured models (such as the curriculum-based comprehensive school reform (CSR) models reviewed in Chapter 8). Schools using these models can take their time in devising optimal changes for their learning communities and the open-endedness of process reforms may become an excuse to procrastinate. Overall, process-oriented reform models provide a viable option for schools that want to take a community-based approach to reform, but these schools face a number of key challenges in successfully implementing the model so as to make meaningful changes in reading instruction. Some methods for overcoming these challenges are described below.

The Research Base

Comprehensive school reforms are based on research on schools. The process-oriented models emphasize teacher professional development and inquiry as the locus of change, placing many of the key decisions about reform strategies in the hands of teachers and reform teams. In the early development of these reform models, the model providers relied on confirmatory research studies that were conducted by affiliated researchers. Some of the more established process-oriented reforms have a long history in certain schools and districts, and this history has allowed opportunities for nonaffiliated researchers to study these reform models. The Policy Center has conducted research on process-oriented models as part of both the Indiana reading studies and the Michigan CSR studies.

Research by Model Providers

The developmental period for Accelerated Schools, initiated in the 1980s, was funded by a grant from the Chevron Corporation to Stanford University and to satellite centers at other universities that piloted the model. The early studies that compared test scores in funded and comparison schools were conducted by researchers affiliated with the Accelerated Schools Satellite Center in Texas (Knight & Stallings, 1995; McCarthy & Still, 1993). These studies indicated that the two accelerated schools studied showed more improvement than a comparison school. However, most of the other research projects did not focus on achievement outcomes but rather on the community building process that was central to the model design (e.g., Finnan, St. John, Slovacek, & McCarthy, 1996; Miron, St. John, & Davidson, 1998; St. John, Griffith, & Allen-Haynes, 1997). These studies found that successful implementation involved more than going through the steps of the reform process; it required a collective commitment to reform. Schools that built this shared sense of community were more likely to show improved student outcomes than were schools that lacked this broad commitment.

The ATLAS Communities model was implemented as part of the New American Schools initiative in the 1990s. The model targeted curriculum more explicitly than did some of the earlier models (e.g., Accelerated Schools and School Development Program) but held to a process focus. The published research has looked most closely at the curriculum developed with the model (Gardner, 1999; Janet, 1999; Muncey, Payne, & White, 1999; Rogers, 1999; Squires, 1999). There is some preliminary research indicating that implementation of the ATLAS Communities model is associated with improved reading scores in elementary schools (Slavin & Fashola, 1998). However, studies concentrating on test scores and other types of outcomes have not been widely disseminated.

Modern Red Schoolhouse was also developed as part of the new American Schools initiative in the 1990s (New American Schools, 1999). It is a standards-driven reform that has not been widely studied by educational researchers. Some schools using this model have shown improvement in reading scores (Slavin & Fashola, 1998), but the evidence remains anecdotal.

The School Development Program was established well before other comprehensive reform models. It offered a community-oriented reform model that centered on the development of children. The model developers used action research in creating the model design (Comer, 1996; Comer, Ben-Avie, Haynes, & Joyner, 1999) but have not placed a substantial emphasis on test scores. Its reading reform component—Essentials of Literacy—focuses on creating a balanced approach to reading for students who are pulled out (School Development Program, 1999b) and thus it can be characterized as a targeted reading reform coupled with process-oriented school reform. While the original research on SDP showed improvement on standardized tests in New Haven schools, most of the recent research with control schools has produced mixed results (Slavin & Fashola, 1998).

The Policy Center's Studies

Research using the framework introduced in this volume has been conducted in the Indiana reading studies and the Michigan CSR studies. Key findings from both sets of studies are summarized below.

The Indiana reading studies included some Accelerated Schools in the comparison group.[3] In regression analyses with a large number of controls for school characteristics, the Accelerated Schools Project showed higher pass rates on ISTEP+, the standardized reading and language arts tests in the third grade (St. John, Manset, et al., 2001). The analyses also indicated that this effect was attributable to parental involvement, a component of reform that is heavily emphasized in the ASP model. This study provides further evidence that implementation of the Accelerated Schools Project is accompanied by improvement in student learning outcomes.

The Michigan CSR study used the conceptual framework introduced in Chapter 3, but asked a generalized set of questions about classroom practices rather than focusing only on reading. In these studies, the process CSR models were compared to curriculum models in a series of multinomial logistic regressions (St. John, Musoba, et al., 2002). The analyses indicated that the process models were modestly associated (a .1 significance level) with reductions in special education referrals. This modest difference could be related to explicit emphasis placed on process, which could mean that curriculum change might take longer in schools using process models because they leave choices about curriculum reform strategies to teachers and reform teams. The curriculum and professional development factors (discussed in the Guidance section of Chapter 6) had a more substantial direct effect on both retention and special education referrals than did this type of model.

Meeting Standards

The earliest process models did not explicitly include standards when they were first developed (e.g., Accelerated Schools and School Development Program), which is understandable as they were created before the new emphasis on standards emerged. However, these models have adapted by incorporating an emphasis on meeting standards as an integral part of the reform process. The New American Schools models pays very explicit attention to standards, and the Modern Red Schoolhouse includes *backmapping*, a program feature that directly links the reform process to state standards.

Schools using process models can address all state reading standards by emphasizing them in the reform process. However, the focus on standards can become a dominant force in the reform process, making it easier to follow district curriculum guides than to develop new innovative approaches.

Politics of Reform

The process-oriented reforms place a substantial emphasis on teacher involvement and professional development. Most of these reforms implicitly view teachers as the locus of the reform process. Many of these models are among those frequently chosen through the federal CSR program, so choosing a school-wide process-oriented reform presents an alternative that merits consideration for many schools. However, the heavy emphasis on teacher involvement creates complexity at each level of governance.

Perhaps the most important issue for teachers to consider if they are interested in making a commitment to a process model is whether all the teachers are willing to put time into the process to make the model work. In general, these reform models encourage teachers to collaborate on restructuring the curriculum. There is evidence from multi-school studies that collaboration on curriculum is associated with improvement in student outcomes, but extensive teacher involvement in governance can have the reverse effect (St. John, Musoba, et al., 2002). So, even when teacher involvement is encouraged teachers need to keep their focus on using inquiry to improve curriculum and instruction rather than on resolving political issues in the school.

Principals play a crucial role in process-oriented reforms. In some schools, principals can have difficulty delegating responsibility to teachers (St. John et al., 1997). When teachers feel their involvement and their ideas are not really wanted and that principals actually want teachers to follow their lead, then it is less likely that teachers will take risks. They may feel that if they show initiative, they will be vulnerable as they will be challenging the school leadership. When principals support teachers' inquiry into their own teaching, these reforms are more likely to become a catalyst for meaningful change, including improvement on test scores (St. John, Meza, Allen-Haynes, & Davidson, 1996). Unfortunately, when principals are successful, they may be moved to other schools that need help, and this can set the reform process back.

At the district level, the process-oriented method can pose a problem unless districts are willing to exempt schools from some of the district requirements that constrain innovation. In a sense, districts should be prepared to treat schools that choose process-oriented reforms much like "charter" schools with respect to district curriculum policies. If districts are serious about giving teachers the freedom to innovate, they need to remove some of the constraints from the process. There is evidence that district offices have been slow to approve changes in policies for CSR schools (St. John, Musoba, et al., 2002), a factor that could inhibit change, especially in those schools using process-oriented reform models.

Integrating Inquiry

Most of the process models actively support inquiry; the Accelerated Schools Project includes *inquiry* as a key feature of the school-wide process and promotes *inquiry learning* as a classroom instruction feature. ATLAS schools engage the school as a whole in a process of *taking stock* and using *study groups* as well as introducing *inquiry learning* in classroom instruction. The School Development Program emphasizes *teacher professionalism* as philosophy, *teacher collaboration* as a professional development method, and the use of *collaborative teams* in the classroom. Thus, while the Accelerated School Project places the most explicit emphasis on inquiry, the other process reforms also have features that essentially involve teachers in collaboration. These collaborative processes can be enhanced if an inquiry-based approach is used. Therefore, we recommend that schools adopting process models also use teacher inquiry to improve curriculum and teaching.

The process reform models depend on teachers to develop strategies that work for their children. The School Development Project and Modern Red Schoolhouse place heavy emphasis on using student *performance assessment* to guide the classroom change process (see reviews above) whereas the Accelerated Schools Projects stresses the use of classroom inquiry to achieve this aim (Hopfenberg, Levin, & Associates, 1993). Both of these approaches encourage teachers to focus on how students are learning in the classroom and to adapt their practices to enable all children to learn. Thus, teachers must be willing to engage in inquiry within their own classrooms if a process reform model is going to work well. This means that teachers should be aware of this component of the reform process when they select one of these reform strategies.

Building Community

When process reforms work well, they create a strong sense of community within schools. However, if school leaders do not embrace the underlying concepts of teacher empowerment, if district offices constrain the reform process by rigidly enforcing district curriculum standards, or if teachers do not want to put in the time required by an inquiry-based reform approach, the process reform can flounder. The sense of community will remain elusive when this happens. Thus, process reform strategies—whether chosen from the widely used reform models or developed locally—provide a clear choice. They emphasize professionalism and teacher involvement as the core elements of the reform process, but they do not provide a set script for achieving the desired reforms.

NOTES

1. Regional mentoring centers are most often located in a university or a state department of education. Indiana schools are associated with the Dayton Satellite Center for Accelerated Schools, located at the University of Dayton.

2. The Coalition of Essentials Schools (CES) advocates authentic teaching/learning focusing on the depth of over the breadth of knowledge. CES promotes professional development through action research and reflective practice. The School Development Program (reviewed in this chapter) focuses on child development and involving the community in the development of a school climate conducive to academic success. Project Zero focuses on applying multiple intelligence theory to schools through authentic assessment and teaching. The Education Development Center develops innovative curriculum and professional development that emphasize inquiry and project-based learning.

3. These studies surveyed all schools funded as part of the Early Reading Intervention Grants and a random sample of other elementary schools in the state. While Accelerated Schools were not included among the funded schools, they were included in the comparison group.

8
Curriculum-Based Reforms

Curriculum-based reforms are comprehensive school reform models that are centered on a particular curriculum, or an approach to curriculum reform. Like process-oriented reforms, these models are designed to improve the educational outcomes of all students. Along with the curriculum are various structural or organizational changes that are geared to increase the effectiveness of schools' educational programs. For example, at the high school level the America's Choice model requires schools to adopt a school-within-a-school configuration that breaks the large high school into smaller, separate, and autonomous academies. These reforms often require changes in instructional practices that are associated with the prescribed curriculum used by the model.

Some curriculum-based reforms focus primarily on one academic area (such as reading/language arts), but most include curricula for multiple content areas. Schools may adopt one or more of these curricular areas as part of their comprehensive school reform. For example, Success for All was initially a reading and writing curriculum. In recent years the model has incorporated a math program and a science/social studies program. Some schools adopt only part of the reform, typically the reading and writing curriculum.

In this *Guide* we review four curriculum-based reforms. Success for All prescribes both a comprehensive curriculum and a specific set of teaching methods. America's Choice (8.1) prescribes a comprehensive set of standards in English, language arts, mathematics, science, and applied learning that serves to outline the school's curriculum. In addition the model prescribes a portion of the actual curriculum. However, the America's Choice model does not prescribe the instructional methods; the school determines what practices to use to implement the curriculum.

Different Ways of Knowing (8.2) is distinctive among the curriculum-based models reviewed here. It introduces an approach to curriculum and instruction that is based on an understanding of the ways students learn. However, while teachers using this model must adapt curriculum, it doesn't replace the existing curriculum.

Lightspan Achieve Now (8.3) offers a very different approach to curriculum-based reform. It provides a technology-based reform model that is systematic and assessment-based but that also increases teachers' discretion and flexibility in meeting the learning needs of individual children.

Success for All (8.4) provides both a comprehensive curriculum in reading (and math and science) and a specific set of teaching methods. It is a widely reviewed and researched reform model.

All students in the school are served by these reforms. They are implemented at all grade levels, creating a consistent instructional approach for all students as they progress through the grades in the school.

Curriculum-based reforms target changing classroom instruction for all students. Thus, schools serving a substantial number of students at-risk of academic failure, that are seeking to change the educational program for all students in the school, would be well suited for a curriculum-based reform. Schools that are having success with a great number of students and seek to improve the educational program of only the struggling students at the school would be better suited for a targeted intervention. The curriculum-based reforms often require a significant departure in curricular materials and instructional methods. The school must invest in both materials and extensive professional development. Thus, to be successful, the school should have a high level of understanding of and commitment to the reform.

This chapter reviews four curriculum-based reform models: America's Choice (8.1), Different Ways of Knowing (8.2), Lightspan Achieve Now (8.3), and Success for All (8.4). We conclude with guidance for educators interested in using a curriculum-based model as a strategy for early literacy reform.

8.1. AMERICA'S CHOICE ■

Reviewed by Siri Ann Loescher and Stacy Jacob

The America's Choice reform design is associated with the National Center on the Education and the Economy (NCEE). NCEE founded the New Standards project in 1991 to develop internationally benchmarked content and performance standards. The New Standards' Performance Standards (New Standards) were piloted in schools, as were related performance-based reference exams and professional development. The America's Choice design was developed based on New Standards work in schools and has been associated with the New American Schools Development Corporation since 1992. The model addresses all levels of schools, although the kindergarten–eighth grade-model varies in design from the high school model.

Program Description

The America's Choice reform design focuses on achieving high standards for all students. The model seeks to enable all students to be fluent readers by the end of third grade and competent readers and writers when entering middle school; they should be prepared for algebra by the beginning of eighth grade and ready to complete college-level work by high school graduation. To reach these goals, the model's features are a blend of some prescription and some process. Prescriptive aspects include a set of standards and reference exams that organize and suggest a curriculum. In addition, the model provides sets of core assignments (components of a curriculum) based on the standards. The process aspect of the reform includes the training of teachers to develop *standards-based instruction* for those parts of the curriculum that are not prescribed.

America's Choice was designed to help all students achieve internationally benchmarked standards in English. One of the main tenets of the English program is that by the end of the third grade, all students will be fluent readers. America's Choice is concerned with thwarting student failure through *acceleration* rather than remediation. Early recognition of failing students and intervention (through extra instruction) are important parts of this model. The program features of America's Choice (Figure 8.1) are summarized in the next sections.

School-Wide Processes

The America's Choice model requires a one-year exploration and *buy-in* process prior to implementation. After deciding to adopt the model, the school creates and fills several positions related to the reform that serve as *on-site facilitators* (see Professional Development). This group serves as the *reform team* and plans and facilitates the implementation of the model at the school.

The reform design includes a *taking stock* initiative to establish baseline implementation data. The process involves collecting and analyzing examples of student performance. These data provide *study groups/teacher* with referent points (current student performance) to be compared to the work required by students in order to achieve the New Standards. Throughout implementation of the model, teacher study groups focus on teaching and learning issues related to student progress toward learning standards (see Professional Development and Implemented Theory/ Philosophy). *Formative program evaluation* occurs annually as part of a process to adapt the reform in the coming year.

Two program features are related to the New Standards and how they guide the activities of the reform. First, the standards themselves provide *instructional guidance,* shaping the type of professional development sought by the school and focusing the *reflective practice* of the study groups. Second, the standards organize the curriculum and the instruction at the school, providing *systematic learning* that is articulated throughout the grade levels and across subject areas within the school.

America's Choice reconfigures several structures of the school to foster a learning community within the classroom and the school, where students and teachers work closely together toward achievement of the standards. *Looping* at the elementary level keeps the classroom teacher and class together through two or more grades. This both increases the teacher's knowledge of each student's strengths and needs and builds caring relationships among students and among the teacher and the students. In the middle and high schools, *school-within-a-school* configurations are used. The same students attend classes together and share the same teachers. Each group consists of two to four hundred students. The model recommends that each school have its own separate faculty and head teacher and operate with some independence. The high school

Figure 8.1 America's Choice Reform Features

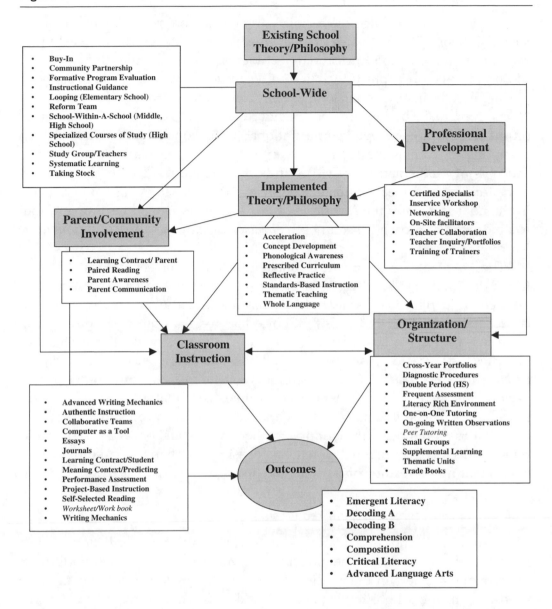

is divided into Upper/Lower Divisions with the lower division focusing on the college preparatory core curriculum, and the upper division broken into various *specialized courses of study* which may include an International Baccalaureate Program, Advanced Placement courses, or an academic Career Academy. America's Choice also provides for a dropout recovery program for students needing educational alternatives.

The community is often involved through *community partnerships* designed to find ways to strengthen the links between success in school and success in the larger community. Examples of such partnerships include business collaborations in the development of career academies and community recognition of the value of diplomas earned, due to the rigorous curriculum, through employment or scholarship opportunities.

Implemented Theory/Philosophy

The America's Choice model places emphasis on two primary areas of learning theory. The first is *acceleration*, which emphasizes enrichment activities rather than remediation to ensure that students gain basic skills and can apply those skills in more sophisticated tasks. *Concept development* is key to this model, placing greater instructional emphasis on conceptual learning with embedded "facts/content." The Performance Standards used by America's Choice build on the standards developed by the national professional organizations in each discipline, including the highly conceptually organized National Council of Teachers of Mathematics (NCTM) standards. The model also emphasizes *thematic teaching* as a means of enhancing relevance and achieving applied learning standards. Finally, the America's Choice early reading and writing program is a balanced approach based in both *phonological awareness* and *whole language* learning theories.

The America's Choice model is rooted in several theories of reform. Primary to the design is *standards-based instruction*—the idea that instruction should be derived from rigorous learning standards. Teachers use a partially *prescribed curriculum* provided by America's Choice and receive training in developing *standards-based instruction* to complete the curriculum. However the model does not prescribe specific instructional methods. Instead it encourages *reflective practice*, in which teachers study the model's standards and curricula, research various instructional methods and determine what methods would be best suited at their school to address the standards, and seek professional development in those methods. Furthermore, teachers work collaboratively to plan and review specific instructional practices, focusing on changes in student outcomes that might result from specific methods.

Professional Development Reform Features

In America's Choice, *certified specialists* work with *on-site facilitators* including a literacy coordinator. The model uses a *training of trainers* method to train the school's teachers in the model. *Inservice workshops* and *networking* are also used to help the school implement the model. The model requires extensive professional development. Throughout the reform the school determines its professional development needs in terms of teaching methods designated by the teachers as appropriate for implementing the *standards-based instruction* (e.g., *project-based instruction* might be well suited for a specific set of standards).

Professional development is also fostered through *reflective practice* and *teacher collaboration*. Opportunities for collaboration are provided through weekly grade-level and subject area meetings where teachers focus on methods, lesson planning and assessment of student work. Teachers share *teacher inquiry/portfolios* of their best lessons.

The facilitators are key during the adaptation and implementation process of the design. Various school-wide work sessions are required by the model, including an annual session based on student performance data; the goal of the session is to help students succeed on the reference exams that are based on the New Standards. Additional support is given to the school through national conferences that provide *networking* opportunities among schools and districts implementing the program.

Parent/Community Involvement Reform Features

Parent involvement is also emphasized in the America's Choice model. Families are kept informed about school progress and the students' success at school through parent conferences and *parent awareness* activities. *Parent communication* is ongoing and is established through a notebook the student carries daily between home and school; in it, both parents and teachers write notes, questions, and observations about the student's progress.

America's Choice requires students to read at least twenty-five books a year as a part of the reading/language arts program. Parents may be involved in this effort in several ways. In the younger grades, *paired reading* may be expected at home. *Learning contracts/parent* may also be expected in the form of a home reading record.

Organizational/Structural Features

The organizational features of the America's Choice model are related to organizing classrooms and school-wide efforts aimed at helping students meet the New Standards as evidenced by their performance on a referent exam. The schools use these exams as *diagnostic procedures* to indicate students who may need additional help; they also give teachers information about the whole class (and school) so that instruction can be adjusted to ensure student success. Additionally, *ongoing written observations, frequent assessments, and cross-year portfolios* are used to monitor student progress.

One of the main goals of America's Choice is to make sure that all children can read fluently by third grade, so the K–3 years are emphasized with a specific literacy program. It emphasizes a *literacy-rich environment* including the use of *trade books* and bridges into other subject areas through *thematic units. Small groups, peer tutoring*, and *one-on-one tutoring* are used to ensure student success. *Supplemental learning* is provided as needed after school, in Saturday school, and in summer school.

Classroom Instructional Features

Assessment is viewed as crucial in achieving successful *standards-based instruction.* Thus, *performance assessments* are used in America's Choice to guide instructional methods. The model emphasizes *authentic instruction* for its students to increase relevance of learning. In addition, *computer as a tool, collaborative teams*, and *project-based instruction* are used to provide concept-rich, interactive instruction.

The America's Choice language arts curriculum emphasizes an approach in which reading and writing are equally important and taught simultaneously. At all levels, meaning acquisition and *critical literacy* are important. For example, *meaning context/predicting* is used as a tool in both reading and writing to deepen students' understanding of language. Sentence comprehension and structures of text are reinforced with *writing mechanics* and *advanced writing mechanics*. Concurrently, classroom reading using *trade books* and *self-selected reading* are supplemented at home with a *learning contracts/student* in which students agree to read twenty-five books during the school year.

America's Choice encourages teachers to build on student interests in its reading and writing methods. Students often choose topics and themes for *essays* and *journals* as well as select the books to be read for the learning contract.

Targeted Literacy Outcomes

The America's Choice reform design is based on internationally bench-marked standards that are very comprehensive in content and skill coverage. However, the instruction can take many forms based on the school in which it is implemented. At the heart of America's Choice is that every child becomes a fluent reader by the third grade. In addition, America's Choice strives to create learners who have both the reading and writing ability to be successful later in their school career—first in a college preparatory curriculum and later in college. This model expects that elementary and middle school programs promote *emergent literacy, decoding A* (context free), *decoding B* (meaning oriented), *comprehension, composition,* and *critical literacy.* The model's use of high-level standards linked with assessment suggests *critical literacy* (reading critically across the curriculum). The high school version of the reform should enhance learning of *advanced language arts.*

REFERENCES AND CONTACTS:
America's Choice

References

Educational Research Service. (1998). *Blueprints for school success: A guide to New American Schools designs.* Arlington, VA: Author.

National Center on Education and the Economy. (1998a). *New Standards performance standards: English language arts, mathematics, science applied learning. Volume 1: Elementary school.* Washington, DC: Author.

National Center on Education and the Economy. (1998b). *New Standards performance standards: English language arts, mathematics, science applied learning. Volume 2: Middle school.* Washington, DC: Author.

National Center on Education and the Economy. (1998c). *New Standards performance standards: English language arts, mathematics, science applied learning. Volume 3: High school.* Washington, DC: Author.

National Center on Education and the Economy. (2000). *America's Choice comprehensive reform designs.* Washington, DC: Author

New American Schools. (1999). *Working toward excellence: Examining the effectiveness of New American school designs.* Alexandria, VA: Author.

Contact Information

National Center on Education and the Economy
700 11th Street, NW, Suite 750
Washington, DC 20005
Phone: (202) 783-3668
Fax: (202) 783-3672
Email: schooldesign@ncee.org
Web Site: www.ncee.org

8.2. DIFFERENT WAYS OF KNOWING ■

Reviewed by Glenda D. Musoba

Different Ways of Knowing (DWoK) was developed at the Galef Institute based on the theories of multiple intelligence proposed by Harvard psychologist Howard Gardner. DWoK attempts to address the educational needs of all students by presenting thematic studies that capitalize on students' natural curiosity and various learning styles. Frequent use of the arts is believed to be critical in helping students make meaning. Based on *constructivist learning* theory, thematic, child-centered learning techniques are used in all areas. Curriculum modules presented to address multiple intelligences integrate multiple subjects and are built around social studies themes. The professional development of teachers and their ongoing growth is a key component of the reform.

DWoK does not include a specific approach or program that targets literacy. Instead it promotes a holistic approach to teaching and learning that is applied to literacy as it is to all teaching areas. DWoK recommends that teachers integrate the various forms of intelligence into their lessons, and this is the reason we classified this model as a curriculum-based reform. While DWoK offers a curriculum component, making it a more prescribed reform, its constructivist principles and teaching strategies that focus on higher order thinking skills are associated with process-oriented reforms.

Program Description

Teachers who want to participate in DWoK are required to attend trainings before they can use the DWoK curriculum modules; however, they are not required to use any of the modules and may adapt the techniques they learn to other materials. DWoK emphasizes an art- and literacy-rich learning environment. DWoK provides multimedia materials and books in addition to the curriculum ideas for using the arts in all subject areas. DWoK modules are built around social studies themes but the teaching strategies can be utilized in any subject area. Schools using DWoK that are specifically interested in increasing students' literacy skills have the flexibility to adapt the modules to incorporate additional material related to specific literacy skills (see Figure 8.2).

Figure 8.2 Different Ways of Knowing: Program Reform Features

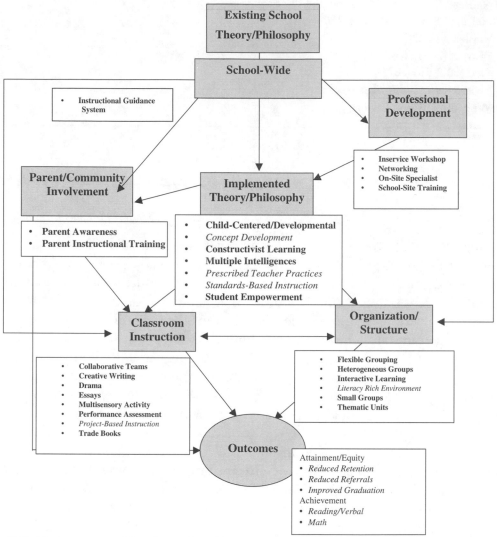

Bolded features are part of the reform; *italicized features* are sometimes adopted by schools implementing the reform.

School-Wide Features

DWoK has a strong emphasis on interdisciplinary, thematic, arts-infused, active learning. This philosophy permeates all activities and rises to the level of an *instructional guidance system* because it directs the professional development, teaching strategies, and curriculum and engenders a common instructional language. In addition, it can influence school organization and staffing decisions.

Implemented Theory/Philosophy

DWoK emphasizes classroom activities in which students play a part in directing their own learning. This *child-centered/developmental* approach begins with what students already know, invites them to ask questions about what else they would like to know, and provides a structure for them to actively engage in research and extended learning. This represents a *constructivist learning theory* whereby knowledge is constructed on the foundation of what one already knows. Lessons are interdisciplinary and thematic with an emphasis on *concept development*; skills are learned in context and there is a focus on higher order thinking skills. DWoK is built around Gardner's theory of multiple intelligences that suggests different children learn in different ways and have strengths in varied forms of intelligence; therefore, effective learning addresses multiple intelligences and allows students to present their knowledge in a variety of formats. DWoK offers a curriculum, but teachers are not required to use it to participate in the program. DWoK *prescribes teacher practices*. For instance, teachers are to incorporate the arts throughout the subject areas; classrooms are interactive and *thematic*. It integrates different ways of learning as well as multiple subject areas under one theme. The curriculum is content rich and *standards based*, but the local school would need to adapt it to local or state educational standards.

Following a theory of *student empowerment*, students have opportunities to do their own research and select some of their readings; they also take some responsibility for self-assessment of their own learning in DWoK. The teacher's role switches from instructor to facilitator.

Professional Development Features

Professional development is an essential aspect of the reform model. The school and DWoK staff commit to three years of professional development support. *Inservice workshops* and *school-site training* in the form of three-day summer orientations, institutes, and leadership training, as well as three or four all-day workshops throughout the year, provide the foundation of training. *On-site specialists* in DWoK teaching strategies and the arts provide *inservices*, visit classrooms, and work with teachers from five times per year to monthly. DWoK advocates believe this training is essential to putting the theory of multiple intelligences into practice. Ultimately the specialist team will train school personnel as coaches to ensure continuation of the practices. In conjunction with the formal training, opportunities for *networking*, either online or in person as teacher support groups, are also key.

Parent Involvement

Parents are informed of the philosophy of DWoK and the changes occurring in the school to heighten *parent awareness* of school reform. While not providing a variety of structures, DWoK emphasizes through the training materials the value of having informed parents who understand the program. *Parent instructional training* is available to parents in the theory and practice of DWoK. Parents are invited to all institutes and *inservices* that the faculty attends to enable them to provide support for their children's education both at home and in the schools.

Organizational/Structural Features

Thematic units form the foundation of DWoK lessons. Units combine social studies, science, math, English, and language arts around one common theme allowing students to see the interconnectedness of knowledge rather than learn discrete skills. DWoK classrooms use *flexible grouping* strategies for students depending on the intent of the lesson or task. *Small groups* are common as well as independent work, groups of mixed ability (*heterogeneous groups*) working together, or whole class activities such as singing. DWoK classrooms are *interactive learning* environments in which teachers guide discussions and students work together conducting research and preparing presentations. Instruction is built around thematic units usually with a social studies theme but integrating multiple subjects. Classrooms are *literacy-rich environments* with materials available through DWoK or other sources; these environments provide students with research resources as well as literature and cultural artifacts related to themes.

Classroom Instructional Features

The most distinctive feature of DWoK classrooms is their *multisensory activities*. Based on the theory of multiple intelligences, students learn through dance, *drama, creative writing*, singing, *essays*, writing dramas or songs, and other activities. The arts are believed to be associated with alternative intelligences and enhanced student outcomes in language arts achievement. *Trade books*, literature, and other multisensory materials enrich the classroom environment and engage students in learning. Each module addresses the multiple ways students learn and provides them with multiple ways to demonstrate their learning. *Performance assessments* can include presentations, readings, dramas, songs, research papers, and projects. Teachers may use small group *project-based instruction* to allow students to research an area of interest more deeply. Students often work in *collaborative teams*. The group process allows students to help one another and lets teachers take a facilitator role as they guide students in their exploration of knowledge.

Targeted Literacy Outcomes

The DWoK approach focuses on multidisciplinary approaches and constructivist and developmental learning. There is an emphasis on deriving meaning from new knowledge by relating it to what the student already knows and presenting it in various ways. The emphasis on thematic lessons would suggest a greater emphasis on *emergent literacy, decoding B, comprehension, composition*, and *critical literacy*.

Research observers noted that teachers using the DWoK model showed an increase in the time they spent on literacy instruction in their classrooms. In addition, opportunities for *creative writing* (including poetry with DWoK's emphasis on the arts), classroom reports and presentations, and research writing are all tasks that have been linked with increases in student's literacy skills. Language arts achievement rose 8 percentage points on a national standardized test in one confirmatory study of DWoK conducted in California (Catterall, 1995). In the same study, scores in reading were not significantly different from those of students at peer schools.

REFERENCES AND CONTACTS:
Different Ways of Knowing

References

Catterall, J. S. (1995). *Different Ways of Knowing 1991–94 National Longitudinal Study Final Report: Program effects on students and teachers.* Los Angeles: UCLA Graduate School of Education and Information Studies.

Petrosko, J. M., Hovda, R., Kyle, D., Wang, C., & Sogin, D. (1997). *Different Ways of Knowing: Effects on elementary teaching and learning in Kentucky.* Washington, DC: Policy Studies Associates.

Contact Information

The Galef Institute
5670 Wilshire Blvd.
20th Floor
Los Angeles, California 90036-5623
Phone: (323) 525-0042
Fax: (323) 525-0408
     (800) 473-8883
Email: DWoKnet@galef.org
Web Site: www.DWoKnet.galef.org

8.3. LIGHTSPAN ACHIEVE NOW ■

Reviewed by Siri Ann Loescher, Osman Cekic, and Stacy Jacob

The Lightspan Achieve Now program is unique among the comprehensive school reforms included in this review in two ways. First, the program is primarily a technology-based content area reform (reading and math). Second, the designers are a for-profit organization. The K–8 program was initially designed as a supplemental program to enhance student learning in reading and math by providing extended time-on-task and by increasing parent involvement in student learning. The extended learning program used various Lightspan computer-based activities that targeted skill acquisition; they could be used either in the classroom or as a stand-alone, supplemental program (e.g., an after-school computer lab). Now the program utilizes computer software, Internet resources, and printed materials. The home involvement program includes training parents, lending hardware (Sony's PlayStation), and sending home Lightspan Adventures (learning games) coordinated with students' schoolwork.

Program Description

With the advent of the Comprehensive School Reform (CSR) movement, the designers developed ways that the Lightspan Achieve Now model could assist schools in their systemic restructuring efforts. The model provides processes for studying student performance in relation to state learning standards in order to develop and implement *standards-based instruction*. In this process, the Lightspan materials become articulated into the schools' reading and math curricula. In addition, the design promotes the use of various professional development, organizational, and instructional features geared toward increasing student achievement. In addition, the designers continue to incorporate various technology- and Internet-based resources to assist schools in using the Lightspan model to meet learning standards. For example, Lightspan's Web site links specific state standards to available materials and ideas such as lesson plans, portfolio and journal ideas, online resources, and Lightspan Adventure games.

It is important to differentiate the use of Lightspan as a supplemental program for improving skills through extended learning time and home involvement from the implementation of Lightspan for comprehensive school reform. As a supplemental program it could be implemented in isolation from the core work of the school and have little impact on the overall school. This review considers only the school-wide implementation of the Lightspan Achieve Now program.

The Lightspan program uses state reading standards to create *standards-based instruction*, incorporating various Lightspan materials and resources, in order to increase students' reading outcomes. The training in developing *standards-based instruction* not only ensures that the school approaches reading instruction with intentionality, but it also encourages teachers to consider incorporating various methods into classroom instruction that will enhance student learning. For example, journaling activities are to increase students' conceptual understanding of both abstract and concrete ideas. While the model encourages the incorporation of various Lightspan materials into the curriculum, the reading program is designed to augment rather than supplant the school's existing literacy/reading program. As a school-wide program, the model retains the emphasis of the original design on extending learning time and parents' involvement. One of Lightspan's main objectives is to encourage interaction among students, parents, and teachers toward a common goal: student achievement. The Lightspan Achieve Now program features are depicted in Figure 8.3.

School-Wide Features

On deciding to adopt the Lightspan Achieve Now program, a school—which to this point has worked with a sales representative—is assigned a Lightspan consultant (a *certified specialist*) who works as a professional development facilitator. Additionally, a *reform team* is created—members of the faculty who work with the consultant to plan the implementation of the Lightspan program. The *reform team* ensures that the process is tailored to the needs of the school and encourages ownership of the project by the school.

The Lightspan design promotes a systematic approach to creating and continually improving *standards-based instruction*. This process involves a recurring

Figure 8.3 Lightspan Achieve Now Program Features

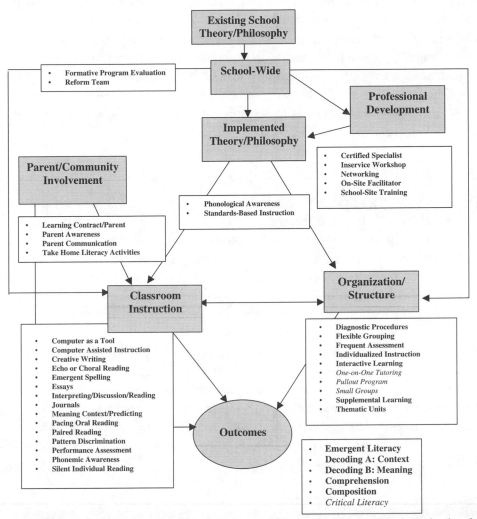

Bolded features are part of the reform; *italicized features* are sometimes adopted by schools implementing the reform.

cycle of research on student outcomes compared to learning standards; planning and implementing instruction based on that research; and assessing student outcomes through more research. To begin this cycle, schools gather baseline data on student outcomes that are used to guide the reform efforts. Each year the school conducts a two-part *formative program evaluation*. The staff conducts a self-implementation survey that provides feedback to the school about the degree of program implementation. Concurrently the Lightspan consultant gathers student outcome data that are reported to the school and to the designers. The results of these evaluations are used by the schools to refine their reform efforts.

Implemented Theories/Philosophies

The Lightspan design's primary theory of learning is *standards-based instruction*. The design emphasizes that all students' learning can be increased through a cycle of standards-based research/planning/implementation and assessment of instruction. The design also advocates using varied instructional methods to encourage student engagement, address individual students' needs, and provide all students with the opportunity to achieve the learning standards.

The Lightspan reading materials at the early grades are based on a *phonological awareness* approach to literacy acquisition. The program reinforces these methods through the parent component in which parents are trained to support students' home use of the Lightspan Adventures. However, because Lightspan tailors its materials and services to schools (and the schools' state standards), the approach to reading and literacy is modified accordingly.

Professional Development Features

The school-wide approach to implementing Lightspan relies on a strong professional development program. Teachers are trained through *school-site training* and additional *inservice workshops* both in developing *standards-based instruction* as a means for school improvement and in using various technological resources as instructional methods. Each school works with a *certified specialist* (a Lightspan consultant) who provides professional development. Schools dedicate a staff person as a part-time *on-site facilitator* to assist the consultant and to provide classroom-level support to the faculty.

Because of its technology base, electronic *networking* is an especially salient feature. Teachers are encouraged to share ideas and lesson plans as well as to participate in online forums geared toward teachers, parents, and students at the Lightspan Internet site. At this Web site are many additional resources to provide teachers with ongoing support for implementing the program. Included are links to topic-oriented Web sites, online learning communities, and other interactive features.

Parent/Community Involvement Features

Because Lightspan was originally developed as a homework replacement program geared toward increasing parent involvement in student learning, parent involvement features play an important, supportive role in the design. Engaging parents is key to the home involvement component. Both *parent awareness* and *parent communication* are used to strengthen home and school connections on which active partnerships are built. When the home involvement materials are coordinated with classroom work, parents become active participants in the effort to improve student outcomes by reinforcing student (classroom) learning. Parents of a Lightspan student will receive *parent instructional training* so they will be able to operate the video games that are provided for home use and be able to participate with their child in the learning activity. Each family in the Lightspan program receives a Sony PlayStation and video games that help children learn at home. There is an implied *learning contracts/parent* requiring parents to make sure that students work with the Lightspan video games for thirty to sixty minutes a day.

The Lightspan design embraces parents as a valuable resource in the schools' efforts to meet high educational standards. In addition to the home involvement program, the Lightspan Achieve Now model provides various resources directly to parents through the Internet, such as learning activities, educational information (e.g., scholarly articles geared toward parents), and discussion forums.

Organizational/Structural Features

Assessment at the individual student level, the classroom level, and the school-wide level are important to the Lightspan design. In the classroom, *diagnostic procedures* are used to assess students' needs, to which instruction is tailored. *Frequent assessments* are used to determine students' progress toward standards, giving information to the teacher when a change of instructional approach is needed.

Lightspan materials/resources may be used to provide whole group instruction and *individualized instruction* (in learning centers within the classroom). The program encourages *flexible grouping* depending on the needs of the students and the particular standards being addressed. Teachers may use *small groups, one-on-one tutoring,* or *individualized instruction.* Lightspan also encourages approaches directed at increasing student engagement, such as *interactive learning* and *thematic units.*

The design encourages giving students extended time-on-task through technology that is personalized to meet individual needs, thus providing *supplemental learning.* This may take place after school or through a *pullout program.*

Classroom Instructional Features

Several instructional features are directly related to the Lightspan reform design. The model, based on interactive technology, incorporates both *computer as a tool* and *computer-assisted instruction* into the reading program. In addition, the design's emphasis on *standards-based instruction* requires the use of *performance assessments* to give feedback—beyond standardized tests—about student learning.

Technology is used to address emergent reading and decoding skills. Both *phonemic awareness* and *pattern discrimination* are recommended by the model.

In addition, the design promotes various nontechnology instructional methods to encourage literacy acquisition. Students are encouraged to build familiarity and ease with reading through *echo or choral reading* and *pacing oral reading. Paired reading* and *silent individual reading* are used to foster student independence in reading. Several features such as *interpreting/discussion/reading* and *meaning context/predicting* are used to increase meaning-oriented reading.

Lightspan's program emphasizes the importance of developing writing skills as part of literacy acquisition. Students use *emergent spelling* to begin to learn the ways in which words become sentences and sentences become pieces of writing. Later students engage in writing activities such as *journal* writing, *essays,* and *creative writing* that strengthen writing skills and foster critical thinking.

Targeted Literacy Outcomes

Lightspan's focus on providing varied learning opportunities for students in the beginning phases of literacy acquisition, including extended learning time through technology and the home involvement program, should be effective in improving student reading outcomes. The incorporation of features consistent with both phonics instruction and meaning-oriented reading suggests that literacy outcomes should include *emergent literacy, decoding A and B*, and *comprehension*. In addition, the design incorporates various writing features that suggest *composition* outcomes. Because fewer features present in the design are associated with *critical literacy*, the degree to which this would be addressed is based on the state standards the school uses in its school improvement process. Indeed, early reports (information on school performance, reported by the company) suggest reading gains for students at schools using Lightspan, although confirmatory research is not yet available.

REFERENCES AND CONTACTS:
Lightspan Achieve Now

References

Din, F., & Caleo, J. (2000). *Playing computer games versus better learning.* Paper presented at the Annual Conference of the Eastern Educational Research Association, Clearwater, FL, February 16–19, 2000.

Lightspan Partnership. (n.d.). *A shared vision: Title 1 & Lightspan Achieve Now* [Brochure]. San Diego, CA: Author.

Lightspan Partnership. (1999a). *Extending learning and family involvement issues.* Proceedings from the Lightspan Achieve Now Education Summit, New Orleans, LA, January 10, 1999.

Lightspan Partnership. (1999b). *Lightspan in action: A skill-and-content comprehensive school reform demonstration model.* Proceedings from a CSRD Invited Symposium for Lightspan Reform Model Users, San Diego, CA, October 21, 1999.

Lightspan Partnership. (2000). *Lightspan Achieve Now: Implementation self-assessment rubric* [Brochure]. School Version. San Diego, CA: Author.

Northwest Regional Educational Laboratory (NWREL). (1988). *Catalog of school reform models: First edition* [On-line]. Available: www.nwrel.org/scpd/natspec/catalog/

Contact Information

The Lightspan Partnership
10140 Campus Point Drive
San Diego, CA 92121-1520
Phone: (888) 824-8000
Fax: (858) 824-8001
Email: ContactUs@lightspan.com
Web site: www.lightspan.com

8.4. SUCCESS FOR ALL ■

Reviewed by Jeffrey S. Bardzell and Siri Ann Loescher

Success for All (SFA) was initially developed as a comprehensive, school-wide reform design focusing on reading, with the goal of all students reading on grade level by the third grade. The program was developed specifically for schools with high concentrations of at-risk youth where reading levels have traditionally lagged and students often fall significantly below grade level on entering middle school. The program has now expanded to include other subject areas such as math (i.e., Math Wings) and social studies and science (i.e., World Lab). A school may implement any of the programs or all three: Success for All (Reading), Math Wings, and/or World Lab. This description focuses on the reading component of Success for All.

Program Description

Success for All is a systematic intervention that includes a tightly structured program designed to provide students with a specific curriculum. It requires that instructional practices be implemented in a uniform manner across the school to give students a consistent and well-articulated approach to learning. The model incorporates a form of *cooperative learning* intended to promote collaboration among students of varied abilities and to encourage more equal outcomes than traditional methods.

The SFA design's skills-oriented reading program includes content, instructional methods, and related structures that are prescribed. While there may be some room in the design for customizing the program to the school, unlike the more process-oriented reform models, Success for All, when implemented, should look very similar in most schools. SFA's program features (Figure 8.4) are described below.

School-Wide Processes

Implementation of Success for All involves several school-wide features. A school must work through an exploration and *buy-in* process to decide whether the program fits with the philosophy of the school and to determine whether the faculty has the level of commitment necessary to implement the program. Prior to implementation the school establishes a *reform team* to work with the Success for All specialist and facilitator to provide the training and implementation of the program to the school.

The instructional materials, methods for student assessment and assignment to groups, and the coordinated teaching methods provide *systematic learning* to the school. This feature ensures that there are instructional links between the learning goals and student outcomes, and that there is uniformity between them. Moreover, the *systematic learning* intends to build a sense of community in the school, with all faculty working as a team in a coordinated effort.

A *parent/community group* is established at the school to attend to the issue of parent and community involvement and to specific student-related issues

Figure 8.4 Success for All Program Features

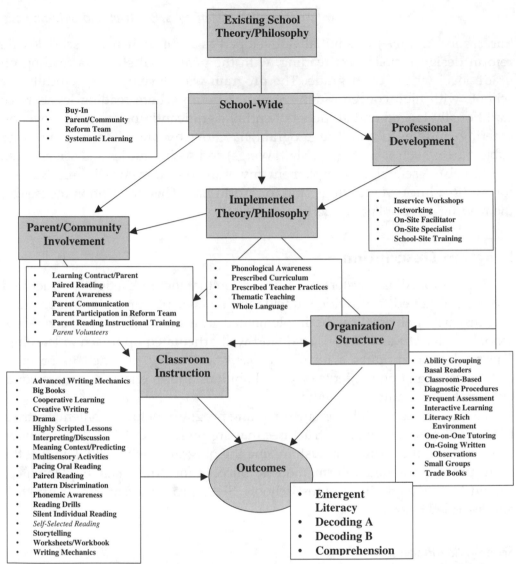

Bolded features are part of the reform; *italicized features* are sometimes adopted by schools implementing the reform.

that are of concern to parents and the community. This group has two functions. First, it ensures that parents and the community are brought into the reform effort, allowing an avenue to raise issues to the school's *reform team*. Second, it provides outreach programs to meet needs identified by the group, such as improving student attendance.

Implemented Theory/Philosophy

The Success for All early reading program intends to build on both *phonological awareness* and *whole language*. The curriculum includes instruction consistent with both approaches to provide a balanced approach to literacy acquisition. To maximize the effectiveness of the instructional program, the SFA model promotes grouping (and frequently regrouping) students based on ability rather than on age or grade. The students are frequently assessed and assigned, or reassigned, to groups according to their ability and are given leveled materials and instruction based on those groupings. SFA uses *thematic teaching* to increase student interest and to connect the reading instruction to other content areas.

Success for All bases its structure of reform on the theory that change in student outcomes will result from changing teachers' practice, and it subscribes to a very specific form of teacher practice. The model design links the *prescribed curriculum* to the *prescribed teacher practices* as a total package to lessen the degree of variation in implementation and to ensure that change in teacher practice will occur. As in any prescribed model, success of the program relies on fidelity of implementation.

Professional Development

Because the SFA reform involves a great number of changes in the classroom, the initial year of implementation requires a large investment in professional development. Before the year starts, a *school-site training* is held to train the school staff in the model. Additional *inservice workshops* are sponsored during the school year to assist teachers with building the capacity to implement Success for All in their classrooms.

Each school has an *on-site specialist* and an *on-site facilitator* who spend time at the school regularly to provide support, conduct classroom observations, and evaluate program implementation. Professional development also includes *networking* opportunities for schools at regional and national conferences.

Parent/Community Involvement

To make sure that parents are involved from the onset, there is *parent participation in the reform team*. To increase parent involvement, Success for All uses *parent awareness* activities to inform parents about the program, instructional methods, and ways they may participate in the school, such as opportunities for *parent volunteers*.

Parents are asked to become direct participants in the reform efforts of the school through several features that require coordinated efforts between the school and the home. Regular direct contact is made through *parent communication* to update parents on students' performance and to let the parents know in advance the work that will be assigned to students. Parents are also given *parent instructional training*, so that time at home doing *paired reading* will model and supplement the classroom instruction.

Organizational/Structural Features

The numerous structural features of Success for All enable the systematic coverage of a broad range of activities. With *ability grouping,* teachers can provide *interactive learning* with some customized instruction without relying too heavily on *one-on-one tutoring*. Students spend time daily reading in *small groups* with reading teachers and tutors. First grade students who are struggling to succeed are given tutoring priority.

The *literacy-rich environment* and *trade books* are included to foster a love of reading in students and to provide a meaning-oriented component that supplements some of the skills-oriented activities often used in connection with *basal readers* for younger children. For older children, *trade books* are used.

Children in the program are carefully monitored with *ongoing written observations*; they are regularly tested using *diagnostic procedures* and *frequent assessment* so students can be regrouped based on their progress and school communities can be informed about the effectiveness of their instructional methods.

Classroom Instruction Features

Success for All uses numerous classroom instructional features that range from *worksheets/workbooks* and *reading drills* to *creative writing* and *drama*. Success for All is designed with the idea that a great variety of activities is needed to ensure near-universal success. Accordingly, meaning-oriented and phonics-oriented instructional features are combined. Thus, features include *phonemic awareness* and *pattern discrimination*, as well as *interpreting/discussion* and *meaning context/predicting*.

As a part of its intent to reach every child, the features also include *multisensory activities* and an emphasis on writing. *Writing mechanics* and *creative writing* are emphasized at all levels. In older grades, *advanced writing mechanics* are used.

The reading instruction is geared to develop independent reading skills. In younger grades, *paired reading* and *pacing oral reading* are used, while in older grades, *silent individual reading* takes precedence in the classroom. The idea is to keep children constantly engaged in literacy activities.

Other classroom features include *storytelling, Big Books*, and *collaborative teams*. The lessons themselves are broken into short segments of five to ten minutes each. Many lessons are *highly scripted lessons. Cooperative learning* strategies are prevalent throughout the activities.

Targeted Literacy Outcomes

Success for All is a school-wide reform model and as such its intended outcomes are diverse and comprehensive. Its stated goal is to ensure that all children succeed the first time. In the same vein, it aims to reduce retention and referrals to special education.

SFA is highly prescribed and has been widely researched. Therefore, specific literacy outcomes are quite apparent. Because it includes kindergarten (in some cases a full-day kindergarten) and provides systematic coverage of a broad range of reading skills in grades, the program is designed to affect *emergent literacy*, both types of decoding (*decoding A and B*), *comprehension*, and *composition*.

The program appears to have little in place to foster *critical literacy*, which is the interaction between *comprehension* of new content and metacognition, or the ability to organize and think about new ideas learned through reading.

REFERENCES AND CONTACTS:
Success for All

References

Dianda, M., & Flaherty, J. (1995). *Promising practices, and program adaptations and successes.* Los Alamitos, CA: Southwest Regional Lab. (ERIC Document Reproduction Service No. ED385793)

Heady, R., & Kilgore, S. B. (1996). The Modern Red Schoolhouse. In S. Stringfield, S. M. Ross, & L. Smith (Eds.), *Bold plans for school restructuring: The New American Schools designs* (pp. 207–231). Hillsdale, NJ: Erlbaum.

Madden, N. A., Slavin, R. E., Karweit, N. L., Dolan, L., & Wasik, B. A. (1991). *Success for All: Multi-year effects of a schoolwide elementary restructuring program.* Rep. No.18. Baltimore, MD: Center for Research on Effective Schooling for Disadvantaged Students, Johns Hopkins University.

Madden, N. A., Slavin, R. E., Karweit, N. L., Livermon, B. J., & Dolan, L. (1989). *Success for All: First-year effects of a comprehensive plan for reforming urban education.* Rep. No. 30. Baltimore, MD: Center for Research on Elementary and Middle Schools, Johns Hopkins University.

Madden, N. A., Slavin, R. E., & Simons, K. (1999). *Math Wings: Effects on student mathematics performance.* Rep. No. 39. Baltimore, MD: Center for Research on the Education of Students Placed at Risk, Johns Hopkins University.

Ross, R. M., & Smith, L. J. (1994). Effects of Success for All model on kindergarten through second-grade reading achievement, teachers' adjustment, and classroom-school climate at an inner city school. *The Elementary School Journal, 95*(2), 121–138.

Slavin, R. E., & Madden, N. A. (1996). *Roots & Wings program design* [On-line]. Available: www.successforall.net/curriculum/rwprogdescr.htm

Slavin, R. E., & Madden, N. A. (1999). *Roots & Wings: Effects of whole-school reform on student achievement.* Rep. No. 36. Baltimore, MD: Center for Research on the Education of Students Placed at Risk, Johns Hopkins University.

Slavin, R. E., Madden, N. A., Karweit, N. L., Donald, L. J., & Wasik, B. A. (1992). *Success for All: A relentless approach to prevention and early intervention in elementary schools.* Arlington, VA: Educational Research Service.

Contact Information

Awareness Department
The Success for All Foundation
200 West Towsontown Boulevard
Baltimore, MD 21204-5200
Phone: (800) 548-4998
Fax: (410) 324-4444
Email: sfa@successforall.net
     Info@successforall.net
Web Site: www.successforall.net

■ GUIDANCE FOR EDUCATORS

A growing number of model providers promote comprehensive reform that focuses on implementing predefined processes, and this is the reason we classify the diverse array of models in one group. We originally classified Lightspan Achieve Now as a process model because it used computers to supplement its curriculum (St. John, Loescher, & Associates, 2002); on subsequent review, however, we reclassified it as a curriculum model because most of the program features emphasized instruction and organization/structure in the classroom (St. John, Musoba, et al., 2002).

When a school selects a curriculum-based model, the planners need to make sure that teachers understand the implications of the choice for their own classrooms. Many process reforms leave room for teachers to adapt their practices, but most of the curriculum-based models dictate the strategy that teachers are to use. If teachers buy in to the model, it has a greater chance of success.

The Research Base

Some curriculum-based reform models have a long history; others are newer and lack a substantial confirmatory research base. The model designs reviewed here are based on research and the model providers often work with researchers to refine their model designs. The reviewed models represent a range of approaches, from structured curricular models (e.g., Success for All) to computer-based models (i.e., Lightspan Achieve Now). We review the status or research on the models reviewed in this section, and then summarize the Policy Center's studies that examined the effects of these models.

Research by Model Providers

The reading component of America's Choice is based on commonly accepted reading standards (National Center on Education and the Economy, 1998). It is a newer model design that has not been fully tested in the field, although it has some anecdotal evidence of success (Slavin & Fashola, 1998). Therefore schools and school districts should examine research on related reforms. It is important that the evidence from the Comprehensive School Reform (CSR) evaluations be released when completed, as a means of facilitating informed choices in schools.

Different Ways of Knowing emphasizes higher order thinking. Its reading program emphasizes *comprehension, composition,* and *critical literacy,* but not *decoding* and *emergent literacy.* The early research indicates positive student outcomes (Catterall, 1995; Petrosko, Hovda, Kyle, Wang, & Sogin, 1997), but more research is needed, especially with respect to early reading outcomes.

Lightspan Achieve Now is a computer-based model that has been adapted to facilitate comprehensive reform (see review), but the research on the model is still limited. Since schools are selecting this method as part of the CSR process, there should be more evidence about the relative effects of this model available in the near future.

Success for All is the most widely evaluated comprehensive reform model. Most of the published studies show improvement in early reading (Slavin & Fashola, 1998; Snow et al., 1998). However, the major part of this research was conducted by Robert Slavin and his colleagues as part of the model development process. Some of the field-based research results have been more mixed. The Policy Center's studies, reviewed below, are illustrative.

The Policy Center's Studies

The Policy Center's studies on reading and literacy reform in Indiana included Success for All in the sample, but not the other models reviewed above. The Michigan CSR studies have examined schools with all the reform models reviewed here, along with other curriculum-based reform models.

The Indiana reading studies had ambiguous findings about Success for All. One study provided effect size analyses in reading, controlling for school characteristics. The effect size analyses examined reading scores three years after the start of the intervention. These analyses provided further evidence that Success for All was associated with higher pass rates on standardized reading tests by third graders in high poverty schools (Manset, St. John, Chung, & Simmons, 2000).

The Indiana reading studies also included a set of regression analyses that controlled for school characteristics and other outcomes. This study considered a larger number of schools, combining three years of data on these schools. These analyses indicated that Success for All was associated with low pass rates on standardized tests but low special education referral rates (St. John, Manset, Chung, & Worthington, 2001). This report speculated that the emphasis on mainstreaming in Success for All could explain both effects. If more special needs students are in the regular classroom (i.e., the special education referrals are low), then more students who have trouble with reading will take standardized tests (and thus will lower the average classroom scores). Another possible explanation is that schools in the study had been in the program for three years.

The Policy Center's study of Michigan's CSR schools included schools using Different Ways of Knowing, Lightspan, and Success for All in curriculum-based models. This study revealed more substantial change in classroom practices in schools that used curriculum models than in schools that used process models, such as Accelerated Schools or Modern Red Schoolhouse (St. John, Musoba, et al., 2002). Using a multinomial logistic regression analysis, the researchers found that the classroom models also had a modestly significant (.1 alpha) association with reductions in retention across grade levels, compared to process models. Thus, the Policy Center's studies add evidence that curriculum models seem to be related to improving achievement in larger percentages of students than is seen with process models. However, still more research is needed on this latest wave of reform and the results need to be more widely disseminated.

Meeting Standards

An advantage of curriculum-based reforms is that they provide schools with curriculum that is aligned with standards. However, these reforms do not always address all the common standards in reading. For example, literary criticism is not emphasized in Success for All, so teachers would need to build this emphasis into the reading program in Grades 4 and 5. In contrast, Different Ways of Knowing may not sufficiently emphasize decoding and phonics. However, if schools supplement the reform model, they can fully address all standards.

Politics of Reform

The classroom-based reforms provide viable options for schools and school districts that seek reading curriculum and instructional methods closely aligned with common reading standards. These models are often preferred over process reforms by district administrators because they are less ambiguous. However, they have political limitations related both to their support by teachers and their capacity to address broader reform issues in schools.

District administrators who have a preference for a curriculum-based model should verify that the teachers understand the model and buy into it. These models can constrain teachers by requiring them to adopt particular practices and demanding that they learn new methods. If teachers do not support the new model enthusiastically, they will experience the imposition of its methods as oppressive. If teachers can visit schools that are using the model before the decision is made to adopt the model at their school—and if they are allowed to move to another school if they find they cannot work with the model—the chances for a successful implementation will be greatly improved. In our site visits to schools with comprehensive models, we have often found enthusiastic teachers, but this is not always the case. Therefore it is crucial that teacher professionalism be valued as part of the transition process when these models are adopted.

Because these models emphasize classroom activities, they do not always include the process features that enable schools to deal with community issues. Success for All does include a community focus, but most of the other models do not. Thus, schools choosing curriculum-based models may want to address a wider range of issues than are routinely included in such models.

Integrating Inquiry

Placing an emphasis on teacher inquiry can enhance the reform process, especially as it relates to addressing the community issues facing schools. In a sense, Success for All encourages inquiry through parent and community groups. However, inquiry is not heavily emphasized in the curriculum models and teachers should be aware of this limitation.

Perhaps the greatest challenge for schools choosing curriculum-based reform models is to address the reform issues that are not included in the model. For example, some of the components required for federal CSR funding are overlooked in the curriculum-based models (St. John, Musoba, et al., 2002). Therefore, we recommend that teachers in schools adopting curriculum-based reform models use inquiry to address challenges outside their reform models.

Building Community

The curriculum-based reforms provide schools with an opportunity to build community through collective action on a common educational approach. Most of the models include reading and language arts programs that address most of the common standards for reading. It is crucial that teachers buy into the methods. However, these reforms have a growing record of success in improving early reading instruction.

9

Research-Based Reform

A confluence of forces now supports systematic efforts to reform reading in elementary schools. There are numbers of proven reform models available as well as many opportunities for schools to receive government funding to implement one of these reforms or to develop a reform locally. The reform strategies range from targeted interventions for children who are having trouble learning to read in the regular classroom to comprehensive reforms that bring structured curriculum into the school. Soon after teachers begin studying the possible options, however, they discover that there are conflicting opinions about the efficacy of different approaches to reading reform, differences that could undermine their efforts to select and implement an effective reading reform strategy. Each reform approach has strengths and limitations, so it is crucial that educators choose strategies that help them address the specific challenges they face in their schools.

This book has introduced a framework and language for deconstructing and comparing reading reform models. Most reform models have a core theory or philosophy around which the model is organized. Many have a professional development component that provides opportunities for teachers to learn about the method. Some have methods of involving parents in their child's learning process. All the models, however, include instructional and structural/organizational features that involve teachers in new approaches to reading instruction. The specific program features in each of these areas vary across models. This volume has defined the features common to many of the better known reading reform models as a way to inform educators, thus allowing them to choose reform strategies that complement and enhance their schools' approaches to reading instruction.

This concluding chapter pulls together key understandings, summarizing the critical ones that can help guide educators engaged in reading reform. First, we revisit the research base, focusing on the dynamic nature of research, policy, and practice. Then we consider the politics of reform, focusing on practical issues facing teachers as they adjust to changes in the reading programs in their elementary schools. Finally, we conclude by briefly discussing ways the reading reform process can become a learning process for the entire school community.

LEARNING FROM RESEARCH ■

The research literature on reading is not monolithic. There is no single approach to reading, nor is there a single approach to research. Most researchers use research methods designed to confirm their own hypotheses rather than to objectively examine competing hypotheses about reading reform. In the Policy Center's studies on reading interventions and comprehensive reforms, we developed a framework that allowed us to simultaneously examine multiple hypotheses about reading reform. Previous chapters have summarized findings from our research that pertain to different reform strategies as well as to specific reform models. There are, however, a few major claims about reading improvement that are frequently used to build political rationales for reading reform:

- The direct instruction hypothesis argues that direct instruction in letter/sound relationships (i.e., direct phonic instruction) can improve early reading.
- The comprehensive reform hypothesis argues that comprehensive and cohesive approaches are essential to improving reading outcomes.
- The professional development hypothesis argues that providing teachers the opportunity to collaborate on classroom strategies is essential for improving educational outcomes.

Not only does each of these hypotheses have a substantial research base, but each also captures an aspect of the problem facing school-based efforts to reform reading. Most of the reform models reviewed in this volume include a form of direct instruction (i.e., explicit instruction in either *decoding A* or *decoding B*), take a reasonably comprehensive approach, and can be implemented in a way that encourages collaborative professional development. The Policy Center's research also provides further insight into each of these hypotheses, as it cross-cuts claims about reading reform. We review each hypothesis and the related Policy Center research below, as well as consider the implications for school-based reform efforts.

Direct Instruction

The proponents of direct instruction argue that teachers should demonstrate effective use of direct instruction "before investing in more complex solutions" (Foorman, Francis, Fletcher, Schatschneider, & Mehta, 1998, p. 27). Experimental research compares reading instruction with phonics to similar instructional methods that exclude phonics (Foorman, Fletcher, Francis, & Schatschneider, 2000; Snow, Burns, & Griffin, 1998). Based on this type of research, several states have required elementary teachers to emphasize direct instruction in phonics (Allington & Woodside-Jiron, 1999). For many schools the major debate about phonics instruction is not whether there is a need for direct instruction in letter-sound relationships but rather how this form of instruction should be integrated into a comprehensive and cohesive reading program in Grades 1–5.

The Policy Center's studies indicate a complex relationship between direct/explicit approaches[1] and other factors that had a direct relationship with literacy-related outcomes. In two studies using a single year of survey results, we found that direct/explicit approaches were associated with higher retention rates and with higher pass rates on reading tests in Grade 3 (Manset-Williamson, St. John, Hu, & Gordon, 2002; St. John, Manset-Williamson, et al., in press). These studies indicated a trade-off between high pass rates and student failure. Placing too much emphasis on direct approaches without integrating an emphasis on text-connected approaches[2] that engage learners increased the failure rate in early elementary grades.

In a follow-up study we used three years of survey data to examine the effects of government funding, the type of reform model, and instructional practices. We found that direct/explicit approaches were not significantly associated with either outcome when multiple years of funding and the types of reading programs were controlled for (St. John, Manset, Chung, & Worthington, 2001). This finding suggests that sustained efforts to implement comprehensive reforms could overcome this key limitation of using direct/explicit approaches.

Direct instruction in letter-sound relationships and related methods is associated with high pass rates on standardized reading tests in early elementary grades, but a balanced approach to early reading instruction is needed to engage all children in learning to read. Consistent with the plethora of prior studies that focus on direct instruction, the Policy Center's research provides modest support for arguments that direct instruction in phonics improves student achievement on standardized tests. However, the Policy Center's studies also reveal a limitation of overemphasis on direct methods without engaging all children in the learning process.

Comprehensive Reform

The comprehensive reform hypothesis holds that comprehensive, cohesive approaches to reading instruction are needed to engage all children and to improve educational outcomes (Clay, 1993; Taylor, Anderson, Au, & Raphael, 2000). This argument is also represented in Comprehensive School Reform (CSR), a federal strategy for total school reform that is promoted by the federal government through Title I (Wong, in press). The National Research Council's review (Snow et al., 1998) gave better reviews to some types of comprehensive models (e.g., Success for All) than others (e.g., Reading Recovery). Thus, while a diverse array of reformers have argued in support of the comprehensive approach, not all comprehensive report models are the same. Therefore educators should carefully study optional strategies to identify approaches that are likely to work in their school.

The Policy Center's studies have examined the effects of different types of reading interventions and comprehensive reform models, controlling for patterns of teaching practice and external funding (St. John et al., 2001). The results of these studies indicate that different reform models have different effects at different points in time. Some reforms, like Literacy Collaborative, were associated with higher reading achievement and equity outcomes (i.e., lower retention and referral). Other reforms had mixed effects. For example, Success for All was associated with greater equity in learning (i.e., lower special education referrals) and with lower pass rates on reading achievement tests. Thus our studies, like the other reviews (Slavin & Fashola, 1998; Snow et al., 1998), indicate that there are differences across reform models. However, rather than claiming any one reform approach is superior, we attempted to illuminate strengths and weaknesses of different approaches. There is growing evidence that no single reform approach works well in every setting. Teachers need to be engaged in and supportive of the school's reading strategy—and the strategy needs to address real challenges in the school.

Our conclusion from the review of this and other research has been that schools should be careful to select a reform model that complements and enhances the reading programs that already exist in their schools. If a school adopts an entirely new reading program, then all of the teachers need to be trained in the new approach. This volume was designed to enable schools to make informed choices about reading interventions.

Professional Development

The role of professional development for teachers should not be overlooked in efforts to choose a comprehensive reform model. Advocates of professional development argue that teachers should have time to collaborate on developing new strategies that can improve educational outcomes (e.g., Bull & Buechler, 1996; Guskey & Sparks, 1997). However, most prior research on reading has not explicitly considered the role of teacher collaboration and other forms of professional development.

Two of the Policy Center's studies support the notion that professional development plays an integral role in the school improvement process. First, the Indiana reading studies found that when teachers have time to collaborate, their schools have an increased capacity to keep children learning on grade level (i.e., both lower retention and low referral rates) (St. John et al., 2001). We also found that multiple years of funding for reading interventions was associated with improved outcomes, enabling schools to overcome the trade-off between test scores and pass rates. Second, the Michigan CSR research indicated that teacher collaboration on classroom practices was associated with improved educational outcomes (St. John et al., 2002). Not only does this finding confirm some of the earlier arguments about professional development, but it suggests that teacher collaboration could explain some the positive effects of comprehensive report models observed in earlier studies. Thus, there is growing and compelling evidence that comprehensive reform of reading programs can be a success, especially if these reforms engage teachers in collaboration that focuses on student learning

A Complex Process

This review of the three major reform claims and related research allows us to look across them. When we do so, it is apparent that reading reform is a complex process. While there is substantial evidence to support the argument that direct instruction is essential to reading reform, direct instruction is only part of the solution for schools with children who are struggling with learning to read. Direct methods may promote higher pass rates on standardized tests, although this is hardly a "success" if more children are failing to stay on grade level. Using a more comprehensive and cohesive approach that emphasizes engaging all children in learning to read can help schools overcome this shortcoming. Comprehensive approaches seem to work best when teachers are engaged through collaboration on instructional improvement processes that focus on learning outcomes. This not only means there is some research to support all three cross-cutting claims about reading reform, but the evidence suggests that all three claims are intertwined.

■ THE POLITICS OF REFORM

This *Guide* was written to enable teams of educators from schools and school districts to make informed choices about strategies for improving their early reading programs. However, when schools involve teachers in selecting a reform model, these choices should not be made in a vacuum. Many private firms are involved in marketing reform models to schools and school districts. These marketing efforts can also have an influence on state legislatures and state education officials. In this context the process of choosing a reform can seem political, even when school districts involve teachers in the selection of the reading reform models they will use. However, involving teachers in the process of selecting a reform model can increase *buy-in* to the reform process, which reduces resistance and increases the chances that the reform will be fully implemented.

Choosing a Reform Model

This *Guide* provides a resource for teams of educators who are actively engaged in planning for reading reform. It can be used to inform the choice of a reading reform model, but it is not intended as a catalogue. Rather, it was structured to facilitate a research-based planning process.

Once a study team is formed in a school or school district, they can use this *Guide* to organize a process for selecting a reform model. Chapter 2 provides a step-by-step process the study team can use to study their own school, review options, and develop a new strategy. The three phases are as follows:

- Assess reading-related outcomes to determine the extent to which reading achievement (i.e., pass rates on standardized tests) and equity outcomes (i.e., the percentage of students learning on grade level) are challenges in the district.
- Set a new direction establishing a vision for school reform.
- Design (or select) an intervention, building consensus around the reform strategy.

With this type of research base, it is possible for teachers and site administrators to make informed choices about the types of reading reform strategies that would make the most sense for their schools. When school districts attempt to establish a reform framework, they should leave some discretion to schools. It is important to recognize these points:

- Targeted reading interventions that pull students out of the classroom work best in schools that are successful in teaching most children to read. It is crucial in these schools that the intervention process provided by the targeted reading intervention be integrated with the regular classroom reading program. Students who are pulled out of the classroom should encounter complementary methods of instruction when they return to the regular classroom.
- Classroom-wide reading interventions are appropriate in schools where there are incongruities in the reading programs. For example, if students are learning to decode but are not learning to comprehend, it may be important to adopt a reading program that integrates reading instruction across grade levels.
- Inquiry-based reading reforms work well in schools where there is a high level of collaboration among teachers. In fact, many of the reform models reviewed in this volume include a focus on teacher collaboration and inquiry.
- Process-oriented comprehensive reforms provide opportunities for schools to engage in a school-wide restructuring process that includes reading as well as other types of curriculum reform. When schools undergo process-oriented reforms it is crucial that most or all teachers be engaged in the process of reviewing and selecting reform models.
- Curriculum-based comprehensive reforms enable teachers to change a school's curriculum using a defined set of methodologies. If there is sufficient need and *buy-in*, these reforms can lead to substantial change.

Thus, there is no one reform solution that fits all schools. District administrators must understand that different types of reading solutions will be needed in different schools. Taking a facilitative approach in the district office, an approach that involves coaching and mentoring rather than control and direction, may also be required, especially given the central role of teacher collaboration.

It is desirable that teachers be engaged in selecting reform models, but this does not always happen. Even when teachers are involved in these processes, they can be politically influenced. For example, in Indiana the Reading Recovery program and Waterford have favored positions in the state funding process. Faculty in the Reading Recovery program at Purdue University lobbied the legislature for special funding for Reading Recovery, while the Waterford program successfully lobbied the legislature for explicit recognition in the legislation enabling program funding. Further, the Indiana Department of Education has actively promoted Four Blocks as a preferred approach for the past five years. All these forces have an influence on the choices teachers make about reforms and school administrators make about reform models. Politics are part of the process of reform. It is nearly impossible to avoid political forces when developing reform strategies in schools and school districts—and some of these political forces are enabling for teachers—but it is still important to involve teachers in making choices about reading reform models because they are responsible for reading instruction.

Implementing a Reform Model

Any single reform model or set of approaches a school selects will be part of the solution, but schools will inevitably face challenges that are well beyond the parameters of the chosen approach. Whether or not a team of teachers has been involved in choosing or developing the school's reading program, the reform probably will not address all components of the comprehensive reading program the school needs. Therefore, we recommend that teachers and administrators focus on the following criteria (restated from Chapter 1) as they implement reading reforms:

- *Recognize the complexity of reading*: Reading demands a remarkably complex set of skills. It is not easy for all students to master all those skills. Placing too much emphasis on one type of skill, such as decoding, can undermine development of comprehensive reading skills.
- *Use a comprehensive, balanced approach*: Because of the variations in experiences of school children, different types of reading material and reading methods are needed by different children. The focus on decoding (i.e., phonics and phonemic awareness) must be balanced with strategies for engaging and interesting children. Selecting literature that is meaningful to students helps engage children in the process of learning to decode.
- *Focus on the underlying development of children*: Reading skills are acquired as part of a developmental process. Interest in stories—oral and written—creates interest in letters and sounds. Predicting how a story will unfold motivates children to read for comprehension. Paying attention to the ways children learn the basic skills of reading enables teachers to engage more children in learning to read.
- *Use a coherent intervention strategy in the classroom and the school*: A school's intervention in reading should add coherence to the ways reading is taught across grade levels. Children need multiple pathways through literacy acquisition: not all children learn to decode, comprehend, and like reading in the same ways, but all children need to acquire these skills. Providing reading instruction that interests all children and enables them to learn to recognize letters and words requires a coherent approach that integrates targeted interventions with regular classroom reading instruction.
- *Integrate inquiry into the intervention*: When teachers routinely assess learning in their classrooms, they are better able to adapt their teaching strategies to engage all children. When reading specialists and regular classroom teachers communicate about the patterns they observe, they are better able to create pathways for children through the skill-building process of literacy acquisition.

If teachers keep these basic criteria in mind as they implement a reading program, they can figure out how to adapt the model they have chosen—or that was chosen for them, possibly by peers—to meet the learning needs of children in their classrooms and in their schools. Ideally teachers should view their early reading programs as a learning process, for children, their families, and themselves.

Reform as a Learning Process

Too frequently reading reform is viewed as a mechanistic process. To claim that teaching is as simple as teaching the alphabetic principle, as an example, oversimplifies a complex learning process for children. Similarly the notion that a single reform model or reading program will meet the needs of all children and all schools in a district oversimplifies the complex ways teachers and parents can collaborate in teaching children to read. As a conclusion, we focus on the ways of enabling teachers to learn about reading reform.

INTEGRATING INQUIRY INTO REFORM   ■

An inquiry orientation can help a school evolve and adapt early reading programs in ways that support the learning needs of all the children in an early elementary classroom. The inquiry process can be integrated into the ongoing process of reading reform in at least three ways.

First, classroom inquiry is essential to early reading reform. A culture of learning involves teachers in developing a vision of the reading program, ideally a vision that is shared among teachers in the school. The vision should include a balance between decoding (i.e., phonemic awareness and phonics instruction) and approaches that engage children with literature, from storytelling in kindergarten through literature programs that give children freedom to follow their own reading interests in upper elementary programs. Within the context of a balanced engaging reading program, teachers should integrate classroom assessment (Shepard, 2000). The Policy Center's research on comprehensive school reform in Michigan confirms that frequent use of classroom assessment increases the probability that teachers will enable more children to learn at or above grade level (St. John, Musoba, et al., 2002). Many of the reading reform models reviewed in this book include an explicit emphasis on classroom assessment.

Second, we strongly recommend that teachers in elementary schools organize themselves to engage in an inquiry-based approach to school reform. This volume was constructed to facilitate this type of school-based inquiry process. Chapter 2 outlined the process and provided a survey instrument that can be used to inform assessment and planning. Chapter 3 provided a generic framework and common language about reading that teachers can use when assessing their current practices and envisioning new possibilities. Most of the other chapters reviewed reform models and provided guidance to teams of teachers.

Finally, with this type of inquiry base, schools can use the results of standardized tests and other school indicators to diagnose and define the challenges they face and to adapt and refine their reading programs. Reforming reading is not simply choosing a reading package or reform model. Rather, it is an ongoing process of making informed choices about teaching methods and reform models based on understandings that emerge from classroom assessment and school-wide outcomes.

■ LEARNING WITH CHILDREN

Reading instruction involves both engaging children in reading and helping them to learn the skills that enable them to decode words and recognize their meaning. Teaching children to read engages teachers and parents in learning processes with children. Creating a climate in schools that enables teachers and parents to learn about reading with their children may be difficult, but it is necessary and possible. With the growing research base and the increasing opportunities for public support, elementary school teachers now have more tools than ever before to help children. Our advice for teachers is to seize this opportunity and create learning processes in the classroom and school that provide optimal support for children as they learn how to read.

NOTES

1. Direct/explicit approaches include basal readings, phonics instruction, reading drills and worksheets/workbooks—a pattern of practice in many schools (Manset, St. John, Hu, & Gordon, 2001; St. John, Manset, Chung, Simmons, & Musoba, 2000)

2. Text-connected approaches include independent reading, cooperative learning, creative writing, emergent spelling, paired reading (student-to-student), and reading aloud.

References

Allington, R. L., & Woodside-Jiron, H. (1999). The politics of literacy teaching: How "research" shaped educational policy. *Educational Researcher, 28*(8), 4–12.

Askew, B. J., & Frazier, D. F. (1994). Substantial effects of Reading Recovery interventions on the cognitive behaviors of second grade children and the perceptions of their teachers. *Literacy, Teaching, and Learning, 1*(1), 240–263.

Au, K. H. (1994a). *Oral language developmental continuum.* Portsmouth, NH: Heinemann.

Au, K. H. (1994b). *Reading resource book.* Portsmouth, NH: Heinemann.

Australian Council for Educational Research. (1993a). *The impact of First Steps on the reading and writing ability of year 5 school students.* An interim report to the Curriculum Development Branch Western Australian Ministry of Education.

Australian Council for Educational Research. (1993b). *The impact of First Steps on schools and teachers.* An interim report to the Curriculum Development Branch Western Australian Ministry of Education.

Bull, B., & Buechler, M. (1996). *Learning together: Professional development for better schools.* Bloomington: Indiana Education Policy Center.

Burrup, P. E., Brimley, V., & Garfield, R. R. (1988). *Financing education in a climate of change.* Boston: Allyn & Bacon.

Catterall, J. S. (1995). *Different ways of knowing 1991–94 National longitudinal study.* Los Angeles: University of California, Los Angeles, School of Education and Information Sciences.

Chall, J. S. (1967). *Learning to read: The great debate.* New York: McGraw-Hill.

Clay, M. M. (1991). *Becoming literate: The construction of inner control.* Portsmouth, NH: Heinemann.

Clay, M. M. (1993). *Reading Recovery: A guidebook for teachers in training.* Portsmouth, NH: Heinemann.

Comer, J. P. (Ed.). (1996). *Rallying the whole village: The Comer process for reforming education.* New York: Teachers College Press.

Comer, J. P., Ben-Avie, M. Haynes, & Joyner, E. T. (Eds.). (1999). *Child by child: The Comer process for change in education.* New York: Teachers College Press.

Connors-Tadros, L. (1996). *Effects of Even Start on family literacy: Local and national comparisons.* Baltimore, MD: Johns Hopkins University, Center on Families, Communities, Schools and Children's Learning. (ERIC Document Reproduction Service No. ED396236)

Cunningham, P. M. (1991). Research directions: Multi-method, multilevel, literacy instruction in first grade. *Language Arts, 68,* 578–584.

Cunningham, P. M., Hall, D. P., & Defee, M. (1991). Non-ability-grouped, multilevel instruction: A year in a first-grade classroom. *The Reading Teacher, 44,* 566–571.

Dechamp, P. (1995). *Case studies of the implementation of the First Steps Project in twelve schools.* Western Australia Education Department, Perth. (ERIC Document No. ED419425)

Ellson, D. G., Barber, L., Engle, T. L., & Kampwerth, L. (1965). Programmed tutoring: A teaching aid and a research tool. *Reading Research Quarterly, 1,* 77–127.

Ellson, D. G., Harris, P., & Barber, L. (1968). A field test of programmed and directed tutoring. *Reading Research Quarterly, 3,* 307–367.

Finnan, C., St. John, E. P., Slovacek, S. P., & McCarthy, J. (Eds.). (1996). *Accelerated Schools in action: Lessons from the field.* Thousand Oaks, CA: Corwin.

Foorman, B. R., Fletcher, J. M., Francis, D. J., & Schatschneider, C. (2000). Response: Misrepresentation of research by other researchers. *Educational Researchers, 29*(6), 27–37.

Foorman, B. R., Francis, D. J., Fletcher, J. M., Schatschneider, C., & Mehta, P. (1998). The role of instruction in learning to read: Preventing reading failure in at-risk children. *Journal of Educational Psychology, 90,* 37–55.

Gardner, H. (1999). A disciplined approach to school reform. *Peabody Journal of Education, 74,* 166–173.

Guskey, T. R., & Sparks, D. (1997). Exploring the relationship between professional development and improvement in learning. *Journal for Staff Development, 17*(4), 4–38.

Hiebert, E. (1994). Reading Recovery in the United States: What difference does it make to an age cohort? *Educational Researchers, 23*(9), 15–25.

Honig, B. (2001). *The components of an effective, comprehensive reading program.* Thousand Oaks, CA: Corwin.

Hopfenberg, W. W., Levin, H. M., & Associates. (1993). *Accelerated Schools resource guide.* San Francisco: Jossey-Bass.

Iverson, S., & Tunmer, W. E. (1993). Phonological processing skills and the Reading Recovery program. *Journal of Educational Psychology, 85,* 112–126.

Jacob, B. S. (2001). Getting tough: The impact of high school graduation exams. *Educational Evaluation and Policy Studies, 23,* 99–122.

Janet, W. (1999). Curriculum in ATLAS. *Peabody Journal of Education, 74,* 174–182.

Knight, K., & Stallings, J. A. (1995). The implementation of the Accelerated School model in an urban elementary school. In R. L. Allington & S. A. Walmsley (Eds.), *No quick fix: Rethinking literacy programs in America's elementary schools* (pp. 236–251). New York: Teachers College Press.

Levenstein, P., Levenstein, S., Shiminski, J. A., & Stolzberg, J. E. (1998). Long-term impact of a verbal interaction program for at-risk toddlers: An exploratory study of high school outcomes in the replication of the Mother-Child Home Program. *Journal of Applied Developmental Psychology, 19,* 267–285.

Manset, G., St. John, E., Chung, C. G., & Simmons, A. (2000). *An evaluation of trends in ISTEP+ reading and language arts scores for Indiana's Early Literacy Intervention Grant Program* (Schools Funded 1997–98). Policy Research Report #00-06. Bloomington: Indiana Education Policy Center.

Manset-Williamson, G., St. John, E. P., Hu, S., & Gordon, D. (2002). Early literacy practices as predictors of reading related outcomes: Test scores, test passing rates, retention, and special education referral. *Exceptionality, 10,* 11–128.

Manset-Williamson, G., St. John, E. P., Musoba, G., Gordon, D., Klingerman, K., & Simmons, A. (2001). *Comprehensive school reform: Promising practices and concerns for the inclusion of students with high-incidence disabilities.* Policy Research Report #01-04. Bloomington: Indiana Education Policy Center.

Manset-Williamson, G., & Washburn, S. (In press). Inclusive education in high stakes, high poverty environments: The care of students with learning disabilities in Indiana's urban high schools and the graduation qualifying examination. In L. F. Miron & E. P. St. John (Eds.), *Reinterpreting urban school reform: A critical-empirical review.* Albany: State University of New York Press.

McCarthy, J., & Still, S. (1993). Hillibrook Accelerated Elementary School. In J. Murphy & P. Hallinger (Eds.), *Restructuring schooling: Learning from on-going efforts* (pp. 63–83). Newbury Park, CA: Corwin.

Miron, L. F., & St. John, E. P. (Eds.). (In press). *Reinterpreting urban school reform: A critical-empirical review.* Albany: State University of New York Press.

Miron, L. F., St. John, E. P., & Davidson, B. M. (1998). Implementing school restructuring in the inner city. *Urban Review, 30*(2), 137–166.

Morris, D., Shaw, B., & Perney, J. (1990). Helping low readers in grades 2 and 3: An after-school volunteer tutoring program. *Elementary School Journal, 91,* 133–150.

Muncey, D. E., Payne, J., & White, N. S. (1999). Making curriculum and instruction reform happen: A case study. *Peabody Journal of Education, 74,* 68–110.

National Center for Education Statistics. (2000). *Digest of education statistics.* NCES 2001-0034. Washington, DC: NCES.

National Center on Education and the Economy. (1998a). *New Standards performance standards: English language arts, mathematics, science applied learning. Volume 1: Elementary school.* Washington, DC: Author.

National Center on Education and the Economy. (1998b). *New Standards performance standards: English language arts, mathematics, science applied learning. Volume 2: Middle school.* Washington, DC: Author.

National Center on Education and the Economy. (1998c). *New Standards performance standards: English language arts, mathematics, science applied learning. Volume 3: High school.* Washington, DC: Author.

New American Schools. (1999). *Working toward excellence: Examining the effectiveness of New American Schools designs.* Alexandria, VA: Authors.

Petrosko, J. M., Hovda, R., Kyle, D., Wang, C., & Sogin, D. (1997). *Different ways of knowing: Effects on elementary teaching and learning in Kentucky.* Washington, DC: Policy Studies Associates.

Pinnell, G. S., DeFord, D. E., & Lyons, C.A. (1998). *Reading Recovery: Early intervention for at-risk first graders.* Arlington, PA: Educators Research Service.

Rogers, B. (1999). Conflicting approaches to curriculum: Recognizing how fundamental beliefs can sustain or sabotage school reform. *Peabody Journal of Education, 74,* 29–67.

Rowe, K. J. (1997). Factors affecting students' progress in reading: Key findings from a longitudinal study. In S. Swartz & A. Klein (Eds.), *Research in Reading Recovery* (pp. 53–101). Portsmouth, NH: Heinemann.

Santa, C. (1999). *Early Steps: Learning from a reader.* Kalispell, MT: Scott Publishing.

School Development Program. (1999a). *Applying the principles of child and adolescent development.* New Haven, CT: School Development Program at the Yale Child Study Center.

School Development Program. (1999b). *The SDP essentials of literacy process.* New Haven, CT: School Development Program at the Yale Child Study Center.

Shepard, L. A. (2000). The role of assessment in a learning culture. *Educational Researchers, 29*(7), 4–14.

Slavin, R., Madden, N., Karweit, N., Dolan, L., & Wasik, B. (1990*). Success for All: Effects of variations in duration and resources of a school-wide elementary restructuring program* (Report No. 2). Baltimore, MD: Johns Hopkins University, Center for Research on Effective Schooling for Disadvantaged Students.

Slavin, R. E., & Fashola, O. S. (1998). *Show me the evidence! Proven and promising programs for America's schools.* Thousand Oaks, CA: Corwin Press.

Snow, C., Burns, M., & Griffin, P. (1998). *Preventing reading difficulties in young children.* Washington, DC: National Academy Press.

Squires, D. A. (1999). Changing curriculum and school's structure: Commentary on ATLAS. *Peabody Journal of Education, 74,* 154–160.

St. John, E. P. (In press). *Refinancing the college dream: Access, equity, and justice for taxpayers.* Baltimore, MD: Johns Hopkins University Press.

St. John, E. P., Bardzell, J. S., & Associates. (1999). *Improving early reading and literacy: A guide for developing research-based programs.* Bloomington: Indiana Education Policy Center.

St. John, E. P., Bardzell, J. S., Michael, R., Hall, G., Manoil, K., Asker, E., & Clements, M. (1998) *Indiana's Early Literacy Intervention Grant Program and Implementation Study.* Bloomington: Indiana Education Policy Center.

St. John, E. P., Griffith, A. I., & Allen-Haynes, L. (1997). *Families in schools: A chorus of voices in restructuring.* Portsmouth, NH: Heinemann.

St. John, E. P., Loescher, S. A., & Associates. (2002). *Improving early reading: A resource guide for elementary schools.* Bloomington: Indiana Education Policy Center.

St. John, E. P., Manset, G., Chung, C. G., Simmons, A. B., & Musoba, G. D. (2000). *Research-based reading interventions: The impact of Indiana's Early Literacy Intervention Grant Program.* Policy Research Report #00-07. Bloomington: Indiana Education Policy Center.

St. John, E. P., Manset, G., Chung. C. G., & Worthington, K. (2001). *Assessing rationales for education reforms: A test of the professional development, comprehensive reform, and direct instruction hypotheses.* Policy Research Report #01-03. Bloomington: Indiana Education Policy Center.

St. John, E. P., Manset-Williamson, G., Chung, C. G., Simmons, A. B., Musoba, G. D., Manoil, K., & Worthington, K. (In press). Research-based reading reform: The impact of state-funded intervention on educational outcome in urban elementary schools. In L. F. Miron & E. P. St. John (Eds.) *Reinterpreting urban school reform: A critical-empirical review.* Albany: State University of New York Press.

St. John, E. P., Meza, J., Allen-Haynes, L., & Davidson, B. M. (1996). Building communities of inquiry: Linking teacher research and school restructuring. In C. Finnan et al. (Eds.), *Accelerated schools in action: Lessons from research and practice.* Thousand Oaks, CA: Corwin Press.

St. John, E. P., Michael, R., Chung, C. G., Simmons, A., Worthington, K., Manoil, K., & Loescher, S. (2001). *Indiana's Early Intervention Grant Program Impact Study for 2002–01.* Bloomington: Indiana Education Policy Center.

St. John, E. P., Musoba, G. D., Chung, C. G., Loescher, S. A., Hossler, C. A., & Simmons, A. B. (2002). *Implementing comprehensive school reform: Lessons from Michigan's statewide evaluations, 2001–2002.* Naperville, IL: North Central Regional Educational Laboratory.

Taylor, B. M. (1995). *The early intervention in reading program: Results and issues spanning six years.* Paper presented at the annual meeting of the American Educational Research Association, San Francisco, CA.

Taylor, B. M., Anderson, R. C., Au, K. H., & Raphael, T. E. (2000). Discretion in translation of research to policy: A case from beginning reading. *Educational Researcher, 29*(6), 16-26.

Taylor, B. M., Strait, J., & Medo, M. (1994). Early intervention in reading: Supplemental instruction for groups of low-achieving students provided by first-grade teachers. In E. H. Heibert & B. M. Taylor (Eds.), *Getting reading right from the start: Effective early literacy interventions.* Boston: Allyn & Bacon.

Vygotsky, L. (1978). The prehistory of written language. In M. Martlew (Ed.), *The psychology of written language: Developmental and educational perspectives* (pp. 279–292). Chichester, England: John Wiley.

Wong, K. K. (In press). Federal Title I as a reform strategy in urban schools. In L. F. Miron & E. P. St. John (Eds.), *Reinterpreting urban school reform: A critical-empirical review.* Albany: State University of New York Press.

Index